1/09

Fodor's

D0052278

KAUA'I

1st Edition

Where to Stay and Eat for All Budgets

Must-See Sights and Local Secrets

Ratings You Can Trust

Portions of this book appear in *Fodor's Hawai'i*
Fodor's Travel Publications   New York, Toronto, London, Sydney, Auckland
www.fodors.com

FODOR'S KAUA'I
Editor: Rachel Klein

Editorial Production: Linda K. Schmidt
Editorial Contributors: Joan Conrow, Andrea Lehman, Kim Steutermann Rogers, Cathy Sharpe, Pamela Woolway
Maps and Illustrations: Henry Columb and Mark Stroud, Moon Street Cartography; David Lindroth, Inc.; William Wu; Bob Blake and Rebecca Baer, *map editors*
Design: Fabrizio La Rocca, *creative director*; Guido Caroti, *art director*; Moon Sun Kim, *cover designer*; Melanie Marin, *senior picture editor*
Production/Manufacturing: Angela McLean
Cover Photo (Nā Pali Coast): Kerrick James

First Edition

ISBN 978–1–4000–1774–4

ISSN 1934–550X

SPECIAL SALES
This book is available for special discounts for bulk purchases for sales promotions or premiums. Special editions, including personalized covers, excerpts of existing books, and corporate imprints, can be created in large quantities for special needs. For more information, write to Special Markets/Premium Sales, 1745 Broadway, MD 6-2, New York, NY 10019, or e-mail specialmarkets@randomhouse.com.

AN IMPORTANT TIP & AN INVITATION
Although all prices, opening times, and other details in this book are based on information supplied to us at press time, changes occur all the time in the travel world, and Fodor's cannot accept responsibility for facts that become outdated or for inadvertent errors or omissions. So **always confirm information when it matters,** especially if you're making a detour to visit a specific place. Your experiences—positive and negative—matter to us. If we have missed or misstated something, **please write to us.** We follow up on all suggestions. Contact the Hawai'i editor at editors@fodors.com or c/o Fodor's at 1745 Broadway, New York, NY 10019.

PRINTED IN THE UNITED STATES OF AMERICA

10 9 8 7 6 5 4 3 2 1

Your opinion matters. It matters to us. It matters to your fellow Fodor's travelers, too. And we'd like to hear it. In fact, we *need* to hear it.

When you share your experiences and opinions, you become an active member of the Fodor's community. That means we'll not only use your feedback to make our books better, but we'll publish your name and comments whenever possible. Throughout our guides, look for "Word of Mouth," excerpts of your unvarnished feedback.

Here's how you can help improve Fodor's for all of us.

Tell us when we're right. **We rely on local writers to give you an insider's perspective. But our writers and staff editors—who are the best in the business—depend on you. Your positive feedback is a vote to renew our recommendations for the next edition.**

Tell us when we're wrong. **We're proud that we update most of our guides every year. But we're not perfect. Things change. Hotels cut services. Museums change hours. Charming cafés lose charm. If our writer didn't quite capture the essence of a place, tell us how you'd do it differently. If any of our descriptions are inaccurate or inadequate, we'll incorporate your changes in the next edition and will correct factual errors at fodors.com *immediately.***

Tell us what to include. **You probably have had fantastic travel experiences that aren't yet in Fodor's. Why not share them with a community of like-minded travelers? Maybe you chanced upon a beach or bistro or B&B that you don't want to keep to yourself. Tell us why we should include it. And share your discoveries and experiences with everyone directly at fodors.com. Your input may lead us to add a new listing or highlight a place we cover with a "Highly Recommended" star or with our highest rating, "Fodor's Choice."**

Give us your opinion instantly at our feedback center at ⊕ www.fodors.com/feedback. You may also e-mail editors@fodors.com with the subject line "Hawai'i Editor." Or send your nominations, comments, and complaints by mail to Hawai'i Editor, Fodor's, 1745 Broadway, New York, NY 10019.

You and travelers like you are the heart of the Fodor's community. Make our community richer by sharing your experiences. Be a Fodor's correspondent.

Aloha!

Tim Jarrell, Publisher

CONTENTS

KAUA'I IN FOCUS

UNDERSTANDING KAUA'I

CLOSEUPS

MAPS & CHARTS

ABOUT THIS BOOK

Our Ratings

Sometimes you find terrific travel experiences and sometimes they just find you. But usually the burden is on you to select the right combination of experiences. That's where our ratings come in.

As travelers we've all discovered a place so wonderful that its worthiness is obvious. And sometimes that place is so experiential that superlatives don't do it justice: you just have to be there to know. These sights, properties, and experiences get our highest rating, **Fodor's Choice**, indicated by orange stars throughout this book.

Black stars highlight sights and properties we deem **Highly Recommended,** places that our writers, editors, and readers praise again and again for consistency and excellence.

By default, there's another category: any place we include in this book is by definition worth your time, unless we say otherwise. And we will.

Disagree with any of our choices? Care to nominate a place or suggest that we rate one more highly? Visit our feedback center at ⊕ www.fodors.com/feedback.

Budget Well

Hotel and restaurant price categories from ¢ to $$$$ are defined in the Where to Eat and Where to Stay chapters. Real prices are listed at the end of each restaurant and hotel review. For attractions, we always give standard adult admission fees; reductions are usually available for children, students, and senior citizens. Want to pay with plastic? **AE, D, DC, MC,** and **V** following restaurant and hotel listings indicate if American Express, Discover, Diners Club, MasterCard, and Visa are accepted.

Restaurants

Unless we state otherwise, restaurants are open for lunch and dinner daily. We mention dress only when there's a specific requirement and reservations only when they're essential or not accepted—it's always best to book ahead.

Hotels

Hotels have private bath, phone, and TV, unless we state otherwise. We always list facilities but not whether you'll be charged an extra fee to use them, so when pricing accommodations, find out what's included.

Many Listings
★ Fodor's Choice
★ Highly recommended
⊠ Physical address
✛ Directions
🕮 Mailing address
🕾 Telephone
🖷 Fax
⊕ On the Web
✑ E-mail
🖃 Admission fee
☉ Open/closed times
Ⓜ Metro stations
🖃 Credit cards

Hotels & Restaurants
🏨 Hotel
🛏 Number of rooms
⚲ Facilities
🍽 Meal plans
✕ Restaurant
⚲ Reservations
🏛 Dress code
⚲ Smoking
🍸 BYOB
✕🏨 Hotel with restaurant that warrants a visit

Outdoors
⛳ Golf
⛺ Camping

Other
☺ Family-friendly
🔢 Contact information
⇨ See also
⊠ Branch address
☞ Take note

1

Experience Kaua'i

WORD OF MOUTH

"Kaua'i is pretty laid back, and I love that people don't get all dressed up, they just hang out. Perfect."   —123Go

"We found Kaua'i to be far more laid back and less touristy. We went on garden tours, hikes in the Waimea Canyon, ate at some really good local joints, and got more R&R than I have probably had in my whole life! They still have some of the touristy stuff to do (like lū'aus and helicopter rides), but the scenery and atmosphere overshadowed those."   —kblonkowski

WELCOME TO KAUA'I

Getting Oriented

Despite its small size—550 square mi—Kaua'i has four distinct regions, each with its own unique characteristics. The windward coast, which catches the prevailing trade winds, consists of the North Shore and East Side, while the drier leeward coast encompasses the South Shore and West Side. One main road nearly encircles the island, except for a 15-mile stretch of sheer cliffs called the Nā Pali Coast.

The center of the island—Mt. Wai'ale'ale, completely inaccessible by car and viewable only from above—is the wettest spot on earth, getting about 450 inches of rain per year. ■ TIP→ On Kaua'i, the directions *mauka* (toward the mountains) and *makai* (toward the ocean) are often used. Locals tend to refer to highways by name rather than by number.

Dry, sunny, and sleepy, the West Side includes the historic towns of Hanapēpē, Waimea, and Kekaha. This area is ideal for outdoor adventurers because it's the entryway to the Waimea Canyon and Kōke'e State Park, and the departure point for some Nā Pali Coast boat trips.

Dreamy beaches, green mountains, breathtaking scenery, and abundant rain, waterfalls, and rainbows characterize the North Shore, which includes the towns of Kīlauea, Princeville, and Hanalei.

The East Side is Kaua'i's commercial and residential hub, dominated by the island's largest town, Kapa'a. The airport, harbor, and government offices are found in the county seat of Līhu'e.

Peaceful landscapes, sunny weather, and beaches that rank among the best in the world make the South Shore the resort capital of Kaua'i. The Po'ipū resort area is here along with the main towns of Kōloa, Lāwa'i, and Kalāheo.

KAUA'I PLANNER

Car Rentals

Unless you plan to stay strictly at a resort or do all of your sightseeing as part of guided tours, you'll need a rental car. You can take the bus, but they tend to be slow and don't go everywhere.

■ TIPS➜ **You most likely won't need a four-wheel-drive vehicle anywhere on the island, so save yourself the money. And while convertibles look fun, the frequent, intermittent rain showers and intense tropical sun make hardtops a better (and cheaper) choice.** ■ **Reserve your vehicle in advance, especially during the Christmas holidays. This will not only ensure that you get a car, but also that you get the best rates. Kaua'i has some of the highest gas prices in the islands.**

When You Arrive

All commercial flights land at Līhu'e Airport, about 3 mi east of Līhu'e town. A rental car is the best way to get to your hotel, though taxis and some hotel shuttles are available. From the airport it will take you about 15 to 25 minutes to drive to Wailua or Kapa'a, 30 to 40 minutes to reach Po'ipū, and 45 minutes to an hour to get to Princeville or Hanalei.

Timing Is Everything

If you're a beach lover, keep in mind that big surf can make many North Shore beaches unswimmable during winter months, while the South Shore gets its large swells in summer. If you want to see the humpback whales, February is the best month, though they arrive as early as December and a few may still be around in early April. In the winter, Nā Pali Coast boat tours are sometimes rerouted due to high seas, and the Kalalau Trail can become very wet and muddy or, at times, impassable. Kayaking Nā Pali during winter is simply not an option. If you have your heart set on visiting Kaua'i's famed coast you may want to visit in the drier, warmer months (May–September).

Will It Rain?

Kaua'i is beautiful in every season, but if you must have good beach weather you should plan to visit between June and October. The rainy season runs from November through February, with the windward or east and north areas of the island receiving most of the rainfall. Nights can be chilly from November through March. Rain is possible throughout the year, of course, but it rarely rains everywhere on the island at once. If it's raining where you are, the best thing to do is head to another side of the island, usually south or west.

Guided Activities

When it comes to kayaking, Kaua'i is the island of choice. It's the only island with navigable rivers. A boat tour along Nā Pali Coast is another unique-to-Kaua'i experience. This chart lists rough prices for Kaua'i's top guided activities.

ACTIVITY	COST
Aerial Tours	$125–$370
Boat tours	$80–$175
Deep Sea Fishing	$120–$575
Golf	$8–$195
Lū'au	$58–$95
Kayaking Tours	$60–$200
Scuba Diving	$110–$395
Snorkel Cruises	$80–$175
Surfing Lessons	$55–$150
Whale-Watching	$59–$69

Here Comes the Super Ferry

It's been a hot-button issue for island residents for some time now: the interisland Superferry will begin offering daily service between Kaua'i and O'ahu in July 2007. Going to Kaua'i, the ferry leaves Honolulu at 2:30 PM and docks at Nāwiliwili at 5:30 PM. Leaving Kaua'i, the ferry departs at 6:30 PM and arrives back in Honolulu at 9:30 PM.

For single passengers the cost is $50 one-way off-peak (Tuesday–Thursday) and $60 peak (Friday–Monday). An $8 discount is offered if you book on the Web (www.hawaiisuperferry.com).

Children ages 2 and under travel for $15 all week. For cars and SUVs, one-way fares are $55 off-peak and $65 peak.

Ways to Save

■ Save on produce and flowers by shopping at the farmers' markets held on different days of the week all around the island.

■ Stock up on gas and groceries in Kapa'a and Līhu'e if you're staying on the North Shore or South Side, as prices go up farther from town.

■ Book guided activities, such as Nā Pali Coast boat tours, on the Internet. Individual outfitters' Web sites usually offer discounts for those who book online.

■ Reserve the smallest car for your needs to save money on gas and rental fees.

How to Pack for the Garden Isle

Even if you consider yourself an expert planner and packer, what you'll need on Kaua'i (as well as what to leave home and what to buy once you arrive) isn't necessarily obvious.

The first thing to know is that Kaua'i is very laid-back, even by Hawai'i standards. No one comes to Kaua'i for its nightlife, so evening dress is ultracasual. In fact, you may want to bring some of the oldest items in your closet, especially for outdoor activities. Kaua'i's infamous red mud will stain those spanking-new white sneakers for sure. Chances are you'll be spending lots of time in the water, but don't pack water shoes. When you arrive, stop into one of the local we-sell-everything stores and pick up a pair for about $10. Trust us, you'll want to toss them before you leave. Consider shipping your snorkel gear in advance, as it can be difficult to pack, or just bring your mask and snorkel, and rent fins.

Island Driving Times

It might not seem as if driving from the North Shore to the West Side, say, would take very much time, as Kaua'i is smaller in size than O'ahu, Maui, and certainly the Big Island. But it will take longer than you'd think from glancing at a map, and Kaua'i roads are subject to some pretty heavy traffic. Here are average driving times that will help you plan your excursions accordingly, starting from Ha'ena in the northwest and working clockwise around the island to Waimea in the southwest.

Ha'ena to Hanalei	15 minutes
Hanalei to Princeville	10 minutes
Princeville to Kilauea	12 minutes
Kilauea to Anahola	15 minutes
Anahola to Kapa'a	8 minutes
Kapa'a to Lihu'e	18 minutes
Lihu'e to Po'ipū	25 minutes
Po'ipū to Kalaheo	20 minutes
Kalaheo to Hanapepe	10 minutes
Hanapepe to Waimea	10 minutes

TOP KAUA'I EXPERIENCES

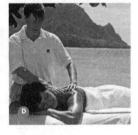

Nā Pali

(A) Some things defy words, and the Nā Pali Coast is one of them. Besides, *beautiful, verdant, spectacular,* and *amazing* lose their meaning after repeated usage, so forget trying to think of words to describe it, but don't forget to experience Kaua'i's remote, northwest coastline any which way—by air, water, or trail, preferably all three.

Waimea Canyon Drive

(B) From its start in the west Kaua'i town of Waimea to the road's end some 20 uphill miles later at Pu'u O Kila lookout, you'll pass through several microclimates—from hot, desertlike conditions at sea level to the cool, deciduous forest of Koke'e—and navigate through the traditional Hawaiian system of land division called *ahupua'a.*

Hanalei Bay

(C) Families. Honeymooners. Retirees. Surfers. Sunbathers. Hanalei Bay attracts all kinds, for good reason—placid water in the summers; epic surf in the winters; the 2-mi-long and wide, crescent-shape beach year-round; and the green mountain backdrop striated with waterfalls—also year-round but definitely in full force in winter. And did we mention the atmosphere? Decidedly laid-back.

Spas. Spas. Spas.

(D) Kaua'i is characterized by its rural nature (read: quiet and peaceful), which lends itself nicely to the spa scene on the island. The vast majority of spas could be called rural, too, as they invite the outside in—or would that be the inside out? For a resort spa, ANARA Spa is not only decadent but set in a garden. Hart-Felt Massage &Day Spa sits in a grove of old-style plantation homes, and Angeline's traditional Hawaiian spa Mu'olaulani is in her home.

Highway 560

(E) This 10-mi stretch of road starting at the Hanalei Scenic Overlook in Princeville rivals all in Hawai'i and in 2003 was listed on the National Register of Historic Places, one of only about 100 roads nationwide to meet the criteria. Indeed, the road itself is said to follow an ancient Hawaiian walking trail that skirts the ocean. Today, Route 560 includes 13 historic bridges and culverts, most of which are one lane wide. Be patient.

River Kayaking

(F) The best part about kayaking Kaua'i's rivers is that you don't have to be experienced. There are no rapids to run, no waterfalls to jump, and therefore, no excuses for not enjoying the scenic sights from the water. On the East Side, try the Wailua River; if you're on the North Shore, don't miss the Hanalei River. But if you have some experience and are in reasonably good shape, you may choose to create a few lifetime memories and kayak Nā Pali Coast.

Sunshine Markets

(G) Bananas. Mangos. Papayas. Lemons. Limes. Lychees. The best and freshest fruits, vegetables, flowers—and goat cheese—are found at various farmers' markets around the island. Just don't get there too late in the day—all the best stuff goes early.

WHEN TO GO

ONLY IN HAWAI'I HOLIDAYS

If you happen to be in the Islands on March 26 or June 11, you'll notice light traffic and busy beaches—these are state holidays not celebrated anywhere else. March 26 recognizes the birthday of Prince Jonah Kūhio Kalaniana'ole, a member of the royal line who served as a delegate to Congress and spearheaded the effort to set aside homelands for Hawaiian people. June 11 honors the first island-wide monarch, Kamehameha I; locals drape his statues with lei and stage elaborate parades. May 1 isn't an official holiday, but it's the day when schools and civic groups celebrate the quintessential Island gift, the flower lei, with lei-making contests and pageants. Statehood Day is celebrated on the third Friday in August (Admission Day was August 21, 1959). Most Japanese and Chinese holidays are widely observed. On Chinese New Year, homes and businesses sprout bright-red good-luck mottoes, lions dance in the streets, and everybody eats *gau* (steamed pudding) and *jai* (vegetarian stew). Good Friday is a state holiday in spring, a favorite for family picnics.

Long days of sunshine and fairly mild year-round temperatures make Hawai'i an all-season destination. Most resort areas are at sea level, with average afternoon temperatures of 75°F–80°F during the coldest months of December and January; during the hottest months of August and September the temperature often reaches 90°F. Only at high elevations does the temperature drop into the colder realms, and only at mountain summits does it reach freezing.

Most travelers head to the Islands in winter, specifically during Christmas and spring break. From mid-December through mid-April, visitors from the mainland and other areas covered with snow find Hawai'i's sun-splashed beaches and balmy trade winds appealing. This high season means that fewer travel bargains are available; room rates average 10%–15% higher during this season than the rest of the year.

Rainfall can be high in winter, particularly on the North and East Shores of the island. Generally speaking, you're guaranteed sun and warm temperatures on the West Side and South Shore no matter what time of year.

Climate

Moist trade winds drop their precipitation on the North Shore and East Side of the islands, creating tropical climates, while the South Shore and West Side remain hot and dry.

Average maximum and minimum temperatures for Kaua'i are listed at left; the temperatures throughout the Hawaiian Islands are similar.

Forecasts Weather Channel Connection ⊕ www.weather.com.

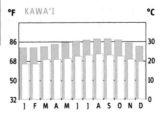

GREAT 1-DAY ITINERARIES

As small as Kaua'i may be, you still can't do it all in one day: hiking Kalalau Trail, kayaking Wailua River, showering in a waterfall, watching whales at Kīlauea Lighthouse, waking to the sun's rise above Keālia, touring underwater lava tubes at Tunnels, and shopping for gifts at Kōloa Town shops. Rather than trying to check everything off your list in one fell swoop, we recommend choosing your absolute favorite and devoting a full day to the experience.

A Bit of History

Because of the Hawaiians' beliefs in nature, much of what you see in Kaua'i today is built on sacred ground. If you're interested in archaeological remains where sacred ceremonies were held, focus on the Wailua River area. Your best bet is to take a riverboat tour—it's full of kitsch, but you'll definitely walk away with a deeper understanding of ancient Hawai'i. Then, head to Līhu'e's Kaua'i Museum, where you can pick up a memento of authentic Hawaiian artistry at the gift shop. End your day at Gaylord's restaurant and meander through the historic Kilohana Plantation sugar estate.

Adventure Galore

For big-time adventure, kayak Nā Pali Coast or spend a day learning to fly a microlight. For those whose idea of adventure is a good walk, take the flat, coastal trail along the East Side—you can pick it up just about anywhere starting at the northern end of Wailua Beach, heading north. It'll take you all the way to Anahola, if you desire. After it's all over, recuperate with a massage by the ocean—or in the comfort of your own room, so you can crash immediately afterward.

A Day on the Water

Start your day before sunrise and head west, to Port Allen Marina. Check in with one of the tour boat operators—who will provide you with plenty of coffee to jumpstart your day—that cruise Nā Pali Coast and then head across the Kaulakahi Channel to snorkel the fish-rich waters of Ni'ihau. Slather up with sunscreen and be prepared for a long—and sometimes big—day on the water and enjoy a couple of mai tais on the return trip. Something about the sun and the salt air combines to manifest an interesting combination of fatigue—so don't plan anything in the evening. It also creates massive hunger, so stop at Grinds in Hanapēpē on the way home.

Coastal Drives

If you're staying on the East Side or North Shore, the best drive for ocean vistas is, hands down, Highway 560. Stop here for a few snapshots, then head down the hill, across the one-lane bridge—taking in the taro fields—and through the town of Hanalei and on to the end of the road at Ke'e Beach. If you're up for it, enjoy a bit of unparalleled hiking on the Kalalau Trail, go snorkeling, or simply soak up the sun on the beach, if it's not too crowded. If you're staying on the South Shore or West Side, follow Highway 50 west. You'll start to catch distant ocean vistas from the highway as you head out of the town of Kalāheo and from the coffee fields of Kaua'i Coffee. Stop here for a sample. You'll come closer to the ocean—and practically reach out and touch it—after you pass through Hanapēpē and, especially, Waimea. Although this isn't great swimming water—unprotected, no reef—there is a long stretch of beach here perfect for walking, running, and pure meandering. Once the paved road ends—if you're brave and your car

rental agreement allows—keep going and you'll eventually come to Polihale, a huge, deserted beach. It'll feel like the end of the world here, so it's a great place to spend a quiet afternoon and witness a spectacular sunset. Just be sure to pack plenty of food, water, and sunscreen before you depart Kekaha—and gas up the car.

Shop Till You Drop

You know, you could actually see a good many of the island's sights by browsing our favorite island shops. Of course, you can't see the entire island, but this itinerary will take you through Kapaʻa and north to Hanalei. Don't miss Marta's Boat—high-end clothing for mom and child—across from Foodland in Waipouli. Just a few blocks north, Kela's Glass has great art pieces. Island Hemp & Cotton Cool is a unique clothing shop featuring a nice selection of hemp apparel for him and, mostly, her. Then, a leisurely drive north will reveal the rural side of Kauaʻi. If you enjoy tea, sake, or sushi, stop at Kīlauea's Kong Lung, where you can stock up on complete place settings for each. Then, head on down the road to Hanalei. If you're inspired by surf, stop in Hanalei Surf Company. Our favorite for one-of-a-kind keepsakes—actually antiques and authentic memorabilia—is Yellow Fin Trading Company, and we never head into Hanalei without stopping at On the Road to Hanalei.

Relax Kauaʻi-Style

If you're headed to Kauaʻi for some peace and quiet, you'll want to start your day with yoga at Yoga Hanalei or Kapaʻa's Bikram Yoga Kauaʻi. If you're staying on the South Shore, try yoga on the beach (actually a grassy spot just off the beach) with longtime yoga instructor Joy Zepeda (www.aloha-yoga.com). If it happens to be the last Sunday of the month, you might then head to the Lāwaʻi International Center (www.lawaicenter.org) for an afternoon stroll among 88 Buddhist shrines. If it's not the last Sunday of the month, head north to Limahuli Gardens for a stroll among native plants. Then, watch the sun slip into the sea on any west-facing beach and call it a day with a glass of wine.

Have a Little Romance

We can't think of a better way to ensure a romantic vacation for two than to pop a bottle of champagne and walk the Māhāʻulepū shoreline at sunrise, hand in hand with a loved one. Make this a Sunday and follow your walk with brunch at the Grand Hyatt. Then, spend the afternoon luxuriating with facials, body scrubs, and massage in the Hyatt's ANARA Spa's new Garden Treatment Village, in a private, thatched hut just for couples. That'll put you in the mood for a wedding ceremony or renewal of vows on the beach followed by a sunset dinner overlooking the ocean at the Beach House restaurant. Can it get any more romantic than this?

WEDDINGS & HONEYMOONS

There's no question that Hawai'i is one of the country's foremost honeymoon destinations. Romance is in the air here, and the white, sandy beaches, turquoise water, swaying palm trees, balmy tropical breezes, and perpetual summer sunshine put people in the mood for love. It's easy to understand why Hawai'i is a popular wedding destination as well, especially as the cost of airfare has gone down and new resorts and hotels entice visitors. A destination wedding is no longer exclusive to celebrities and the superrich. You can plan a traditional ceremony in a place of worship followed by a reception at an elegant resort, or you can go barefoot on the beach and celebrate at a lū'au. There are almost as many wedding planners on the islands as real estate agents (because of the recent boom), which makes it easy to wed in paradise, and then, once the knot is tied, stay and honeymoon as well. What makes Kaua'i such an attractive wedding and honeymoon destination is its seclusion. And the lush and green surroundings are evocative of, oh, the Garden of Eden.

The Big Day

Choosing the perfect place. When choosing a location, remember that you really have two choices to make: the ceremony location and where to have the reception, if you're having one. For the former, there are beaches, bluffs overlooking beaches, gardens, private residences, resort lawns, and, of course, places of worship. It really depends on you. As for the reception, there are these same choices, as well as restaurants and even lū'au. If you decide to go outdoors, remember the seasons—yes, Hawai'i has seasons. If you're planning a winter wedding outdoors, be sure you have a backup plan (such as a tent), in case it rains. Also, if you're planning an outdoor

wedding at sunset—which is very popular—be sure you match the time of your ceremony to the time the sun sets. If you choose indoors, be sure to ask for pictures of the environs when you're planning. You don't want to plan a pink wedding, say, and wind up in a room that's predominantly red. Or maybe you do. The point is, it should be your choice.

Now, as for the exact location—Na Aina Kai, Anini Beach, Hanalei Pier, Mahaulepu Beach, Allerton Gardens, say—we recommend you discuss this at length with your wedding officiant or wedding planner, which brings us to our next point.

Finding a wedding planner. If you're planning to invite more than the person marrying you and your loved one to your wedding ceremony, seriously consider an on-island wedding planner who can help select a location, design the floral scheme and recommend a florist as well as a photographer, plan the menu and choose a restaurant, caterer, or resort, and suggest any special Hawaiian traditions to incorporate into your ceremony. And more: Will you need tents? Of course, a cake. Music. Maybe transportation. Lodging. Many planners have relationships with vendors, providing packages—which mean savings.

If you're planning a resort wedding, most have on-site wedding coordinators; however, there are many independents around the island and even those who specialize in certain types of ceremonies—by locale, size, religious affiliation, and so on. A simple "Kauai weddings" Google search will reveal dozens. What's important is that you feel comfortable with your coordinator. Ask for references—and call them. Share your budget. Get a proposal—in

writing. Ask how long they've been in business, how they charge, how often you'll meet with them, and how they select vendors. Request a detailed list of the exact services they'll provide. If your idea of your wedding doesn't match their services, try someone else. If you can afford it, you might want to consider meeting the planner in person.

Getting your license. The good news about marrying in Hawai'i is that no waiting period, no residency or citizenship requirements, and no blood tests or shots are required. However, both the bride and groom must appear together in person before a marriage license agent to apply for a marriage license. You'll need proof of age—the legal age to marry is 18. Upon approval, a marriage license is immediately issued and costs $60, cash only. Your officiant will want to see the license, because it authorizes a marriage to take place. After the ceremony, your officiant will mail the marriage license to the state. Approximately 120 days later, you will receive a copy in the mail. (For $10 extra, you can expedite this process. Ask your marriage license agent when you apply for your license.) For more detailed information, visit www.hawaii.gov or call 808/241-3498.

Also—this is important—the person performing your wedding must be licensed by the Hawai'i Department of Health. Be sure to ask. First things first: Make an appointment with a marriage license agent by calling the Department of Health at 808/241-3495.

Wedding attire. In Hawai'i, basically anything goes, from long, formal dresses with trains to white bikinis. Floral sundresses are fine, too. For the men, tuxedos are not the norm; a pair of solid-colored slacks with a nice aloha shirt is. In fact, tradition in Hawai'i for the groom is a plain white aloha shirt (they do exist) with slacks or long shorts and a colored sash around the waist. If you're planning a wedding on the beach, barefoot is the way to go.

If you decide to marry in a formal dress and tuxedo, don't expect to find such on Kaua'i. It's possible but not easy. Instead, make your selections on the mainland and hand-carry them aboard the plane. Yes, it can be a pain, but ask your wedding gown retailer to provide a special carrying bag. After all, you don't want to chance losing your wedding dress in a wayward piece of luggage. For fittings, again, that's something you'll want to take care of before you arrive on Kaua'i.

Local customs. When it comes to traditional Hawaiian wedding customs, the most obvious is the lei exchange in which the bride and groom take turns placing a lei around the neck of the other—with a kiss. Bridal lei are usually floral, whereas the groom's is typically made of maile, a green leafy garland that drapes around the neck and is open at the ends. Brides often also wear a haku lei—a circular floral headpiece. Other Hawaiian customs include the blowing of the conch shell, hula, chanting, and Hawaiian music.

The Honeymoon

One island or more? Ever since airlines started flying direct from the West Coast of the mainland to the neighboring islands, fewer and fewer people have been island hopping, especially if their visit is a week or less, and although the flights from island to island are quite short, the time adds up. Consider the recent increased security measures and the fact that most interisland flights—say from Kaua'i to the Big Island—still go through Honolulu, often requiring a plane change. If you're staying a week or less, it just isn't worth it, especially after the stresses of planning a wedding.

Choosing your nest. Do you want champagne and strawberries delivered to your room each morning? A maze of a swimming pool in which to float? A five-star restaurant in which to dine? Then a resort is the way to go. If, however, you prefer the comforts of a home, try a bed-and-breakfast. A B&B is also good if you're on a tight budget or don't plan to spend much time in your room. On the other hand, maybe you want your own private home in which to romp naked—or just laze around recovering from the wedding. Maybe you want your own kitchen in which to whip up a gourmet meal for your loved one. Maybe your entire family is joining you on your honeymoon. In that case, a private vacational rental home is the answer. Or maybe a condominium resort. That's another beautiful thing about Hawai'i: the lodging accommodations are almost as plentiful as the beaches, and there's one to match your tastes and your budget.

Romance on Kaua'i. Romance on Kaua'i rains down like the mists over Mt. Wai'ale'ale—continually. It might be the sparkle of the sun reflecting off the ocean's surface, the glow of the sky after sunset, the way a shadow drapes the mountain—all these things conspire to create romance anywhere on Kaua'i. But certain experiences are undoubtedly über-romantic. Take, for example, a swim in a secluded waterfall pool—accessible only by helicopter—or a sunset walk along the beach in Hanalei. Make sure to witness the full moon rise over the ocean at Keālia Beach (don't forget the wine) and to have a picnic lunch at the nearly-always-deserted beach, Polihale, at the road's end on the west side. The other thing not to miss? On a clear, summer night, stars pop out like fireworks one after another. It doesn't get more romantic than that.

KIDS & FAMILIES

With dozens of adventures, discoveries, and fun-filled beach days, Hawai'i is a blast with kids. Even better, the things to do here do not appeal only to small fry. The entire family, parents included, will enjoy surfing, discovering a waterfall in the rain forest, and snorkeling with sea turtles. And there are plenty of organized activities for kids that will free parents' time for a few romantic beach strolls.

Choosing a Place to Stay

Resorts: All of the big resorts make kids' programs a priority, and it shows. When you are booking your room, ask about "kids eat free" deals and the number of kids' pools at the resort. Also check out the size of the groups in the children's programs, and find out whether the cost of the programs includes lunch, equipment, and activities.

On the North Shore the best bet is the Princeville Resort, where kids can spend the day (without their parents) sightseeing or the evening at the movies. The Kaua'i Marriott Resort is a good choice on the East Side, and on the South Shore both the Hyatt Regency Kaua'i and Sheraton Kaua'i Resort have kids' programs.

Condos: Condo and vacation rentals are a fantastic value for families vacationing in Hawai'i. You can cook your own food, which is cheaper than eating out and sometimes easier (especially if you have a finicky eater in your group), and you'll get twice the space of a hotel room for about a quarter of the price. If you decide to go the condo route, be sure to ask about the size of the complex's pool (some try to pawn a tiny soaking tub off as a pool) and whether barbecues are available. One of the best parts of staying in your own place is having a sunset family barbecue by the pool or overlooking the ocean.

On the North Shore, one of the most popular places for those with kids is North Country Farms, for its value and amenities. There are kitchenettes, and the common area is packed with videos and puzzles. There's also Hanalei Bay Resort, which offers kids' programs. On the South Shore, Outrigger Kiahuna Plantation is a family favorite, with an excellent location that includes a very swimmable beach adjacent to a grassy field great for picnics.

Ocean Activities

Hawai'i is all about getting your kids outside—away from TV and video games. And who could resist the turquoise water, the promise of spotting dolphins or whales, and the fun of boogie boarding or surfing?

On the Beach: Most people like being in the water, but toddlers and school-age kids tend to be especially enamored of it. The swimming pool at your condo or hotel is always an option, but don't be afraid to hit the beach with a little one in tow. There are several beaches in Hawai'i that are nearly as safe as a pool—completely protected bays with pleasant white-sand beaches. As always, use your judgment, and heed all posted signs and lifeguard warnings.

Calm beaches to try include Anini Beach and Hanalei Bay Beach Park on the North Shore, Lydgate State Park and Kalapaki Beach on the East Side, Poipu Beach Park on the South Shore, and Salt Pond Beach Park on the West Side.

On the Waves: Surf lessons are a great idea for older kids, especially if mom and dad want a little quiet time. Beginner lessons

are always on safe and easy waves and last anywhere from two to four hours.

The Blue Seas Surf School is best for beginners, and you can book your kids a 1½-hour lesson for $65.

The Underwater World: If your kids are ready to try snorkeling, Hawai'i is a great place to introduce them to the underwater world. Even without the mask and snorkel, they'll be able to see colorful fish darting this way and that, and they may also spot turtles and dolphins at many of the island beaches.

Get your kids used to the basics at Lydgate State Park on the island's East Side, where there's no threat of a current. For guided snorkel tours, SeaFun Kaua'i will show kids of all ages how to identify marine life and gives great beginner instruction.

Land Activities

In addition to beach experiences, Hawai'i has rain forests, botanical gardens (the Big Island and Maui have the best), numerous aquariums (O'ahu and Maui take the cake), and even petting zoos and hands-on childrens' museums that will keep your kids entertained and out of the sun for a day.

On the North Shore, kids will love Na Aina Kai, a garden with a 16-foot-tall Jack and the Beanstalk bronze sculpture, gecko maze,

treehouse, kid-size train, and tropical jungle, and on the East Side is Smith's Tropical Paradise, a 30-acre botanical garden.

Horseback riding is a popular family activity, and most of the tours on Kaua'i move slowly, so no riding experience is required. Kids as young as two can ride at Esprit de Corps.

When it rains on Kaua'i, kids aren't subject to staying indoors. ATV tours are the activity of choice. Try Kaua'i ATV tours, which has two-passenger "Mud Bugs" to accommodate families with kids ages five and older.

After Dark

At nighttime, younger kids get a kick out of lū'aus, and many of the shows incorporate young audience members, adding to the fun. The older kids might find it all a bit lame, but there are a handful of new shows in the islands that are more modern, incorporating acrobatics, lively music, and fire dancers. If you're planning on hitting a lū'au with a teen in tow, we highly recommend going the modern route. We think the best lū'au for kids on Kaua'i is a Lū'au Kilohana, in Lihue. All guests arrive by horse-drawn carriage, and there's a bit of a history lesson, too, as the grounds were once a sugar-plantation manager's estate.

CRUISING THE HAWAIIAN ISLANDS

Cruising has become extremely popular in Hawai'i. For first-time visitors, it's an excellent way to get a taste of all the islands; and if you fall in love with one or even two, you know how to plan your next trip. It's also a comparatively inexpensive way to see Hawai'i. The limited amount of time in each port can be an argument against cruising—there's enough to do on any island to keep you busy for a week, so some folks feel shortchanged by cruise itineraries.

Cruising to Hawai'i

Until 2001 it was illegal for any cruise ships to stop in Hawai'i unless they originated from a foreign port, or were including a foreign port in their itinerary. The law has changed, but most cruises still include a stop in the Fanning Islands, Ensenada, or Vancouver. Gambling is legal on the open seas, and your winnings are tax-free; most cruise ships offer designated smoking areas and now enforce the U.S. legal drinking age (21) on Hawai'i itineraries.

Carnival Cruises. They call them "fun ships" for a reason—Carnival is all about keeping you busy and showing you a good time, both on board and on shore. Great for families, Carnival always plans plenty of kid-friendly activities, and their children's program rates high with the little critics. Carnival offers itineraries starting in Ensenada, Vancouver, and Honolulu. Their ships stop on Maui (Kahului and Lahaina), the Big Island (Kailua-Kona and Hilo), O'ahu, and Kaua'i. ☎ 888/227–6482 ⊕ www.carnival.com.

Celebrity Cruises. Celebrity's focus is on service, and it shows. From their waitstaff to their activity directors to their fantastic Hawaiian cultural experts, every aspect of your trip has been well thought out. They cater more to adults than children, so this may not be the best line for families. Celebrity's Hawai'i cruises depart from Los Angeles and stop in Maui (Lahaina), O'ahu, the Big Island (Hilo and Kailua-Kona), and Kaua'i. ☎ 800/647–2251 ⊕ www.celebrity.com.

Holland America. The grande dame of cruise lines, Holland America has a reputation for service and elegance. Holland America's Hawai'i cruises leave and return to San Diego, CA, and stop on Maui (Lahaina), the Big Island (Kailua-Kona and Hilo), O'ahu, and for half a day on Kaua'i. ☎ 877/724–5425 ⊕ www.hollandamerica.com.

Norwegian Cruise Lines. Norwegian has traditionally been one of the more casual cruise lines and offers a variety of service, activity, and excursion options. The latest addition to their fleet, *Pride of Hawai'i,* has expensive suites; but all the boats maintain a family-friendly focus (there are no casinos). The only line with ships not required to stop in foreign ports, NCL Pride itineraries originate either in San Francisco, Kahului (Maui), or Honolulu and include stops on Maui (Kahului), O'ahu, the Big Island (Hilo and Kailua-Kona), and Kaua'i (Nāwiliwili). ☎ 800/327–7030 ⊕ www.ncl.com.

Princess Cruises. Princess strives to offer affordable luxury. Their prices start out a little higher, but you get more bells and whistles (more affordable balcony rooms, nice decor, more restaurants to choose from, personalized service). They're not fantastic for kids, but they do a great job of keeping teenagers occupied. Princess' Hawaiian cruise is 15 days, round-trip from Los Angeles, with a service call in En-

senada. The *Island Princess* stops in Maui (Lahaina), the Big Island (Hilo and Kailua-Kona), Oʻahu, and Kauaʻi. ☎*800/774–6237* ⊕ *www.princess.com.*

Royal Caribbean. Royal Caribbean's cruises originate in Los Angeles only, and stop in Maui (Lahaina), Kauaʻi, Oʻahu, and the Big Island (both Hilo and Kailua-Kona). In keeping with its reputation for being all things to all people, Royal Caribbean offers a huge variety of activities and services on board and more excursions on land than any other cruise line. ☎*800/521–8611* ⊕ *www.royalcaribbean.com.*

Cruising Within Hawaiʻi

If you'd like to cruise from island to island, Norwegian is the only major cruise line option. For a different experience, Hawaiʻi Nautical offers cruises on smaller boats.

Norwegian Cruise Lines. Norwegian is the only major operator to offer interisland cruises in Hawaiʻi. Three of their ships cruise the islands—*Pride of Aloha* (older, Hawaiian-themed, priced lowest), *Pride of Hawaiʻi* (brand new, the most chic of the three, suites available, Hawaiian themed, slightly pricier), and *Pride of America* (Vintage Americana theme, very new, big family focus with lots of connecting staterooms and suites). All three offer 7-day itineraries within the islands, stopping on Maui, Oʻahu, the Big Island, and overnighting in Kauaʻi; the *Pride of America* offers guests two additional itineraries, one that includes more time on Maui and the other more time at sea. ☎ *800/327–7030* ⊕ *www.ncl.com.*

Hawaiʻi Nautical. Offering a completely different sort of experience, Hawaiʻi Nautical provides private multiple-day interisland cruises on their catamarans, yachts, and sailboats. Prices are higher, but service is completely personal, right down to the itinerary. ☎ *808/234–7245* ⊕ *www.hawaiinautical.com.*

TIPS

❶ On all but the *Pride of America*, *Pride of Hawaiʻi*, and *Pride of Aloha* cruises (operated by Norwegian Cruise Lines), you must bring a passport as you will be entering foreign ports of call.

❷ Think about booking your own excursions directly. You'll often pay less for greater value. For example, if you want to take a surfing lesson on Oʻahu, visit one of the beachside shacks to find excellent instructors who offer better deals to individuals than they do to the cruise lines.

❸ Tendering in Maui can be a tedious process—if you want to avoid a little bit of the headache (and hours waiting in the sun), be sure to book an excursion there through the ship and you'll have smooth sailing.

❹ Most Mainland cell phones will work without a hitch on board between the islands and at all Hawaiian ports of call.

Exploring Kaua'i

WORD OF MOUTH

"Having been to three of the islands, my vote is for Kaua'i. North Shore of this island was heaven on earth. Really it was paradise . . . People are friendly. It's not crowded or too commercialized, and there are so many beaches to explore. This island is lush! You cannot go wrong with the North Shore of Kaua'i."

—Momof5

Updated by
Kim
Steutermann
Rogers

EVEN A NICKNAME LIKE "THE GARDEN ISLAND" fails to do justice to Kaua'i's beauty. Verdant trees grow canopies over the few roads, and brooding mountains are framed by long, sandy beaches, coral reefs, and sheer sea cliffs. The main road tracing Kaua'i's perimeter takes you past much more scenery than would seem possible on one small island. Chiseled mountains, thundering waterfalls, misty hillsides, dreamy beaches, lush vegetation, and small towns make up the physical landscape. Perhaps the most stunning piece of scenery is a place no road will take you— the breathtakingly beautiful, magical Nā Pali Coast, which runs along the northwest side of the island.

For adventure seekers, Kaua'i offers everything from difficult hikes to helicopter tours. The island has top-notch spas, golf courses, and its beaches are known to be some of the most beautiful in the world. Even after you've spent days lazing around drinking mai tais or kayaking your way down a river, there's still plenty to do, as well as see: plantation villages, a historic lighthouse, wildlife refuges, a fern grotto, a colorful canyon, and deep rivers are all easily explored.

■ TIP➔ While exploring the island, try to take advantage of the many roadside scenic overlooks to pull off and take in the constantly changing view. And don't try to pack too much into one day. Kaua'i is small, but travel is slow. The island's sights are divided into four geographic areas, in clockwise order: the North Shore, the East Side, the South Shore, and the West Side.

Geology

Kaua'i is the oldest and northernmost of the main Hawaiian Islands. Five million years of wind and rain have worked their magic, sculpting fluted sea cliffs and whittling away at the cinder cones and caldera that prove its volcanic origin. Foremost among these is Wai'ale'ale, one of the wettest spots on Earth. Its 480-inch annual rainfall feeds the mighty Wailua River, the only navigable waterway in Hawai'i. The vast Alaka'i Swamp soaks up rain like a sponge, releasing it slowly into the watershed that gives Kaua'i its emerald sheen.

Flora & Fauna

Kaua'i offers some of the best birding in the state, due in part to the absence of the mongoose. Many nēnē (the endangered Hawaiian state bird) reared in captivity have been successfully released here, along with an endangered forest bird called the puai'ohi. The island is also home to a large colony of migratory nesting seabirds, and has two refuges protecting endangered Hawaiian water birds. Kaua'i's

> **WORD OF MOUTH**
>
> "Don't let the rain issue keep you from going to Kaua'i. I think people tend to make way too much of the rain being a negative thing on Kaua'i. It isn't your typical mainland dreary, soaking, cold, depressing-type rain. It's normally more of a refreshing, cooling, pleasurable shower-type rain that comes and goes and usually results in the most beautiful rainbows you've ever experienced. I find the many daily rain showers actually a very enjoyable part of the Kaua'i experience."
>
> –dfarr

most noticeable fowl, however, is the wild chicken. A cross between jungle fowl (moa) brought by the Polynesians, and domestic chickens and fighting cocks that escaped during the last two hurricanes, they are everywhere, and the roosters crow when they feel like it, not just at dawn. Consider yourself warned.

History

Kaua'i's residents have had a reputation for independence since ancient times. Called "the separate kingdom," Kaua'i alone resisted King Kamehameha's charge to unite the Hawaiian Islands. In fact, it was only by kidnapping Kaua'i's king, Kaumuali'i, and forcing him to marry Kamehameha's widow that the Garden Isle was joined to the rest of Hawai'i. That spirit lives on today as Kaua'i residents resist the lure of tourism dollars captivating the rest of the islands. Local building rules maintain that no structure may be taller than a coconut tree, and Kaua'i's capital city Līhu'e is still more small town than city.

Legends & Mythology: The Menehune

Although all of the islands have a few stories about the menehune—magical little people who accomplished great big feats—Kaua'i is believed to be their home base. The Menehune Fishpond, above Nawilwili Harbor, is a prime example of their work. The story goes that the large pond (initially 25 mi in diameter) was built in one night by thousands of menehune passing stones from hand to hand. A spy disrupted their work in the middle of the night, leaving two gaps that are still visible today (drive to the pond on Hulemalu Road, or kayak up Huleia Stream).

> **WORD OF MOUTH**
>
> "Another good stop is the Kīlauea Lighthouse and Wildlife Refuge. Incredible views! This really should not be missed. You can check out binoculars for free and scan the ocean and north shore. Lots of wildlife. There are many areas marked off for nesting birds. My boys really enjoyed discovering and quietly watching the chicks resting underneath the shrubs."
> —wtm003

THE NORTH SHORE & NĀ PALI COAST

The North Shore of Kaua'i includes the environs of Kīlauea, Princeville, Hanalei, and Hā'ena. Traveling north on Route 56 from the airport, the coastal highway crosses the Wailua River and the busy towns of Wailua and Kapa'a before emerging into a decidedly rural and scenic landscape, with expansive views of the island's rugged interior mountains. As the two-lane highway turns west and narrows, it winds through spectacular scenery and passes the posh resort community of Princeville before dropping down into Hanalei Valley. Here it narrows further and becomes a federally recognized scenic roadway, replete with one-lane bridges (the local etiquette is for five or six cars to cross at a time, before yielding to those on the other side), hairpin turns, and heart-stopping coastal vistas. The road ends at Kē'ē, where the ethereal rain forests and fluted sea cliffs of Nā Pali Coast Wilderness State Park begin.

Nā Pali Coast is considered the jewel of Kaua'i, and for all its greenery, it would surely be an emerald. After seeing the coast, many are at a loss

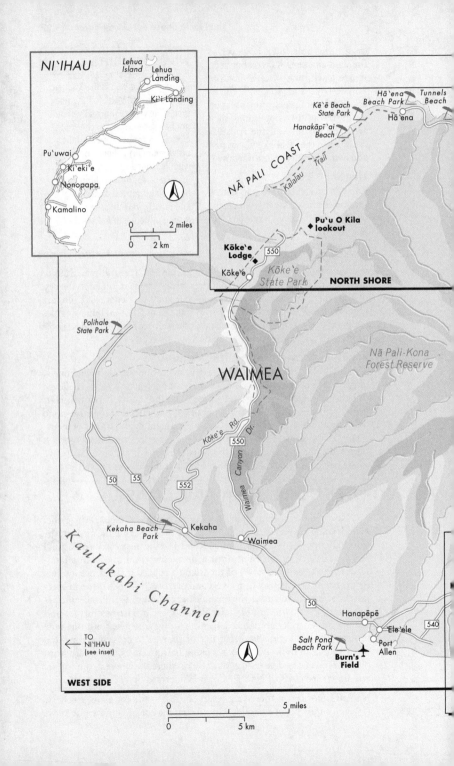

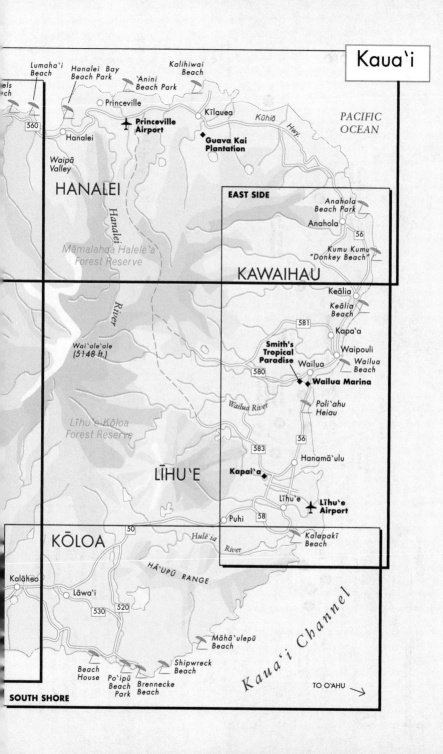

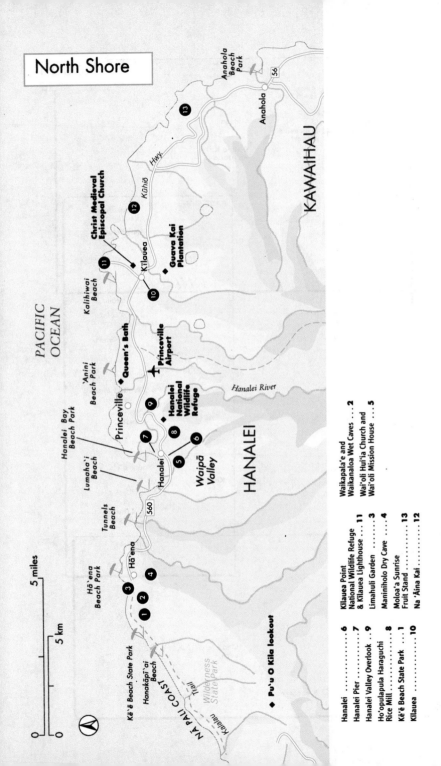

North Shore

PACIFIC OCEAN

KAWAIHAU

HANALEI

NA PALI COAST

Christ Medieval Episcopal Church

Guava Kai Plantation

Queen's Bath

Princeville Airport

Hanalei National Wildlife Refuge

Pu'u O Kila lookout

Kūhiō Hwy.

Hwy. 56

Anahola Beach Park

Anahola

Kīlauea

Kalihiwai Beach

'Anini Beach Park

Princeville

Hanalei Bay Beach Park

Lumaho'i Beach

Hanalei River

Waipā Valley

Hanalei

Tunnels Beach

560

Hā'ena

Hā'ena Beach Park

Kē'ē Beach State Park

Hanakāpi'ai Beach

Kalalau Trail

Wilderness State Park

5 miles

5 km

Hanalei 6
Hanalei Pier 7
Hanalei Valley Overlook .. 9
Ho'opulapula Haraguchi
Rice Mill 8
Kē'ē Beach State Park ... 1
Kīlauea 10

Kīlauea Point
National Wildlife Refuge
& Kīlauea Lighthouse ... 11
Limahuli Garden 3
Maniniholo Dry Cave ... 4
Moloa'a Sunrise
Fruit Stand 13
Na 'Āina Kai 12

Waikapala'e and
Waikanaloa Wet Caves ... 2
Wai'oli Hui'ia Church and
Wai'oli Mission House ... 5

for words, because its beauty is so overwhelming. Others resort to poetry. Pulitzer Prize–winning poet W.S. Merwin wrote a book-length poem, "The Folding Cliffs," based on a true story set in Nā Pali. "Nā Pali" means "the cliffs," and while it sounds like a simple name, it's quite an apt description. The coastline is cut by a series of impossibly small valleys, like fault lines, running to the interior, with the resulting cliffs seeming to fold back on themselves like an accordion-folded fan made of green velvet.

> **WORD OF MOUTH**
>
> "We did the stroll and ride tour [of Na 'Āina Kai Botanical Gardens], and it is just amazing. Hundreds of acres of tropical gardens, a formal garden, a desert garden, a children's garden, and throughout all of them, wonderful sculptures. We also saw two adolescent Albatross here!"   –daydreamin

In winter Kaua'i's North Shore receives more rainfall than other areas of the island. Don't let this deter you from visiting. The clouds drift over the mountains of Nā Molokama creating a mysterious mood and then, in a blink, disappear, and you're rewarded with mountains laced with a dozen waterfalls or more. The views of the mountain—as well as the sunsets over the ocean—from The Living Room, adjacent to the lobby of the Princeville Resort, are fantastic.

The North Shore attracts all kinds. It was once home, or so they say, to a mythical people, called Menehune. In the late 1960s, Howard Taylor, brother to actress Elizabeth Taylor, allowed a few men to camp on his property. They invited friends who invited more friends until the number reached well over 100 and the area became known as "Taylor Camp." Some lived in tents, others under tarps, a good number even built makeshift tree houses. Eventually, state officials bulldozed the camp. Today, the North Shore attracts the likes of Taylor's sister—Hollywood celebrities—and surfers. In fact, Andy Irons, three-time world surfing champion, grew up riding waves along the North Shore; when he's not traversing the globe in search of waves, he lives and surfs here.

Main Attractions

❻ **Hanalei.** Crossing the historic one-lane bridge into Hanalei reveals Old World Hawai'i, including working taro farms, poi making, and evenings of throwing horseshoes at Black Pot Beach Park—found unmarked (as most everything is on Kaua'i) at the east end of Hanalei Bay Beach Park. Although the current real estate boom on Kaua'i has attracted mainland millionaires building estate homes on the few remaining parcels of land in Hanalei, there's still plenty to see and do. It's *the* gathering place on the North Shore. Add restaurants, shops, and people-watching to the list here, and you won't find a single brand name, chain or big-box store around—unless you count surf brands like Quiksilver and Billabong. The beach and river offer swimming, snorkeling, Boogie boarding, surfing, snorkeling, and kayaking. Those hanging around at sunset often congregate at the Hanalei Pavilion where a husband-and-wife, slack-key-guitar-playing combo are longtime fixtures. There's an old rumor that the local newspaper, the *Garden Island*, quashed, that says Hanalei was the inspiration for the song *Puff the Magic Dragon* performed by the 1960s singing sensation Peter, Paul & Mary. Even with the newspaper's exposé, Hawai'i Movie Tours caps off their daylong visit of famous Kaua'i movie sites on the Hanalei Pier with a guide pointing out the shape of the dragon carved into the mountains encircling the town. ⊠ *Rte. 560, 3 mi north of Princeville Shopping Center.*

❾ Hanalei Valley Overlook. Dramatic mountains and a patchwork of neat taro farms bisected by the wide Hanalei River make this one of Hawai'i's most picturesque sights. The fertile Hanalei Valley has been planted in taro since perhaps AD 700, save for a century-long foray into rice that ended in 1960. (The historic Haraguchi Rice Mill is all that remains of the era.) Many taro farmers lease land within the 900-acre Hanalei National Wildlife Refuge, helping to provide wetland habitat for four species of endangered Hawaiian water birds. ⊠ *Rte. 56, across from Foodland, Princeville.*

⓫ Kīlauea Point National Wildlife Refuge & Kīlauea Lighthouse. A beacon for *FodorśChoice* sea traffic since it was built in 1913, this National Historic Landmark ★ has the largest clamshell lens of any lighthouse in the world. It's within a national wildlife refuge, where thousands of seabirds soar on the trade winds and nest on the steep ocean cliffs. Endangered nēnē geese, red-footed boobies, Laysan albatross, wedge-tailed shearwaters, white- and red-tailed tropicbirds, great frigatebirds, Pacific golden plovers (all identifiable by educational signboards) along with native plants, dolphins, humpback whales, huge winter surf, and gorgeous views of the North Shore add to the drama of this special place, making it well worth the modest entry fee. The gift shop has a great selection of books about the island's natural history and an array of unique merchandise, with all proceeds benefiting education and preservation efforts. ⊠ *Kīlauea Lighthouse Rd., Kīlauea* ☎ *808/828–0168* ⊕ *www.fws.gov/pacificislands/ wnwr/kkilaueanwr.html* ☞ *$3* ⊙ *Daily 10–4.*

⓭ Moloa'a Sunrise Fruit Stand. Don't let the name fool you; they don't open at sunrise. (More like 7:30 AM, so come here after you watch the sun rise elsewhere.) And it's not just a fruit stand. Breakfast is light—bagels, granola, smoothies and, of course, coffee (even espresso, cappuccino and latte) and tropical-style fresh juices (pineapple, carrot, watermelon, guava, even sugar cane). This is also a great stop to pick up sandwiches to go, although then you wouldn't enjoy the friendliness of Meow, the resident cat. Select local produce is always available, although not the variety as you'll find at the island's Farmers' Markets. What makes this fruit stand stand out is the fresh, natural ingredients like multigrain and spelt breads and nori as a wheat-free bread alternative. ⊠ *Just past mile marker 16 mauka on 56 Hwy* ☎ *808/822–1441* ⊙ *Mon–Sat 7:30–6 and Sun 10–6.*

★ ☾ ⓬ Na 'Āina Kai. One small sign along the highway is all that promotes this onetime private garden gone awry. Ed and Joyce Doty's love for plants and art now spans 240 acres, includes 13 different gardens, a hardwood plantation, a canyon, lagoons, Japanese Tea House, a Poinciana maze,

Views of the Kalalau Valley from Kalalau Lookout, Kōke'e State Park.

(top left) Naupaka, Limahuli Garden. (top right) Ficus carica roots.
(bottom) Sunset from Ke'e Beach.

(top) Mt. Waiʻaleʻale. (bottom) Sailing a 48-foot cruising yacht off the Nā Pali Coast North Shore.

(top) A surfer waits for a wave at sunset. (bottom) Windsurfing.

Queen's Bath near Princeville on the North Shore.

(top) Hawaiian sunset. (bottom) Waimea Canyon.

(top) Hula dancers. (bottom) Diver with a Hawaiian monk seal.

Hiker, Hanakapi'ai Valley, Nā Pali Coast.

waterfall, and a sandy beach. Throughout are more than 70 bronze sculptures, reputedly one of the nation's largest collections. Now a nonprofit organization, the latest project is a children's garden with a 16-foot-tall Jack and the Beanstalk bronze sculpture, gecko maze, tree house, kid-size train and, of course, a tropical jungle. Located in a residential neighborhood and hoping to maintain good neighborly relations, the garden limits tours (guided only). Tour lengths vary widely, from 1½ to 5 hours. Reservations strongly recommended. ⊠ *Rte. 56 north of mile marker 21, turn makai on Wailapa Rd. and follow signs* ☏ *808/828–0525* ⊕ *www.naainakai.org* ☏ *$25 for 1½-hr stroll to $70 for 5-hr hiking tour* ☉ *Tues.–Fri., call ahead for hours.*

Also Worth Seeing

★ ❶ **Kēʻē Beach State Park.** This stunning, and often overcrowded, beach marks the start of majestic Nā Pali Coast. The 11-mi **Kalalau Trail** begins near the parking lot, drawing day hikers and backpackers. Another path leads from the sand to a stone hula platform dedicated to **Laka**, the goddess of hula, which has been in use since ancient times. This is a sacred site that should be approached with respect; it's inappropriate for visitors to leave offerings at the altar tended by students in a local hula halau (school). Local etiquette suggests observing from a distance. Most folks head straight for the sandy beach and its idlyllic lagoon, which is great for snorkeling when the sea is calm. ⊠ *Drive to western end of Rte. 560.*

❿ **Kīlauea.** A former plantation town, Kīlauea town itself maintains its rural flavor in the midst of unrelenting gentrification encroaching all around it. Especially noteworthy are its historic lava-rock buildings, including **Christ Memorial Episcopal Church** on Kolo Street and the Kong Lung Company on Keneke Street, now an expensive shop. ⊠ *Rte. 56, 23 mile marker.*

OFF THE BEATEN PATH

GUAVA KAI PLANTATION – This 480-acre farm is one of the world's most productive guava plantations and a major player in the island's push toward diversified agriculture. That's surprising considering its low-key location in a country neighborhood. Wander around the orchard and then see how the fruit is processed into jellies, juices, marinades, and other goodies, all sold at the visitor center. ⊠ *North of mile marker 23 on Rte. 56; turn mauka onto Kuawa Rd., near Kīlauea, and follow sign* ☏ *808/828–6121* ⊕ *www.guavakai.com* ☏ *Free* ☉ *Daily 9–5.*

❼ **Hanalei Pier.** Imagine a white-tablecloth, candlelight dinner seemingly perched in the middle of Hanalei Bay. It could be your special celebration—wedding, anniversary, birthday. Built in 1892, the historic Hanalei Pier is a landmark seen from miles across the bay. During the day, kids use it as a diving board, fishermen fish, picnickers picnic. In 1957, the pier was featured in the award-winning movie *South Pacific.* Day or moonlight night, it's a treat. ⊠ *In Hanalei, turn makai at Aku Rd. and drive 1 block to Weli Weli Rd. Turn right. Drive to end of road, park and walk left to beach.*

❽ **Hoʻopulapula Haraguchi Rice Mill.** Rice once grew in the taro fields of Hanalei valley for almost 80 years—beginning in the 1880s and ending in the early 1960s. Today, its history remains in the form of the Haraguchi

Continued on page 42

NĀ PALI COAST: EMERALD QUEEN OF KAUA'I

If you're coming to Kaua'i, Nā Pali ("cliffs" in Hawaiian) is a major must-see. More than 5 million years old, these sea cliffs rise thousands of feet above the Pacific, and every shade of green is represented in the vegetation that blankets their lush peaks and folds. At their base, there are caves, secluded beaches, and waterfalls to explore.

The big question is how to explore this gorgeous stretch of coastline. You can't drive to it, through it, or around it. You can't see Nā Pali from a scenic lookout. You can't even take a mule ride to it. The only way to experience its magic is from the sky, the ocean, or the trail.

FROM THE SKY

If you've booked a helicopter tour of Nā Pali, you might start wondering what you've gotten yourself into on the way to the airport. Will it feel like being on a small airplane? Will there be turbulence? Will it be worth all the money you just plunked down?

Your concerns will be assuaged on the helipad, once you see the faces of those who have just returned from their journey: Everyone looks totally blissed out. And now it's your turn.

Climb on board, strap on your headphones, and the next thing you know the helicopter gently lifts up, hovers for a moment, and floats away like a spider on the wind—no roaring engines, no rumbling down a runway. If you've chosen a flight with music, you'll feel as if you're inside your very own IMAX movie.

Pinch yourself if you must, because this is the real thing. Your pilot shares history, legend, and lore. If you miss something, speak up: pilots love to show off their island knowledge. You may snap a few pictures (not too many or you'll miss the eyes-on experience!), nudge a friend or spouse and point at a whale breeching in the ocean, but mostly you stare, mouth agape. There is simply no other way to take in the immensity and greatness of Nā Pali but from the air.

⇨ *See Chapter 5 for helicopter-tour information.*

Helicopter flight over Nā Pali Coast

2

NĀ PALI COAST: EMERALD QUEEN OF KAUA'I

GOOD TO KNOW	WHAT YOU MIGHT SEE
Helicopter companies depart from the north, east, and west shores. Our advice? Choose your departure location based on its proximity to where you're staying.	▪ Nu'alolo Kai (an ancient Hawaiian fishing village) with its fringed reef
If you want more adventure—and air—choose one of the helicopter companies that flies with the doors off.	▪ The 300-foot Hanakāpī'ai Falls
Some companies offer flights without music. Know the experience you want ahead of time. Some even sell a DVD of your flight, so you don't have to worry about taking pictures.	▪ A massive sea arch formed in the rock by erosion
	▪ The 11-mile Kalalau Trail threading its way along the coast
Wintertime rain grounds some flights; plan your trip early in your stay in case the flight gets rescheduled.	▪ The amazing striations of a'a and pāhoehoe lava flows that helped push Kaua'i above the sea

IS THIS FOR ME?	
Taking a helicopter trip is the most expensive way to see Nā Pali—as much as $280 for an hour-long tour.	
Claustrophobic? Choose a boat tour or hike. It's a tight squeeze in the helicopter, especially in one of the middle seats.	
Short on time? Taking a helicopter tour is a great way to see the island.	

FROM THE OCEAN

Nā Pali from the ocean is two treats in one: spend a good part of the day on (or in) the water, and gaze up at majestic green sea cliffs rising thousands of feet above your head.

There are three ways to see it: a mellow pleasure-cruise catamaran allows you to kick back and sip a mai tai; an adventurous raft (Zodiac) tour will take you inside sea caves under waterfalls, and give you the option of snorkeling; and a daylong outing in a kayak is a real workout, but then you can say you paddled 16 miles of coastline.

Any way you travel, you'll breathe ocean air, feel spray on your face, and see pods of spinner dolphins, green sea turtles, flying fish, and, if you're lucky, a rare Hawaiian monk seal.

Nā Pali stretches from Ke'e Beach in the north to Polihale beach on the West Side. If your departure point is Ke'e, your journey will start in the lush Hanakāpī'ai Valley. Within a few minutes, you'll see caves and waterfalls galore. About halfway down the coast just after the Kalalau Trail ends, you'll come to an immense arch—formed where the sea eroded the less dense basaltic rock—and a thundering 50-foot waterfall. And as the island curves near Nu'alolo State Park, you'll begin to notice less vegetation and more rocky outcroppings.

⇨ *See Chapter 4 for more boat-tour information.*

(left and top right) Kayaking on Nā Pali Coast
(bottom right) Dolphin on Nā Pali Coast

2

NĀ PALI COAST: EMERALD QUEEN OF KAUA'I

GOOD TO KNOW	WHAT YOU MIGHT SEE
If you want to snorkel, choose a morning rather than an afternoon tour—preferably during a summer visit—when seas are calmer.	■ Hawai'i's state fish—the humuhumunukunukuapuaa—otherwise known as the Christmas wrasse
If you're on a budget, choose a non-snorkeling tour.	
If you want to see whales, take any tour, but be sure to plan your vacation for December through March.	■ Waiahuakua Sea Cave, with a waterfall coming through its roof
If you're staying on the North Shore or East Side, embark from the North Shore. If you're staying on the South Shore, it might not be worth your time to drive to the north, so head to the West Side.	■ Tons of marine life, including dolphins, green sea turtles, flying fish, and humpback whales, especially in February and March
IS THIS FOR ME?	
Boat tours are several hours long, so if you have only a short time on Kaua'i, a helicopter tour is a better alternative.	■ Waterfalls—especially if your trip is after a heavy rain
Even on a small boat, you won't get the individual attention and exclusivity of a helicopter tour.	
Prone to seasickness? A large boat can be surprisingly rocky, so be prepared.	

FROM THE TRAIL

If you want to be one with Nā Pali—feeling the soft red earth beneath your feet, picnicking on the beaches, and touching the lush vegetation—hiking the Kalalau Trail is the way to do it.

Most people hike only the first 2 miles of the 11-mile trail and turn around on Hanakāpī'ai Trail. This 4-mile round-trip hike takes three to four hours. It starts at sea level and doesn't waste any time gaining elevation. (Take heart—the uphill lasts only a mile and tops out at 400 feet; then it's downhill all the way.) At the half-mile point, the trail curves west and the folds of Nā Pali Coast unfurl.

Along the way you'll share the trail with feral goats and wild pigs. Some of the vegetation is native; much is introduced.

After the 1-mile mark the trail begins its drop into Hanakāpī'ai. You'll pass a couple of streams of water trickling across the trail, and maybe some banana, ginger, the native uluhe fern, and the Hawaiian ti plant. Finally the trail swings around the eastern ridge of Hanakāpī'ai for your first glimpse of the valley and then switchbacks down the mountain. You'll have to boulder-hop across the stream to reach the beach. If you like, you can take a 4-mile, round-trip fairly strenuous side trip from this point to the gorgeous Hanakāpī'ai Falls.

⇨ *See Chapter 5 for more Kalalau Trail hiking information.*

(left) Awaawapuhi mountain biker on razor-edge ridge
(top right) Feral goats in Kalalau Valley
(bottom right) Nā Pali Coast

2

NĀ PALI COAST: EMERALD QUEEN OF KAUA'I

GOOD TO KNOW

Wear comfortable, amphibious shoes. Unless your feet require extra support, wear a self-bailing sort of shoe (for stream crossings) that doesn't mind mud. Don't wear heavy, waterproof hiking boots.

During winter the trail is often muddy, so be extra careful; sometimes it's completely inaccessible.

Don't hike after heavy rain—flash floods are common.

If you plan to hike the entire 11-mile trail (most people do the shorter hike described at left) you'll need a permit to go past Hanakāpī'ai.

IS THIS FOR ME?

Of all the ways to see Nā Pali (with the exception of kayaking the coast), this is the most active. You need to be in decent shape to hit the trail.

If you're vacationing in winter, this hike might not be an option due to flooding—whereas you can take a helicopter or boat trip year-round.

WHAT YOU MIGHT SEE

- Big dramatic surf right below your feet

- Amazing vistas of the cool blue Pacific

- The spectacular Hanakāpī'ai Falls; if you have a permit don't miss Hanakoa Falls, less than ½ mile off the trail

- Wildlife, including goats and pigs

- Zany-looking ōhi'a trees, with aerial roots and long, skinny serrated leaves known as hala. Early Hawaiians used them to make mats, baskets, and canoe sails.

family whose antecedents threshed, hulled, polished, separated, graded and bagged rice in their 3,500-square-foot rice mill that was once demolished by fire and twice by hurricanes. Rebuilt to the exacting standards of the National Register of Historic Places, the mill is open today for tours on a very limited schedule. The family still farms—taro—on the onetime rice patties and also operates the Hanalei Taro & Juice kiosk in Hanalei town. Reservations required for tour. ✉ Located next to Kayak Kauai right as you enter Hanalei town 5-5070 Kuhio Hwy. ☎ 808/651–3399 ⊕ www.haraguchiricemill.org ✉ $65 ⊗ Sat. for tours only; kiosk daily 10–5 except Sun.

❸ **Limahuli Garden.** Narrow Limahuli Valley, with its fluted mountain peaks and ancient stone taro terraces, creates an unparalled setting for this botanical garden and nature preserve. Dedicated to protecting native plants and unusual varieties of taro, it represents the principles of conservation and stewardship held by its founder, Charles "Chipper" Wichman. Limahuli's priomordial beauty and strong mana (spiritual power) eclipse the extensive botanical collection. It's one of the most gorgeous spots on Kaua'i and the crown jewel of the National Tropical Botanical Garden, which Wichman now heads. Call ahead to reserve a guided tour, or tour on your own. Be sure to check out the quality gift shop and revolutionary compost toilet and be prepared for walking a somewhat steep hillside. ✉ Rte. 560, Hā'ena ☎ 808/826–1053 ⊕ www.ntbg.org ✉ Self-guided tour $15, guided tour $25 (reservations required) ⊗ Tues.–Fri. and Sun. 9:30–4.

❹ **Maniniholo Dry Cave.** According to legend, Maniniholo was the head fisherman of the Menehune, the possibly real, possibly mythical first inhabitants of the island. As they were preparing to leave Kaua'i and return home (wherever that was), Maniniholo called some of his workers to Hā'ena to collect food from the reef. They gathered so much that they couldn't carry it all, and left some near the ocean cliffs, with plans to retrieve it the following day. It all disappeared during the night, however, and Maniniholo realized that imps living in the rock fissures were the culprits. He and his men dug into the cliff to find and destroy the imps, leaving behind the cave that now bears his name. Across the highway from Maniniholo Dry Cave is **Hā'ena State Park.** ✉ Rte. 560, Hā'ena.

❷ **Waikapala'e and Waikanaloa Wet Caves.** Said to have been dug by Pele, goddess of fire, these watering holes used to be clear, clean, and great for swimming. Now stagnant, they're nevertheless a photogenic example of the many haunting natural landmarks of Kaua'i's North Shore. Waikanaloa is visible right beside the highway. Across the road from a small parking area, a five-minute uphill walk leads to Waikapala'e. ⊠ *Western end of Rte. 560.*

⑤ Wai'oli Hui'ia Church. Designated a National Historic Landmark, this little church—affiliated with the United Church of Christ—doesn't go unnoticed right alongside Rte. 560 in downtown Hanalei, and its doors are usually wide open (from 9 to 5, give or take) inviting inquisitive visitors in for a look around. Like the Wai'oli Mission House, it is an exquisite representation of New England architecture meets Hawaiian thatched buildings. During Hurricane 'Iniki's visit in 1992 which brought sustained winds of 160 mph and wind gusts up to 220 mph, this little church was lifted off its foundation but, thankfully, lovingly restored. Services held at 10 AM on Sundays with many hymns sung in Hawaiian. ⊠ *Located at 3mm on Hwy. 56* ☎ *808/826–6253.*

⑤ Wai'oli Mission House. This 1837 home was built by missionaries Lucy and Abner Wilcox. Its tidy New England architecture and formal koa wood furnishings epitomize the prim and proper missionary influence, while the informative guided tours offer a fascinating peek into the private lives of the island's first white residents. Half-hour guided tours are available. ■ TIP➜ **If no one is there when you arrive, don't despair; just ring the bell.** ⊠ *Kūhiō Hwy., Hanalei* ☎ *808/245–3202* ✉ *Donations accepted* ☉ *Tues., Thurs., and Sat. 9–3.*

THE EAST SIDE

The East Side encompasses Līhu'e, Wailua, and Kapa'a; it's also known as the "Coconut Coast," as there was once a coconut plantation where today's aptly named Coconut Marketplace is located. A small grove still exists on both sides of the highway. Mauka, a fenced herd of goats keep the grass tended; on the makai side, you can walk through the grove, although it's best not to walk directly under the trees. Falling coconuts hit hard. Līhu'e is the county seat and the whole East Side is the island's center of commerce, so early morning and late afternoon drive times (or rush hour) can get congested. (Because there's only one main road, if there's a serious traffic accident the entire roadway may be closed, with no way around. Not to worry; it's a rarity.) Continuing straight from the airport, the road leads to the middle of Līhu'e. To the left and right are fast-food restaurants, Wal-Mart, Kmart, Borders Books and Music—most recently a Home Depot, Costco, and Starbucks, too— and a variety of county and state buildings. The avid golfer will like the three golf courses in Līhu'e—all within a mile or so of each other.

Turn to the right out of the airport for the road to Wailua. A bridge— under which the very culturally significant Wailua River gently flows— marks the beginning of town. Wailua is comprised of a few restaurants and shops, a few mid-range resorts along the coastline and a housing community mauka. It quickly blends into Kapa'a; there's no real demarcation. Kapa'a houses the two biggest grocery stores on the island, side by side: Foodland and Safeway. It also offers plenty of dining options, breakfast, lunch, and dinner, and gift shopping. Old Town Kapa'a was once a plantation town, which is no surprise—most of the larger towns on Kaua'i once were—however this one didn't disappear with the sugar mill and pineapple cannery. Old Town Kapa'a is made up of a collection of wooden-front shops, some built by plantation workers and still run by their progeny today.

Main Attractions

㉖ Kaua'i Museum. Maintaining a stately presence on Rice Street, the historic museum building is easy to find. It features a permanent display, "The Story of Kaua'i," which provides a competent overview of the Garden Island and Ni'ihau, tracing the islands' geology, mythology, and cultural history. Local artists are represented in changing exhibits in the second-floor Mezzanine Gallery. The gift shop alone is worth a visit, with a fine collection of authentic Ni'ihau shell lei, feather hatband lei, handturned wooden bowls, reference books, and other quality arts, crafts, and gifts, many of them locally made. ⊠ *4428 Rice St., Līhu'e* ☎ *808/245–6931* ⊠ *$7* ⊙ *Weekdays 9–4, Sat. 10–4.*

㉘ Kipu Falls. For the truly adventurous, or perhaps voyeuristic, there's Kipu Falls, located on the private property of amazingly tolerant owners. It's rare to find these falls deserted; however, the throngs lining up to jump add to the excitement. Depending upon who you ask, the falls are 25 feet high, but if it's you standing up there, you might say higher. In addition to jumpers, there are swingers, too—those who opt for the rope swing. Both produce squealers and, of course, stallers. A dirt trail leads approximately one-half mile in length to the falls. ■ TIP→ **Wear water footwear when you jump to make climbing back up the cliff—usually supplied with an aluminum ladder by a tour outfitter—less painful.** ⊠ *From Hwy 50, at mile marker 3, turn makai onto Kipu Rd. Take the first right to stay on Kipu Rd. and drive one-half mile, park on side of road and follow dirt trail to falls.*

㋡ ㉓ Lydgate State Park. The park, named for the Reverend J. M. Lydgate, founder of the Līhu'e English Union Church, has a large children-designed and community-built playground, pavilion, and picnic area. It also houses the remains of an ancient site where commoners who broke a royal tabu could seek refuge from punishment. It's part of an extensive complex of sacred archaeological sites that runs from Wai'ale'ale to the sea, underscoring the significance of this region to the ancient Hawaiians. In recent years the community expanded the playground to include a bridge of mazes, tunnels, and slides. It's located a short walk or drive south of the main park, off Nehe Dr. ⊠ *South of Wailua River turn makai off Rte. 56 onto Leho Dr. and makai onto Nalu Rd.* ⊠ *Free* ⊙ *Daily dawn–dusk.*

★ ⑲ 'Ōpaeka'a Falls. The mighty Wailua River produces many dramatic waterfalls, and 'Ōpaeka'a (pronounced oh-pie-kah-ah) is one of the best. It plunges hundreds of feet to the pool below and can be easily viewed from a scenic overlook with ample parking. 'Ōpaeka'a means "rolling shrimp," which refers to tasty native crustaceans that were once so abundant they could be seen tumbling in the falls. ■ TIP→ **Just before reaching the parking area for the waterfalls, turn left into a scenic pullout for great**

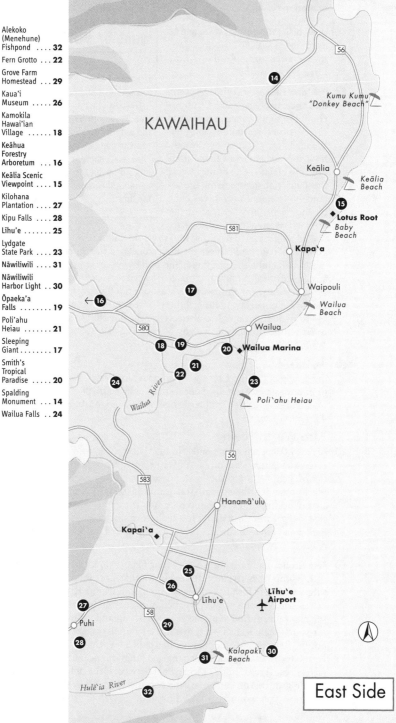

KAWAIHAU

Kumu Kumu
"Donkey Beach"

Keālia

Keālia
Beach

Lotus Root

Baby
Beach

Kapa'a

Waipouli

Wailua
Beach

Wailua

Wailua Marina

Poli'ahu Heiau

Wailua River

Hanamā'ulu

Kapai'a

Līhu'e

Līhu'e
Airport

Puhi

Kalapakī
Beach

Hulē'ia River

East Side

views of the Wailua River valley and its march to the sea. ⊠ *FromRte. 580, turn mauka onto Kuamo'o Rd., drive 1½ mi Wailua.*

㉑ **Poli'ahu Heiau.** Storyboards near this ancient *heiau* (sacred site) recount the significance of the many sacred structures found along the Wailua River. It's unknown exactly how the ancient Hawaiians used Poli'ahu Heiau—one of the largest pre-Christian temples on the island—but legend says it was built by the Menehune because of the unusual stonework found in its

WORD OF MOUTH

"'Ōpaeka'a Falls isn't quite as big/impressive as Wailua Falls, but it's just a short distance off the main highway and totally worth a quick stop. Friends of ours did a kayak trip to this waterfall and were able to swim around underneath it. They really enjoyed it, and I think that's probably the best way to experience this waterfall if you have the time."   –Erin 74

walled enclosures. From this site, drive downhill toward the ocean to **pōhaku hānau,** a two-piece birthing stone said to confer special blessings on all children born there, and **pōhaku piko,** whose crevices were a repository for umbilical cords left by parents seeking a clue to their child's destiny, which reportedly was foretold by how his cord fared in the rock. Some Hawaiians feel these sacred stones shouldn't be viewed as "tourist attractions," so always treat them with respect. Never stand or sit on the rocks, or leave any offerings. ⊠ *Rte. 580, Kuamo'o Rd., Wailua.*

㉔ **Wailua Falls.** You may recognize this impressive cascade from the opening sequences of the *Fantasy Island* television series. Kaua'i has plenty of noteworthy waterfalls, but this one is especially picturesque, easy to find, and easy to photograph. ⊠ *End of Rte. 583, Ma'alo Rd., in Kapai'a 4 mi from Rte. 56.*

Also Worth Seeing

㉜ **Alekoko (Menehune) Fishpond.** No one knows just who built this intricate aquaculture structure in the Hule'ia River. Legend attributes it to the Menehune, a possibly real, possibly mythical ancient race of people known for their small stature, industrious nature, and superb stoneworking skills. Volcanic rock was cut and fit together into massive walls 4 feet thick and 5 feet high, forming an enclosure for raising mullet and other freshwater fish that has endured for centuries. ⊠ *Hulemalu Rd., Niumalu.*

㉒ **Fern Grotto.** The Fern Grotto has a long history on Kaua'i. For some reason, visitors seem to like it. It's really nothing more than a yawning lava tube swathed in lush fishtail ferns 3 mi up the Wailua River. Or, at least, it was. Heavy rains in 2006 created mini rock slides crushing much of the plant life, although all the year-round sun and rain works wonders for plant life on Kaua'i—it grows like a baseball slugger on steroids. It's not the first time Mother Nature has paid a less-than-pleasant call; the Fern Grotto was significantly damaged after Hurricane 'Iniki and completely recovered. Smith's Motor Boat Services is the only way to legally see the grotto. You can access the entrance with a kayak, but if boats are there, you won't be allowed to land. ⊠ *Depart from Wailua Ma-*

rina on mauka side of Rte. 56, just south of Wailua River ⊠ *$15* ⊙ *Daily departures 9:30–3:30* ☎ *808/821–6892.*

㉙ Grove Farm Homestead. Guided **Fodor'sChoice** tours of this carefully restored 80-★ acre country estate offer a fascinating, and authentic, look at how upper-class Caucasians experienced plantation life in the mid-19th century. The tour focuses on the original home, built by the Wilcox family in 1860 and filled with a quirky collection of classic Hawaiiana. You can also see the workers' quarters, farm animals, orchards, and gardens that reflect the practical, self-sufficient lifestyle of the island's earliest Western inhabitants. Tours of the homestead are con-

WATERFALL WARNING

The many waterfalls on Kaua'i can be quite alluring; however, it's important we caution you to:

■ Evaluate water conditions before entering—do not enter a waterfall pool during or after heavy rains.

■ Never dive into the pool.

■ Remember the leptospirosis bacteria may be present in fresh water streams and pools.

■ Wear water-friendly shoes in the water; the rocks can be quite slippery entering and exiting the pool.

ducted twice a day, three days per week. To protect the historic building and its furnishings, tours may be canceled on very wet days. ■ TIP→ With a six-person limit per tour, reservations are essential and young children are not encouraged. Reservations required. ⊠ *Rte. 58, Nāwiliwili Rd., Līhu'e* ☎ *808/245–3202* ⊠ *$10* ⊙ *Tours Mon., Wed., and Thurs. at 10 and 1.*

⑱ Kamokila Hawai'ian Village. This village is dramatically located at the base of a long, winding and steep road right beside the Wailua River. Of course, in the days of King Kaumuali'i, there wasn't a road, just access by boat, and so it made the perfect hideout for his war canoes tucked away in this crook of the Wailua River. Today, there's a replica Hawaiian village in place of war canoes—numerous thatched-roof structures and abundant plant life. Yet, the lack of human activity here gives rise to a feeling of abandonment that may explain why Hollywood found it appealing for its movie "Outbreak." ⊠ *Turn mauka on Kuamoo Rd. in Wailua, drive 1½ mi, turn left across from 'Ōpaeka'a Falls* ☎ *808/823–0559* ⊠ *$5* ⊙ *9–5.*

⑯ Keāhua Forestry Arboretum. Tree-lined and grassy, this is a perfect spot for a picnic—there are numerous picnic tables scattered throughout the parklike setting. A shallow, cascading stream makes for a fun spot for kids to splash, although 6+ miles up the mountain from the ocean's edge, the water's a bit chilly here. A one-mile walking trail meanders through mango, monkeypod and eucalyptus trees. This is an exceptionally peaceful place—good for yoga and meditation—that is, unless the resident roosters decide to crow. ■ TIP→ If it looks like rain, do not follow the road across the stream; it often floods, leaving you stranded on the wrong side. ⊠ *In Wailua, take Kuamoo Rd. mauka 6.7 miles* ⊙ *Dawn to dusk.*

⑮ Keālia Scenic Viewpoint. Located between the 9mm and 10mm on Hwy 56 is this ocean overlook, perfect for spotting whales during their winter migration. In fact, on three Saturdays in winter, the Hawaiian Islands

Humpback Whale National Marine Sanctuary conducts its annual whale count from this spot, one of several around the island. If you packed them, bring your binoculars. ■ TIP→ **Make this stop when traveling north, as there is no left turn allowed for those cars traveling south into Kapa'a.**

🐢 ㉗ **Kilohana Plantation.** This estate dates back to 1896, when plantation manager Albert Spencer Wilcox first developed it as a working cattle ranch. His nephew, Gaylord Parke Wilcox, took over in 1936, building Kaua'i's first mansion. Today the 16,000-square-foot, Tudor-style home houses specialty shops, art galleries, and Gaylord's, a pretty restaurant with courtyard seating. Nearly half the original furnishings remain, and the gardens and orchards were replanted according to the original plans. You can tour the grounds for free; children enjoy visiting the farm animals. Horse-drawn carriage rides are available, or you can tour the old Grove Farm Plantation in a sugarcane wagon pulled by Clydesdales. Beginning the summer of 2006, a train now runs 2.5 mi through 104 acres of lands representing the agricultural story of Kaua'i—then and now. ⊠ *3-2087 Kaumuali'i Hwy., Rte. 50, Līhu'e* ☎ *808/245–5608* ⊙ *Mon.–Sat. 9:30–9:30, Sun. 9:30—5:30.*

㉕ **Līhu'e.** The commercial and political center of Kaua'i County, which includes the islands of Kaua'i and Ni'ihau, Līhu'e is home to the island's major airport, harbor, and hospital. This is where you can find the state and county offices that issue camping and hiking permits and the same fast-food eateries and big-box stores that blight the mainland. The county is seeking help in reviving the downtown; for now, once your business is done, there's little reason to linger in lackluster Līhu'e. ⊠ *Rtes. 56 and 50.*

㉛ **Nāwiliwili.** The commercial harbor at Nāwiliwili is a major port of call for container ships, U.S. Navy vessels, and passenger cruise lines. Anglers and recreational boaters use the nearby small boat harbor. This is the main departure point for deep-sea fishing charters. There's protected swimming at Kalapakī Bay, fronting the Marriott resort, although the water quality is questionable at times. With the recent increase in docking cruise ships, Anchor Cove Shopping Center and Harbor Mall have refurbished and offer a good selection of shops and restaurants. ⊠ *Makai end of Wa'apā Rd., Līhu'e.*

㉚ **Nāwiliwili Harbor Light.** On March 1, 1917, the U.S. Government purchased 3.2 acres surrounding this lighthouse from the Līhu'e Plantation Company for all of $8. When it comes to real estate, this could be the bargain of the century. As expected of any lighthouse location, this one is perched on a peninsula with views of the ocean spanning from the Nāwiliwili Harbor, down the rocky coast to Kīpū Kai and out to open ocean. The 2½ mile drive requires a 4WD vehicle and means it's not overrun. Good thing. Sunrises, moon rises, whalewatching, stargazing, boatwatching: You can't beat it. ⊠ *From airport entrance, go south on Rte. 51 for ½ miles. Turn left at stone wall entrance; there is a guard shack here but never any guards. Drive 2½ mi to lighthouse.*

⑰ **Sleeping Giant.** Although its true name is Nounou, this landmark mountain ridge is better known as the Sleeping Giant because of its resem-

SUNSHINE MARKETS

If you want to rub elbows with the locals and purchase fresh produce and flowers at very reasonable prices, head for Sunshine Markets, also known as Kaua'i's farmers' markets. These busy markets are held weekly, usually in the afternoon, at locations all around the island. They're good fun, and they support small, neighborhood farmers. Arrive a little early, bring dollar bills to speed up transactions and plastic shopping bags to carry your produce, and be prepared for some pushy shoppers. Farmers are usually happy to educate visitors about unfamiliar fruits and veggies, especially when the crowd thins. For more information, contact **Sunshine Markets** (☎ 808/241–6303 ⊕ www.kauai.gov).

North Shore. ⊠ *Waipa, mauka of Rte. 560 north of Hanalei after mile marker 3* ⊙ *Tues. 2 PM* ⊠ *Kīlauea Neighborhood Center, on Keneke St. in Kīlauea* ⊙ *Thurs. 4:30 PM* ⊠ *Hanalei Community Center* ⊙ *Sat. 9:30 AM.*

East Side. ⊠ *Vidinha Stadium, Līhu'e, ½ mi south of airport on Rte. 51* ⊙ *Fri. 3 PM* ⊠ *Wailua Homesteads Park, Wailua, turn mauka on Kuamo'o Rd., drive 2½ mi, turn right on Rte. 581/Olohena Rd., drive ½ mi* ⊙ *Tues. 3 PM* ⊠ *Kapa'a, turn mauka on Rte. 581/Olohena Rd for 1 block* ⊙ *Wed. 3 PM.*

South Shore. ⊠ *Ballpark, Kōloa, north of intersection of Kōloa Road and Rte. 520* ⊙ *Mon. noon.*

blance to a very large man sleeping on his back. Legends differ on whether the giant is Puni, who was accidentally killed by rocks launched at invading canoes by the Menehune, or Nunui, a gentle creature who has not yet awakened from the nap he took centuries ago after building a massive temple and enjoying a big feast. ⊠ *Mauka Rte. 56, about 1 mi north of Wailua River, backing Kapa'a.*

NEED A BREAK?

Stop in at **Lotus Root** (⊠ 4-1384 Kuhio Hwy, Kapa'a ☎ 808/823–6658), an offshoot of the wildly popular vegan restaurant Blossoming Lotus, for a healthy and yummy snack. The juice bar and bakery serves pizza by the slice, breakfast burritos, and the outta-this-world Cloud Nine, a juice concoction made with papaya, macadamia nuts, dates, coconut milk, and vanilla rooibos tea.

☺ ⑳ **Smith's Tropical Paradise.** Nestled up next to Wailua Marina along the mighty Wailua River, this 30-acre botanical and cultural garden offers a glimpse of exotic foliage, including fruit orchards, a bamboo rain forest, and tropical lagoons. Take the tram and enjoy a narrated tour or stroll along the mile-long pathways. It's a popular spot for wedding receptions and other large events, and its three-times-weekly lū'au is one of the island's oldest and best. ■ TIP→ **It's very difficult to make a northbound turn onto Kūhiō Highway from this road, so it's best to stop in when you're Līhu'e-bound.** ⊠ *Just south of Wailua River, mauka, on Rte. 56., Kapa'a* ☎ *808/821–6895* ⊕ *www.smithskauai.com* 🎫 *$5.25* ⊙ *Daily 8:30–4.*

⑭ **Spalding Monument.** The area just north of Kapa'a known as Keālia was once planted in sugar. Turn onto Keālia Rd. just after the 10mm for an off-the-beaten track 4½-mile scenic detour. Immediately on your right is a small post office and snack shop and on your left, rodeo grounds often in use on summer weekends. The road ascends and 2½ miles later, you'll reach a grassy area with the concrete remains of a onetime monument that bedecked the former estate of Colonel Zephaniah Spalding. It's a nice spot for a picnic or to simply gaze at the nearby grazing horses. If you're an early riser, this would make a great spot to watch the sun rise; if not, check the local newspaper for the next full moon and bring a bottle of wine. Continue on another 2 bumpy miles, and you'll reconnect with Hwy. 56 near the town of Anahola.

> **ROADSIDE VENDORS**
>
> Lei. Tropical flowers. Corn. Rambutan. Avocados. Huli huli chicken. Kalua pig. It's not uncommon to run across individuals selling flowers, produce and food on the side of the road. Some are local farmers trying to make a living; others are fundraising for the local canoe club. Don't be afraid to stop and buy. Most are friendly and enjoy chatting.

THE SOUTH SHORE

As you follow the main road south from Līhu'e, the landscape becomes lush and densely vegetated before giving way to drier conditions that characterize Po'ipū, the South Side's major resort area. Po'ipū owes much of its popularity to a steady supply of sunshine and a string of sandy beaches, although the beaches are smaller and more covelike compared to West Side beaches. With its extensive selection of accommodations, services, and activities, it attracts more visitors than any other region on Kaua'i. It's also attracting developers with big plans for the onetime sugar fields that are nestled in this region and enveloped by mountains. There are few roads in and out, and local residents are concerned about increased traffic.

Both Po'ipū and nearby Kōloa (site of Kaua'i's first sugar mill) can be reached via Route 520 (Maluhia Road) from the Līhu'e area. Route 520 is known locally as Tree Tunnel Road due to the stand of eucalyptus trees lining the road that were planted at the turn of the 20th century by Walter Duncan McBryde, a Scotsman who began cattle ranching on Kaua'i's South Shore. The canopy of trees was ripped to literal shreds twice—in 1982 during Hurricane 'Ewa and again in 1992 during Hurricane 'Iniki. And, true to Kaua'i, both times the trees grew back into an impressive tunnel. It's a distinctive way to announce, "You are now on vacation," for there's a definite feel of leisure in the air here. There's still plenty to do—snorkel, bike, walk, horseback ride, ATV tours, surf, scuba dive, shop, and dine—everything you'd want on a tropical vacation. From the west, Route 530 (Kōloa Road) slips into downtown Kōloa, a string of fun shops and restaurants, at an intersection with the only gas station on the South Shore.

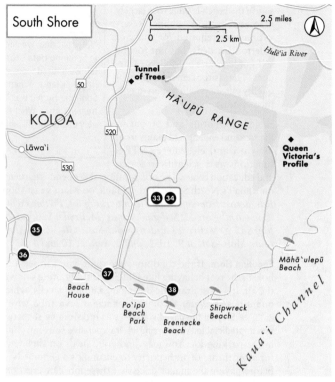

Main Attractions

③③ **Kōloa.** Hawai'i's lucrative foray into sugar was born in this sleepy town, where the first sugar was milled back in 1830. You can still see the mill's old stone smokestack. Little else remains, save for the charming plantation-style buildings that have kept Kōloa from becoming a tacky tourist trap for Poipu-bound visitors. The original small-town ambience has been preserved by converting historic structures along the main street into boutiques, restaurants, and shops. Placards describe the original tenants and life in the old mill town. Look for Kōloa Fish Market, which offers poke and sashimi takeout, and Progressive Expressions, a popular local surf shop. ⊠ *Rte. 520.*

③⑤ **National Tropical Botanical Gardens** (NTBG). Tucked away in Lāwa'i Valley, these gardens include lands and a cottage once used by Hawai'i's Queen Emma for a summer retreat. Visitors can take a self-guided tour of the rambling 252-acre **McBryde Gardens** to see and learn about plants collected from throughout the tropics. The 100-acre **Allerton Gardens,** which can be visited only on a guided tour, artfully display statues and water features that were originally developed as part of a private estate. A secluded cove known as Lāwa'i Kai can be reached through Allerton Gardens (only on tour, with no time for romping around in the sand); the beach is otherwise largely inaccessible to the public. Reservations are required for tours of Allerton Gardens, but not for the self-guided tours of McBryde Gardens. The visitor center has a high-quality gift shop with botany-theme merchandise.

WORD OF MOUTH

"After packing, we decided to go to Spouting Horn nearby. As we left we noticed more storm clouds in the distance. When we got to Spouting Horn it was "spouting" tremendously! What a show (probably due to the distant storms)!"
–CajunStorm

Besides harboring and propagating rare and endangered plants from Hawai'i and elsewhere, NTBG functions as a scientific research and education center. The organization also operates gardens in Limahuli, on Kaua'i's North Shore, and in Hāna, on Maui's east shore. ✉ *Lāwa'i Rd., across from Spouting Horn parking lot, Po'ipū* ☎ *808/742–2623* 🌐 *www.ntbg.org* 🎫 *Self-guided tour (McBryde) $20, guided tour (Allerton) $35* ⏲ *McBryde Gardens Mon.–Sat. 9:30—2:30, Allerton Gardens tours Mon.–Sat. at 9, 10, 1, and 2, Sun. at 10 and 1.*

36 **Spouting Horn.** If the conditions are right, you can see a natural blowhole in the reef behaving like Old Faithful, shooting salt water high into the air. It's most dramatic during big summer swells, which force large quantities of water through an ancient lava tube with great force. ■ TIP→ **Stay on the paved walkways as rocks can be slippery and wave action unpredictable.** Vendors hawk inexpensive souvenirs and other items in the parking lot. You may find good deals on shell jewelry, but ask for a certificate of authenticity to ensure it's a genuine Ni'ihau shell lei before paying the higher price that these intricate creations command. ✉ *At end of Lāwa'i Rd., Po'ipū.*

Also Worth Seeing

34 **Kōloa Heritage Trail.** Throughout the South Shore, you'll find brass plaques and all the details of 14 historical stops along a 10-mile route—bike it, hike it or drive it, your choice. You'll learn about Kōloa's whaling history, sugar industry, ancient Hawaiian cultural sites, the island's volcanic formation and more. Pick up a free self-guided trail map at most any shop in Kōloa Town.

38 **Po'ipū.** Po'ipū has emerged as Kaua'i's top visitor destination, thanks to its generally sunny weather and a string of golden-sand beaches dotted with oceanfront lodgings, including the Sheraton Kaua'i Resort and a half dozen condominium projects. More and more homes in the area are converting to private vacation rentals and B&Bs. (This trend across the island has created a shortage of affordable housing for residents.) Beaches are user-friendly, with protected waters for *keiki* (children) and novice snorkelers, lifeguards, clean restrooms, covered pavilions, and a sweet coastal promenade ideal for leisurely strolls. Some experts even rank Po'ipū Beach Park number one in the nation. That may be a bit of an overstatement, although it certainly does warrant high accolades. ■ TIP→ **In summertime don't be surprised to see a monk-seal mom and her pup on the beach here; the seals seem to like this beach as much as the visitors.** ✉ *Rte. 520.*

2

NEED A BREAK?	Stop in at **Brennecke's Beach Broiler** (⌧ 2100 Ho'ōne Rd., Po'ipū ☎ 808/742–7588). After a day at the beach, chill out with a mango margarita or "world famous" mai tai and a pupu platter from this longtime fixture on the beach in Po'ipū.

㉔ Prince Kūhiō Park. A triangle of grass behind the Prince Kūhiō condominiums honors the birthplace of Kaua'i's beloved Prince Jonah Kūhiō Kalaniana'ole. Known for his kind nature and good deeds, he lost his chance at the throne when Americans staged an illegal overthrow of Queen Lili'uokalani in 1893 and toppled Hawai'i's constitutional monarchy. This is a great place to view wave riders surfing a popular break known as "PKs," and to watch the sun sink into the Pacific. ⌧ *Lāwa'i Rd., Po'ipū.*

THE WEST SIDE

Exploring the West Side is akin to visiting an entirely different world. The landscape is dramatic and colorful: a patchwork of green, blue, black, and orange. The weather is hot and dry, the beaches are long, the sand is dark. Ni'ihau, a private island where only Hawaiians may live, can be glimpsed offshore. This is rural Kaua'i, where sugar is making its last stand and taro is still cultivated in the fertile river valleys. The lifestyle is slow, easy, and traditional, with many folks fishing and hunting to supplement their diets. Here and there modern industry has intruded into this pastoral scene: huge generators turn oil into electricity at Port Allen; scientists cultivate experimental crops of genetically engineered plants in Kekaha; the Navy launches rockets at Mānā to test the "Star Wars" missile defense system; and NASA mans a tracking station in the wilds of Koke'e. It's a region of contrasts that simply shouldn't be missed.

Heading west you pass through a string of tiny towns, plantation camps, and historical sites, each with a story to tell of centuries past. There's Hanapēpē, whose coastal salt ponds have been harvested since ancient times; Kaumakani, where the sugar industry still clings to life; Fort Elisabeth, from which an enterprising Russian tried to take over the island in the early 1800s; and Waimea, where Captain Cook made his first landing in the Islands, forever changing the face of Hawai'i.

From Waimea town you can head up into the mountains, skirting the rim of magnificent Waimea Canyon and climbing higher still until you reach the cool, often-misty forests of Kōke'e State Park. From the vantage point at the top of this gemlike island, 3,200 to 4,200 feet above sea level, you can gaze into the deep verdant valleys of the North Shore and Nā Pali Coast. This is where the "real" Kaua'i can still be found: the native plants, insects, and birds that are found nowhere else on Earth.

Main Attractions

㊺ Hanapēpē. In the 1980s Hanapēpē was fast becoming a ghost town, its farm-based economy mirroring the decline of agriculture. Today it's a burgeoning art colony, with galleries, craft studios, and a lively art-theme street fair on Friday nights. The main street has a new vibrancy enhanced by the restoration of several historic buildings. The emergence of Kaua'i

SIGHTSEEING TOURS

Aloha Kaua'i Tours. You get *way* off the beaten track on these 4WD van excursions. There's the half-day Backroads Tour covering mostly haul-cane roads behind the locked gates of Grove Farm Plantation. The full-day Aloha Kaua'i Tour starts with the Backroads tour and then spends the other half of the day covering the public roads along the Waimea Canyon. Another half-day tour, the Rainforest Tour, follows the Wailua River to its source, Mt. Wai'ale'ale. The expert guides are some of the best on the island. Rates are $70, $125 and $75, respectively. ⊠ *Check in at Kilohana Plantation on Rte. 50 in Puhi, Līhu'e* ☎ *808/245-6400 or 800/452-1113* ⊕ *www.alohakauaitours.com.*

Hawai'i Movie Tours. Hawai'i Movie Tours' minibuses with in-van TV monitors let you see the actual scenes of films while visiting the real locations used for the filming of *Jurassic Park, Raiders of the Lost Ark, South Pacific, Blue Hawaii, Gilligan's Island,* and other Hollywood hits. The standard coastal tour is $111. The four-wheel-drive Off Road Tour is $123 and takes you to film locations on private lands and rugged backcountry areas that are otherwise not easily visited. We recommend this tour primarily for serious movie buffs. ⊠ *4-885 Kūhiō Hwy., Kapa'a* ☎ *808/822-1192 or 800/628-8432* ⊕ *www.hawaiimovietour.com.*

Kaua'i Island Tours. A good general tour company, Kaua'i Island Tours will arrange charter tours around Kaua'i in anything from a passenger car to a 57-person bus. ☎ *808/245-4777 or 800/733-4777.*

Plantation Lifestyles Walking Tour. To see a rapidly vanishing lifestyle that once dominated life in Hawai'i, take the fascinating and unique Plantation Lifestyles Walking Tour through the residential area of a real mill camp in Waimea. Reservations are needed for the complimentary two-hour volunteer-led tour that also stops at other historical sites in Waimea and begins at 9:30 every Monday morning at the West Kaua'i Visitor Center. ☎ *808/338-1332.*

Roberts Hawai'i Tours. The Round-the-Island Tour, sometimes called the Wailua River–Waimea Canyon Tour, gives a good overview of half the island including Fort Elisabeth, 'Ōpaeka'a Falls, and Alekoko (Menehune) Fishpond. Guests are transported in air-conditioned, 17-passenger minivans. The $68 trip includes a boat ride up the Wailua River to the Fern Grotto, and a visit to the lookouts above Waimea Canyon. ☎ *808/245-9101 or 800/831-5541* ⊕ *www.robertshawaii.com.*

Robinson Family Adventures. Gay and Robinson, the island's last sugar grower, offers tours of its plantation and factory. You can go into the fields to hear about how cane is grown and processed into the white, granular stuff we eat so heartily, and you learn about the history of sugar in Hawai'i. One highlight is viewing scenic coastal areas otherwise closed to the public. Tours are offered weekdays at 8:45 and 12:45 for $34. ☎ *808/335-2824* ⊕ *www.gandrtours-kauai.com.*

Coffee as a major West Side crop and expanded activities at Port Allen, now the main departure point for tour boats, also gave the town's economy a boost. ⊠ *Rte. 50.*

★ ③⑨ **Kalalau Lookout.** At the end of the road, high above Waimea Canyon, Kalalau Lookout marks the start of a 1-mi (one-way) hike to **Pu'u o Kila lookout.** On a clear day at either spot you can look down at a dreamy landscape of gaping val-

WORD OF MOUTH

"If you go to the top [of Waimea Canyon], the last mile of the road is closed. We hiked it, about a mile, and were rewarded with an awesome Nā Pali coast view. If it is fogged in, wait five minutes for the clouds to clear off—you won't be disappointed!"   –daydreamin

leys, sawtooth ridges, waterfalls, and turquoise seas, where whales can be seen spouting and breaching during the winter months. If clouds obscure the spectacle, don't despair. They tend to blow through fast, giving you time to snap that photo of a lifetime before the next cloud bank drifts in. You may spot wild goats clambering on the sheer, rocky cliffs, and white tropic birds soaring gracefully on the thermals, their long tails streaming behind them. If it's very clear to the northwest, look for the shining sands of Kalalau Beach, gleaming like golden threads against the deep blue of the Pacific. ⊠ *Waimea Canyon Dr., 4 mi north of Kōke'e State Park.*

★ ④⓪ **Kōke'e State Park.** This 4,345-acre wilderness park is 4,000 feet above sea level, an elevation that affords you breathtaking views in all directions. You can gain a deeper appreciation of the island's rugged terrain and dramatic beauty from this vantage point. Large tracts of native ōhi'a and koa forest cover much of the terrain, along with many varieties of exotic plants. Hikers can follow a 45-mi network of trails through diverse landscapes that feel wonderfully remote—until the tour helicopters pass overhead. **Kōke'e Natural History Museum** is a great place to start your visit. The friendly staff is knowledgeable about trail conditions and weather, while informative displays and a good selection of reference books can teach you more about the unique attributes of the native flora and fauna. You may also find that special memento or gift you've been looking for. ⊠ *Rte. 550* ☎ *808/335–9975* ⊠ *Donations accepted* ☉ *Daily 10–4.*

NEED A BREAK?

There's only one place to buy food and hot drinks, and that's the dining room of rustic **Kōke'e Lodge** (⊠ Kōke'e State Park, 3600 Kōke'e Rd., mile marker 15 ☎ 808/335-6061 ☉ No dinner). They're known for their corn bread—of all things. Peruse the gift shop for T-shirts, postcards, or campy Kōke'e memorabilia.

Also Worth Seeing

★ ④③ **Fort Elisabeth.** The ruins of this stone fort, built in 1816 by an agent of the imperial Russian government named Anton Scheffer, are reminders of the days when Scheffer tried to conquer the island for his homeland, or so one story goes. Another purports Scheffer's allegiance to King Kaumuali'i in his hopeful attempts to regain leadership of his island nation from the grasp of Kamehameha the Great. The crumbling walls of the

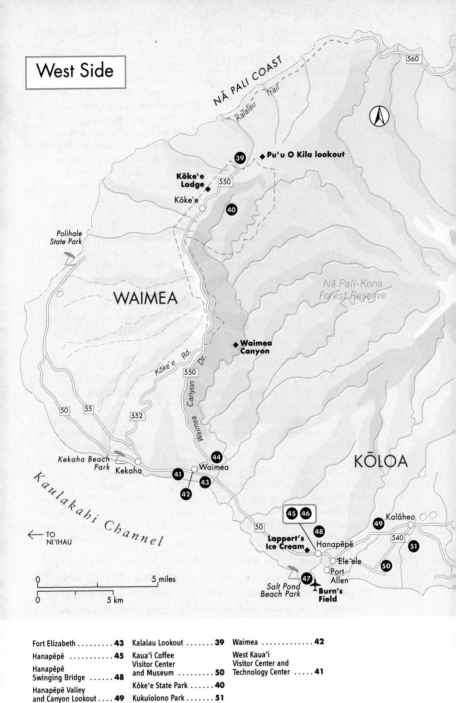

West Side

NĀ PALI COAST

Kalalau Trail

560

39 ◆ Pu'u O Kila lookout

Kōke'e Lodge

550

Kōke'e

40

Polihale State Park

Nā Pali-Kona Forest Reserve

WAIMEA

◆ Waimea Canyon

Kōke'e Rd.

550

Waimea Canyon Dr.

50 55

552

Kekaha Beach Park

Kekaha

44

41 Waimea

43

42

KŌLOA

Kalāheo

49

45 46

50

48

540

51

Kaulakahi Channel

Lappert's Ice Cream

Hanapēpē

'Ele'ele

50

← TO NI'IHAU

Port Allen

0   5 miles

0   5 km

Salt Pond Beach Park

47

Burn's Field

KAUA'I'S OWN GRAND CANYON

Fodor's Choice | Carved over countless centuries by the Waimea River and the forces of wind and rain, Waimea Canyon is a dramatic gorge nicknamed the "Grand Canyon of the Pacific"—and not by Mark Twain, as many people mistakenly think. Hiking and hunting trails wind through the canyon, which is 3,600 feet deep, 2 mi wide, and 10 mi long. The cliff sides have been sharply eroded, exposing swatches of colorful soil. The deep red, brown, and green hues are constantly changing in the sun, and frequent rainbows and waterfalls enhance the natural beauty. This is one of Kaua'i's prettiest spots, and it's worth stopping at both the **Pu'u ka Pele** and **Pu'u hinahina** lookouts. Clean public restrooms and parking are at both.

fort are not particularly interesting, but the informative placards are. ⊠ *Rte. 50, Waimea.*

NEED A BREAK? It's not ice cream on Kaua'i if it's not Lappert's. Guava, mac nut, pineapple, mango, coconut, banana—Lappert's is the ice cream capital of Kaua'i. Warning: Even at the factory store in Hanapēpē, the prices are no bargain. But, hey, you gotta try it. **Lappert's Ice Cream** (⊠ On Hwy. 50 mauka, Hanapēpē ☎ 808/335-6121).

48 Hanapēpē Swinging Bridge. It's not the biggest adventure on Kaua'i, but it's enough to make your heart hop just a bit. It's an historic suspension bridge—although not so historic anymore after it was rebuilt in 1996, because the original was destroyed—like so much of the island—by Hurricane 'Iniki. What is interesting is this bridge is not just for show; it actually provides the only access to taro fields across the Waimea River. If you're in the neighborhood, go for a walk. ⊠ *Located mauka in downtown Hanapēpē next to Banana Patch Studios' parking lot.*

49 Hanapēpē Valley and Canyon Lookout. This dramatic divide and fertile river valley once housed a thriving Hawaiian community of taro farmers, with some of the ancient fields still in cultivation today. From the lookout you can take in the farms on the valley floor with the majestic mountains as a backdrop. ⊠ *Rte. 50.*

46 Hanapēpē Walking Tour. This tour sounds very similar to the Kōloa Heritage Trail—proving good ideas are often imitated. This one, though, is purely a walking tour and much shorter—only 1½ miles in length. Look for 14 plaques with historic photos and stories mounted on buildings throughout Hanapēpē town. Businesses and shops in town sell the maps for $2; however, you can often pick one up for free in many of the area's promotional brochure rack stands. ⊠ *Hanapēpē town.*

50 Kaua'i Coffee Visitor Center and Museum. Two restored camp houses, dating from the days when sugar was the main agricultural crop on the Islands, have been converted into a museum, visitor center, and gift shop.

About 3,400 acres of McBryde sugar land have become Hawai'i's largest coffee plantation. You can walk among the trees, view old grinders and roasters, watch a video to learn how coffee is processed, sample various estate roasts, and check out the gift store. On the way to Waimea Canyon in 'Ele'ele, take Highway 50 and veer right onto Highway 540, west of Kalāheo. The center is 2½ mi from the Highway 50 turnoff. ⊠ 870 Halawili Rd. ☎ 808/335–3237 ⊕ www.kauaicoffee.com ☒ Free ☉ Daily 9–5:30.

> **COFFEE TO GO**
>
> For a reminder of Kaua'i throughout the year, Kaua'i Coffee offers a coffee-of-the-month club. You can choose your favorite brew or go for the flavor-of-the-month. If you're a big lover of the joe, you can even sign up for the twice-a-month-club.

51 **Kukuiolono Park.** Translated as "light of the god Lono," Kukuiolono has serene Japanese gardens, a display of significant Hawaiian stones, and spectacular panoramic views. This quiet hilltop park is one of Kaua'i's most scenic areas and an ideal picnic spot. There's also a small golf course. ⊠ Pāpālina Rd., Kalāheo ☎ 808/332–9151 ☒ Free ☉ Daily 6:30–6:30.

44 **Menehune Ditch.** Archaeologists claim that this aqueduct was built before the first Hawaiians lived on Kaua'i, and it is therefore attributed to the industrious hands of the legendary, tiny Menehune. The way the flanged and fitted cut-stone bricks are stacked and assembled indicates a knowledge of construction that is foreign to Hawai'i, and the ditch is inscribed with mysterious markings. Until someone comes up with a better explanation, the Menehune retain credit for this engineering feat. ⊠ Menehune Rd., Waimea Valley.

47 **Salt Pond Beach Park.** This popular park lies just west of some privately owned salt ponds where Hawaiians continue the traditional practice of harvesting salt (valued for its culinary and medicinal properties). They let the sun evaporate the seawater in mud-lined drying beds, then gather the salt left behind. You can't visit the ponds, but the beach park's protected swimming cove and campgrounds are worth a stop. ⊠ Lele Rd., Hanapēpē.

42 **Waimea.** Most recently Waimea was named to the national "Dozen Distinctive Destinations 2006" list, selected from 93 entries representing 39 states. This serene, pretty town has played a major role in Hawaiian history since 1778, when Captain James Cook became the first European to set foot on the Hawaiian Islands. Waimea was also the place where Kaua'i's King Kaumuali'i acquiesced to King Kamehameha's unification drive in 1810, averting a bloody war. The town hosted the first Christian missionaries, who hauled in massive timbers and limestone blocks to build the sturdy Waimea Christian Hawaiian and Foreign Church in 1846. It's one of many lovely historic buildings preserved by residents who take great pride in their heritage and history. The town itself has the look of the Old West and the feel of Old Hawai'i, with a lifestyle that's decidedly laid-back. Waimea beaches are sunny and sandy, but near-shore waters are often murky with runoff from the Waimea River. It's an ideal place for a refreshment break while sightseeing on the West Side. ⊠ *Rte. 50.*

㊶ West Kaua'i Visitor and Technology Center. Local photos and informational computers with touch screens bring the island's history and attractions to life. Weekly events include lei making, a walking tour, and a craft fair. Call for schedule. ⊠ *9565 Kaumuali'i Hwy. (Rte. 50), Waimea* ☎ *808/ 338–1332* ⊕ *www.wkbpa.org/visitorcenter* 🖃 *Free* ☉ *Daily 9:30–5.*

Beaches

WORD OF MOUTH

"The best activity, the one that comes to mind every time I think of Kaua'i, is sitting on a beach, relaxing, not having to be anywhere at a given time."   —daydreamin

"I'd say that the most secluded and romantic beaches are up in the North Shore. Poipu (South Shore) is a favorite of many people because it is sunny, but it is also much more developed compared to the North Shore, which is more mountainous/jungle-like.
                                              —NorCal_lo

Updated
by Kim
Steutermann
Rogers

ALTHOUGH KAUA'I IS NICKNAMED the Garden Island thanks to the abundance of rain falling near its center, draining mostly to the north, east, and south and creating lush rain forests and foliage that blanket those sides, she could just as easily be dubbed the Sandy Island. That's because Kaua'i has more sandy beaches per mile of coastline than any other Hawaiian island. Totaling more than 50 mi, Kaua'i's beaches make up 44 percent of the island's shoreline—almost twice that of O'ahu, second on this list. It is, of course, because of Kaua'i's age as the eldest sibling of the inhabited Hawaiian Islands, allowing more time for water and wind erosion to break down rock and coral into sand. But not all Kaua'i's beaches are the same. If you've seen one, you certainly haven't seen them all. Each beach is unique unto itself, for that day, that hour. Conditions, scenery, and intrigue can change throughout the day and certainly throughout the year, transforming, say, a tranquil lake-like ocean setting in summer into monstrous waves drawing internationally ranked surfers from around the world in winter.

There are sandy beaches, rocky beaches, wide beaches, narrow beaches, skinny beaches, and alcoves. Generally speaking, surf kicks up on the North Shore in winter and the South Shore in summer, although summer's southern swells aren't nearly as frequent or big as the northern winter swells that attract those surfers. Kaua'i's longest and widest beaches are found on the North Shore and West Side and are popular with beachgoers, although during winter's rains, everyone heads to the dry West Side. The East Side beaches tend to be narrower and have on-shore winds less popular with sunbathers, although fishermen abound. Smaller coves are characteristic of the South Shore and attract all kinds of water lovers year-round, including monk seals.

In Hawai'i, all beaches are public, but their accessibility varies greatly. Some require an easy ½-mi stroll, some require a four-wheel-drive vehicle, others require boulder-hopping, and one takes an entire day of serious hiking. And then there are those "drive-in" beaches onto which you can literally pull up and park your car. Kaua'i is not Disneyland, so don't expect much signage to help you along the way. One of the top-ranked beaches in all the world—Hanalei—doesn't have a single sign in town directing you to the beach. Furthermore, the majority of Kaua'i's beaches are remote, offering no services. ■ TIP→ **If you want the convenience of restrooms, picnic tables, and the like, stick to county beach parks.**

We've divided the island's best beaches into four sections in clockwise order: the North Shore, the East Side, the South Shore, and the West Side. We'll take you from the road's end on the North Shore to the road's end on the West Side, and a bit beyond. If you think of the island as a clock, the North Shore beaches start at about 11; the East Side beaches start around 2, the South Side beaches at 5, and the West Side beaches around 7.

THE NORTH SHORE

If you've ever dreamed of Hawai'i—and who hasn't—you've dreamed of Kaua'i's North Shore. *Lush, tropical,* and *abundant* are just a few words to describe this rugged and dramatic area. And the views to the

BEACH SAFETY ON KAUAʻI

Kauaʻi's waters are beguiling. The Pacific Ocean, despite its tranquil-sounding name, is a *real* ocean deserving real respect. Dangerous conditions can occur at any time of the year at any beach, even in normal surf conditions and under clear, sunny skies. Remember, not all beaches have lifeguards, and even those with lifeguard stands aren't necessarily staffed all day or even year-round. The Hawaiian Lifeguard Association recommends the following:

- Swim only when a lifeguard is present.
- Don't go swimming alone.

- Dive only in water you know is deep.
- Before swimming, always ask the lifeguard about water conditions.
- Watch for beach safety signs, and always heed them.
- If you're ever unsure whether the water is safe, don't go in.

We offer two additional tips:

- Never turn your back on the ocean.
- If lava rock boulders are wet, stay off them. Another wave may wash in and knock you down at a moment's notice.

---

sea aren't the only attraction—the inland views of velvety green valley folds and carved mountain peaks will take your breath away. Rain is the reason for all the greenery on the North Shore, and winter is the rainy season. Not to worry, though; it rarely rains *everywhere* on the island at one time. ■ TIP→ **The rule of thumb is to head south or west when it rains in the north.**

The waves on the North Shore can be big—and we mean huge—in winter, drawing crowds to witness nature's spectacle. By contrast, in summer the waters can be completely serene. The beaches below are listed in order—west to east—from Hanakāpīʻai to Kalihi Wai. ■ TIP→ **Remember to gear up before you head to the beach.** Try one-stop shopping at Ching Young Village in Hanalei, which has several stores that will fill your trunk with goodies such as snorkel gear, surf and body boards, beach chairs, umbrellas, snacks, coolers, and more.

BEACHES KEY

🚻	*Restroom*
🚿	*Showers*
🏄	*Surfing*
🤿	*Snorkel/Scuba*
👨‍👧	*Good for kids*
🅿	*Parking*

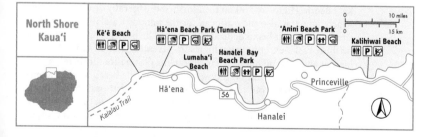

FodorśChoice   **Kalalau.** This oft-described Garden of Eden awaits the intrepid hiker
    ★   who traverses 11 arduous mi along sea cliff faces, through muddy
coastal valleys and across sometimes raging streams—all the while
schlepping food provisions and camping gear in a backpack. The trek
requires 6 to 10 hours of hiking, making it a serious adventure indeed.
With serious planning and preparation, the effort is worth it. Another
option is to paddle in to the beach—summers only, though. Otherwise,
the surf's way too big. The beach is anchored by a *heiau* (a stone platform used as a place of worship) on one end, and a waterfall on the
other. The safest hiking to and swimming at the beach takes place during the summer months when the rains abate, so the trail can dry out,
and when the North Shore's famous winter surf recedes, revealing an
expansive beach cupped by low, vegetated sand dunes and a large
walk-in cave on the western edge. Day hikes into the valley reveal waterfalls, freshwater swimming pools, and wild, tropical fruits, as well
as illegal campers forsaking society. Don't be mistaken: camping permits are required, although this beach and surrounding valley are famous for those on the lamb, including Ko'olau the Leper. In 1893, to
avoid sentence of exile in Kalaupapa, the leper colony on Moloka'i,
Ko'olau hid out in Kalalau until his death, evading for years the local
sheriff and troops shipped in from O'ahu. Located at the end of a trail
with the same name, Kalalau is a remote, wilderness beach along the
15 mi of the spectacular Nā Pali Coast, itself a 6,500-acre state park.
⊠ *Trailhead starts at end of Rte. 560, 7 mi west of Hanalei.*
⊕ *http://www.hawaii.gov/dlnr/dsp/NaPali/na_pali.htm* ⌖ *No facilities.*

FodorśChoice   **Hanakāpī'ai Beach.** If you're not up for the 11-mi haul to Kalalau Beach,
    ★   then hike 2 mi along Nā Pali Coast's Kalalau Trail to Hanakāpī'ai
Beach. It'll take about 1½ hours. Just don't get in the water. Ever. The
waters here are what locals like to call "confused." It has something to
do with the radical change in water depth and sheer cliff walls creating
wicked currents, rogue waves, backwash, undertow, cross waves, and
rip currents. Get the picture? Enjoy a picnic away from the ocean's edge.
In the winter when the surf eats up the beach, this might mean perch-
ing on the lava rock boulders backing the sand. To reach the beach, you'll
have to boulder-hop across the stream. During heavy rains or even just
after, the stream can flood, stranding hikers on the wrong side. This has
resulted in helicopter rescues, so don't cross unless the boulders are vis-
ibly exposed. ⊠ *Trailhead starts at end of Rte. 560, 7 mi west of
Hanalei.* ⊕ *http://www.hawaii.gov/dlnr/dsp/NaPali/na_pali.htm* ⌖ *No
facilities.*

Kē'ē Beach. Highway 560 on the North Shore literally dead-ends at this
beach, which is also the trailhead for the famous Kalalau Trail and the
site of an ancient heiau dedicated to hula. The beach is protected by an
offshore reef—except during high surf—creating a small sandy-bottom
lagoon and making it a popular snorkeling destination. If there's a current, it's usually found on the western edge of the beach as the incom-
ing tide ebbs back out to sea. Makana (a prominent peak also known
as Bali Hai after the blockbuster musical *South Pacific*) is so artfully
arranged, you'll definitely want to capture the memory, so don't forget

your camera. The popularity of this beach makes parking difficult. ■ TIP→ Start extra early or, better yet, arrive at the end of the day, in time to witness otherworldly sunsets sidelighting Nā Pali Coast. ☒ *End of Rte. 560, 7 mi west of Hanalei* ☞ *Toilets, showers, parking lot.*

★ **Hā'ena Beach Park Tunnels.** This is a drive-up beach park popular with campers year-round. The wide bay here—named Mākua and commonly known as Tunnels—is bordered by two large reef systems creating quite favorable waves for surfing during peak winter conditions. In July and August this same beach is usually transformed into lakelike conditions, and snorkelers enjoy the variety of fish life found in a hook-shape reef made up of underwater lava tubes, on the east end of the bay. ■ TIP→ **During the summer months only, this is the premier snorkeling site on Kaua'i.** It's not unusual to find a couple of food vendors parked here selling sandwiches and drinks out of their converted bread vans. ☒ *Near end of Rte. 560, across from lava-tube sea caves, after stream crossing* ☞ *Lifeguard, toilets, showers, food concession, picnic tables, grills/firepits, parking lot, camping.*

Lumaha'i Beach. Famous because it's the beach where Nurse Nellie washed that man out of her hair in *South Pacific,* Lumaha'i Beach's setting is all you've ever dreamed Hawai'i to be. That's the drawing card, and if you're adventurous and safety conscious, a visit here is definitely worth it. The challenges are that it's hard to find, there's little parking, and there's a steep hike in; also, too many people misjudge the waves, even those never intending to set foot in the water. There's a year-round surge of onshore waves, massive sand movements (especially around the river mouth), and a steep foreshore assaulted by strong currents. Like the mythical creature from the deep, rogue waves have actually washed up on lava rock outcroppings and pulled sightseers out to sea. ■ TIP→ **Lumaha'i Beach has the second-highest drowning rate on Kaua'i, behind Hanakāpī'ai.** Our advice: look from the safety of the scenic overlook or walk on *dry* sand only; play in the water at another beach. ☒ *On winding section of Rte. 560 west of Hanalei, east of mile marker 5. Park on makai side of road and walk down steep path to beach.* ☞ *No facilities.*

★ ☺ **Hanalei Bay Beach Park.** This 2-mi, crescent-shape beach surrounds a spacious bay that is quintessential Hawai'i. After gazing out to sea and realizing you have truly arrived in paradise, look landward. The site of the mountains, ribboned with waterfalls, will take your breath away. In winter Hanalei Bay boasts some of the biggest onshore surf breaks in the state, attracting world-class surfers. Luckily, the beach is wide enough to have safe real estate for your beach towel even in winter. In summer the bay is transformed—calm waters lap the beach, sailboats moor in the bay, and outrigger canoe paddlers ply the sea. Pack the cooler, haul out the beach umbrellas, and don't forget the beach toys, because Hanalei Bay is definitely worth scheduling for an entire day, maybe two.

BEST SWIMMING HOLES

You don't have to head to the beach to go swimming, and we're not talking chlorinated swimming pools, either. (There are enough beaches and swimming holes around Kaua'i that you should never have to set foot in chlorine.) But there's a difference between swimming in the ocean at the beach and swimming in these spots. These tend to be more remote, and—as the term *swimming hole* implies—they are enclosed. That doesn't mean they're safer than swimming in the ocean, with its possible rips and currents. Never dive—hidden boulders abound. Wear protective footwear—those boulders can have sharp edges. Stay away during or just after heavy rains and high surf. And, of course, always exercise caution.

Queen's Bath. Listen to us when we tell you not to attempt this in winter. This is one of those places where rogue waves like to roam; unfortunately, so do people. Several have drowned here during North Shore swells, so always check ocean conditions. During summer, this is an experience unlike many others around Kaua'i, as the winter surf recedes, revealing a lava shelf with two good-size holes for swimming—sometimes even snorkeling. Turtles cruise in and out, too, via an underwater entry. It's said that Queen Emma once bathed here; hence, the name. The trail down is short but steep; then there's a section of lava rock scrambling before you get to the swimming holes. Over the years, the county has periodically closed access for safety reasons and

because of residents' complaints. Access is in tony Princeville, amid private residences, so be sure to park only in the designated spot. If it's full, do not park on the street, and do not park on anyone's lawn, or driveway. ⊠ *In Princeville from Ka Haku Rd., turn makai on Punahele and right on Kapi'olani.*

Keāhua Forestry Arboretum. Not the deepest of swimming holes, this is, however, an excellent choice for families. The cascading stream makes for a fun spot for kids to splash. Stay away during heavy rains, as flash flooding does occur. ⊠ *In Wailua, take Kuamoo Rd. mauka 6½ mi.*

Kipu Falls. This is a swimming hole extraordinaire, because as well as swimming, the more adventurous will enjoy leaping off the 25-foot waterfall or entering the water via a swinging rope. Although this is on private property, the owners do not seem to mind. A dirt trail approximately ½ mi in length leads to the falls. From Highway 50, at mile marker 3, turn makai onto Kipu Road. Take the first right to stay on Kipu Road and drive ½ mi, park on the side of the road, and follow the dirt trail to the falls.

Uluwehi Falls. If you paddle upriver a couple of miles and hike a mile or so inland, you'll discover the 120-foot Uluwehi Falls, more commonly known as Secret Falls, with a big swimming area. Now, you could do this on your own—if you're familiar with the river and the trail; however, we recommend hiring one of the many Wailua River kayak guides, so you don't get lost.

■ TIP➔ **Take a walk on the pier. You'll feel like you're walking on water.**
✉ *In Hanalei, turn makai at Aku Rd. and drive 1 block to Weli Weli Rd. Parking areas are on makai side of Weli Weli Rd.* ☞ *Lifeguard, toilets, showers, picnic tables, grills/firepits, parking lot, camping.*

Pu'u Poa Beach. The coastline along the community of Princeville is primarily sea cliffs with a couple of pockets of beaches. The sea cliffs end with a long, narrow stretch of beach just east of the Hanalei River and at the foot of the Princeville Resort. Public access is via 100-plus steps around the back of the hotel; hotel guests can simply take the elevator down to sea level. The beach itself is subject to the hazards of winter's surf, narrowing and widening with the surf height. On calm days, snorkeling is good thanks to a shallow reef system pocked with sand. Sometimes a shallow sandbar extends across the river to Black Pot Beach Park, part of the Hanalei Beach system, making it easy to cross the river. On high surf days, the outer edge of the reef near the river draws internationally ranked surfers. The pool may be off-limits to nonguests, but the restaurants and bars are not. ✉ *Follow Ka Haku Rd. to end; park in public parking on right just before hotel's entrance; cross street for beach access.* ☞ *Parking lot.*

Pali Ke Kua Beach Hideaways. This is actually two very small pocket beaches separated by a narrow rocky point. ■ TIP➔ **Wear aqua socks or water shoes to cross.** The beach area itself is narrow and can all but disappear in wintertime. However, in summer, the steep, rocky trail that provides access reduces the number of beachgoers, helping to create a deserted beach feel. With patches of offshore reef and a combination sandy and rocky bottom, the swimming and snorkeling can be good, although winter's high surf can create dangerous conditions. ✉ *Follow Ka Haku Rd. to end; park in public parking on right just before hotel's entrance; follow dirt trail between parking lot and condominium complex.* ☞ *Parking lot.*

☺ **'Anini Beach Park.** A great family park, 'Anini is unique in that it features one of the longest and widest fringing reefs in all Hawai'i, creating a shallow lagoon that is good for snorkeling and quite safe in all but the highest of winter surf. The reef follows the shoreline for some 2 mi and extends 1,600 feet offshore at its widest point. During times of low tide—usually occurring around the full moon of the summer months—much of the reef is exposed. 'Anini is inarguably the windsurfing mecca on Kaua'i, even for beginners, and it's also attracting the newest athletes of wave riding: kiteboarders. On Sunday afternoons in summer, polo matches in the fields behind the beach park draw a sizable crowd. ■ TIP➔ **Try the Sara Special at the lone food vendor here—'Anini Beach Lunch Shak, which is really a lunch wagon.**
✉ *Turn makai off Rte. 56 onto Kalihi Wai Rd., on Hanalei side of Kalihi Wai Bridge; follow road left to reach 'Anini Rd. and beach.* ☞ *Toilets, showers, food concession, picnic tables, grills/firepits, parking lot, camping.*

> **WORD OF MOUTH**
>
> "For a beautiful beach with very calm waters I recommend 'Anini."
> –annahead

Kalihiwai Beach. A winding road leads down a cliff face to this picture-perfect beach. A jewel of the North Shore, Kalihiwai Beach is on par with Hanalei, just without the waterfall-ribbon backdrop. It's another one of those drive-up beaches, so it's very accessible. Most people park on the sand under the grove of ironwood trees. Families set up camp for the day at the west end of the beach, near the stream, where young kids like to splash and older kids like to Boogie board. This is also a good spot to disembark for a kayaking adventure up the stream. It's not a long paddle, but it's calm, so it's perfect for beginning paddlers. ■ TIP→ Haul in your own; there aren't any for rent on the beach. On the eastern edge of the beach, from which the road descends, there's a locals' favorite surf spot during winter's high surf. The onshore break can be dangerous during this time. During the calmer months of summer, Kalihiwai Beach is a good choice for beginning board riders and swimmers. ⊠ *Turn makai off Rte. 56 onto Kalihiwai Rd., on Kīlauea side of Kalihiwai Bridge.* ☞ *Toilets, parking lot.*

★ **Kauapea Secret Beach.** This beach went relatively unknown—except by some intrepid fishermen, of course—for a long time; hence, the common reference as "Secret Beach." That's easily understood once you stand on the shore of Kauapea with a solid wall of rock 100 feet high, maybe more, cupping the length of the beach and making it fairly inaccessible. For the hardy, there is a steep hike down the western end. Then, if you make the long trek across the beach—toward Kīlauea Point National Wildlife Refuge—and if you arrive just after sunrise, you may witness a school of dolphins just offshore. Usually, they're pretty inactive, resting before they head to deeper feeding waters. You'll also, no doubt, run across a gathering of another kind on the beach—nudists. Because of its remote location, Kauapea has become popular with nude sunbathers. ■ TIP→ Remember, nudity is illegal in Hawai'i. ⊠ *Turn makai on Kalihiwai Rd. just past the turnoff for Kīlauea; take second dirt road to its end; park and follow dirt trail.* ☞ *Parking lot.*

Kāhili Beach. You wouldn't know it today, but Kīlauea Bay was once an interisland steamer landing and a rock quarry. Today, it's a fairly quiet beach, although when the surf closes out many other North Shore breaks, Rock Quarry, directly offshore Kīlauea Stream near the abandoned quarry, is still rideable. For the regular oceangoer, summer's your best bet, although the quickly sloping ocean bottom doesn't make for great snorkeling. The stream estuary is quite beautiful, and the ironwood trees and false kamani growing in the generous sand dunes at the rear of the beach provide protection from the sun. In March 2006, the streambed emptying into the ocean here grew to immense proportion, taking life and property with it, when Ka Loko dam broke, sending a wall of water some say 40 feet high to the sea. ⊠ *Turn makai on Wailapa Rd.; stay to the left at "Y" and follow dirt road to its end.* ☞ *No facilities.*

Larsen's Beach. The long, wide fringing reef offshore is this beach's trademark. Although the waters nearshore are often shallow—too shallow for swimming—the snorkeling can oftentimes be exquisite. ■ TIP→ Wear a rash guard, so you don't scrape your belly! Also, don't touch the prickly

sea urchins. Like many North Shore beaches, this one requires a hike, although it's not as steep as others. ✉ *Turn makai at the north intersection of Koʻlau Rd., drive 1¼ mi to dirt turnoff on left marked with a slender pole and yellow letters "beach access." Park at end of Rd.* ☞ *Parking lot.*

THE EAST SIDE

3

The East Side of the island is considered the "windward" side, a term you'll often hear in weather forecasts. It simply means the side of the island receiving onshore winds. The wind helps break down rock into sand, so there are plenty of beaches here. Unfortunately, only a few of those beaches are protected, so many are not ideal for beginning ocean-goers, though they are perfect for long sunrise ambles. On superwindy days, kite boarders sail along the east shore, sometimes jumping waves and performing acrobatic maneuvers in the air.

The beaches below are listed in order from Keālia in the north to Kalapakī in the south. ■ TIP→ Fill your cooler with sandwiches and drinks at Safeway or Foodland in Kapaʻa before you hit the sand. Snorkel and other beach gear is available at Seasport Divers, Snorkel Bob's, and Play Dirty, among others.

ʻAliomanu Beach. Because of the time change, most visitors to Hawaiʻi awake before the sun rises. Great. Head to the easily accessible and lesser-known ʻAliomanu Beach for a long morning walk and witness that great, orange orb emerging over the ocean's horizon. The waters off ʻAliomanu Beach are protected by the fringing reef 100 yards or so out to sea, making snorkeling as good as many more-popular areas; however, currents can be tricky, especially near the stream tucked in the beach's elbow toward the northern end and at the river mouth on the southern end that demarcates ʻAliomanu Beach from its neighbor Anahola Beach. Start at the river mouth and head north, skirting a seawall midway; aqua shoes are recommended, especially for rounding the rocky point at the northern tip. ■ TIP→ With its shallow waters, this is a popular fishing and family beach, so stick to weekdays if you want quiet, as weekends—especially holidays—draw entire families, complete with dogs, tents, fishing gear, portable grills, and sometimes even portable toilets. ✉ *Turn makai just north of mile marker 14 on ʻAliomanu Rd.; park in dirt parking lot where road bends 90 degrees to the left.* ☞ *Parking lot.*

Anahola Beach Park. Anahola is known as the most Hawaiian of all communities on Kauaʻi, so Anahola Beach Park is definitely a locals' hangout, especially for families with small children. A child's first birthday is considered a big bash (including rented tents, picnic tables, and catered lūʻau food) for family and friends in Hawaiʻi, and this is a popular location for the celebration. The shallow and calm water at the beach road's end is tucked behind a curving finger of land and perfect for young ones. As the beach winds closer to the river mouth, there is less protection and a shore break favorable for Boogie boarders if the trades are light or kona winds are present. Children like to frolic in the river, and pole fishermen often set up at the river mouth. On Tuesdays and Thurs-

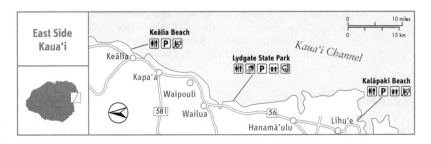

days at 5 PM Puna Dawson's hula hālau meets and welcomes visitors to watch and participate. The sunrise view of Kalalea Mountains with the Anahola River trailing in front of it makes for a good photographic opportunity. ■ TIP→ **During summers, this beach practically turns into a tent community, feeling a bit crowded.** ⊠ *Turn makai just south of mile marker 14 on Anahola Rd. and drive .7 mi.* ☞ *Toilets, showers, picnic tables, grills/firepits, parking lot, camping.*

Donkey Beach. This beach has one of the most unusual names of all on Kaua'i and rarely known by its proper Hawai'ian name, Palikū. Līh'ue Plantation Company kept a herd of mules and donkeys in the pasture adjacent to the beach and used the herd to haul bundles of seed cane and bags of fertilizer through the sugarcane fields, which gave the beach its nickname. It's a popular spot for au naturel sunbathers, and during certain conditions, body boarders and surfers might be spotted offshore. However, the waters here are rough and not recommended for swimming and snorkeling. Instead, we recommend a morning sunrise walk or mountain biking along the easy trail that overlooks the beach. Start at the northern end of Keālia Beach (or in Kapaa town for a longer walk or bike ride) and head north. The trail splinters just past Donkey Beach and then splinters again; however, it does go all the way to Anahola Beach. ■ TIP→ **When you're not sure which fork to take, that's a good sign to turn around or wind up lost in paradise.** ⊠ *Just north of Keālia Kai subdivision entrance on Rte. 56, turn makai into parking lot. Hike down to beach.* ☞ *Parking lot.*

Keālia Beach. A half mile long and adjacent to the highway heading north out of Kapa'a, Keālia Beach attracts body boarders and surfers year-round (possibly because the local high school is just up the hill). Keālia is not generally a great beach for swimming or snorkeling. The waters are usually rough and the waves crumbly because of an onshore break (no protecting reef) and northeasterly trade winds. A scenic lookout on the southern end, accessed off the highway, is a superb location for saluting the morning sunrise or spotting whales during winter. A level dirt road follows the coastline north and is one of the most scenic coastal trails on the island for walking, running, and biking. ■ TIP→ **A local family opened a snack and surf shop across the highway, perfect for a beach break or to rent boards. The toilets here are the portable kind, by the lifeguard stand.** ⊠ *At mile marker 10 on Rte. 56* ☞ *Lifeguard, toilets, parking lot.*

☾ **Baby Beach.** There aren't many swimming beaches on Kaua'i's East Side; however, this one usually ranks highly with mothers of small children, because there's a narrow lagoonlike area between the beach and the near-shore reef perfect for small children. Of course, in winter, watch for east and northeast swells that would not make this such a safe option. There are no beach facilities—no lifeguards, so watch your babies. ⊠ *In Kapaʻa, turn mauka at the Chevron Gas Station onto Keaka Rd, then left on Moamakai Rd. Parking is off-street between Makaha and Panihi Rds.*

Wailua Beach. Some say the first Polynesians to migrate to Hawaiʻi landed at Wailua Beach. At the river's mouth, petroglyphs carved on boulders are sometimes visible during low surf and tide conditions. Surfers, body boarders, and bodysurfers alike enjoy this beach year-round thanks to its dependable waves (usually on the north end); however, thanks to Hawaiʻi's dependable northeast trade winds, these waves are not the "cleanest" for surf aficionados. Many families spend the day under the Wailua Bridge at the river mouth, even hauling out their portable grills and tables to go with their beach chairs. During summer months, outrigger canoe races are often held on the river, which happens to be the largest in all Hawaiʻi. Numerous tour outfitters offer kayaking and hiking expeditions up the river. There are even water-skiing boats for hire and, more popular, twice-hourly tour boats running to the Fern Grotto, an amphitheater-shape cave with perfect acoustics and, as the name implies, ferns growing everywhere, even from the ceiling of the cave. The great news about Wailua Beach is that it's almost impossible to miss; however, parking can be a challenge. ⊠ *The best parking for the north end of the beach is on Papaloa Rd. behind the Shell station. For the southern end of the beach, the best parking is in the Wailua River State Park; to get there, turn mauka on Kuamoʻo Rd. and left into the park, then walk along the river and under the bridge.* ☞ *Lifeguard, toilets, showers, parking lot.*

🕑 **Lydgate State Park.** This is hands down the best family beach park on Kauaʻi. The waters off the beach are protected by a hand-built breakwater creating two boulder-enclosed saltwater pools for safe swimming and snorkeling just about year-round. The smaller of the two is perfect for *keiki* (children). Behind the beach is Kamalani Playground, designed by the children of Kauaʻi and built by the community. Children of all ages—that includes you—enjoy the swings, lava-tube slides, tree house, and more. Picnic tables abound in the park, and a large covered pavilion is available by permit for celebrations. Recently, Kamalani Bridge was built, again by the community and again based on the children's design, as a second playground south of the original. (The two are united by a walking path that will someday go all the way to Anahola Beach Park.) A second, smaller pavilion is the newest addition to the park—built near the bridge—and is surrounded by campsites, perfect for group outings. ■ TIP→ **This park is perennially popular; the quietest times to visit are early mornings and weekdays. If you want to witness a "baby lūʻau," Lydgate State Park attracts them year-round, especially in summers.** ⊠ *Just south of Wailua River, turn makai off Rte. 56 onto Lehu Dr. and left onto Nalu Rd.* ☞ *Lifeguard, toilets, showers, picnic tables, grills/firepits, playground, parking lot, camping.*

🕒 **Kalapakī Beach.** Five minutes south of the airport in Līhu‘e, you'll find this wide, sandy-bottom beach fronting the Kaua‘i Marriott. One of the big attractions is that this beach is almost always safe from rip currents and undertow because it's situated around the backside of a peninsula, in its own cove. There are tons of activities here, including all the usual water sports—beginning and intermediate surfing, body boarding, body-surfing, and swimming—plus, there are two outrigger canoe clubs paddling in the bay and the Nāwiliwili Yacht Club's boats sailing around the harbor. Kalapakī is the only place on Kaua‘i where sailboats—in this case Hobie Cats—are available for rent (at Kaua‘i Beach Boys, which fronts the beach next to Duke's Canoe Club restaurant). Visitors can also rent snorkel gear, surfboards, body boards, and kayaks from Kaua‘i Beach Boys. A volleyball court on the beach is often used by a loosely organized group of local players; visitors are always welcome. ■ TIP➔ **Families prefer the stream end of the beach, whereas those seeking more solitude will prefer the cliff side of the beach.** Duke's Canoe Club restaurant is one of only a couple of restaurants on the island actually on a beach; the restaurant's lower level is casual, even welcoming beach attire and sandy feet, perfect for lunch or an afternoon cocktail. ⊠ *Off Wapa‘a Rd., which runs from Līhu‘e to Nāwiliwili* ⌇ *Toilets, food concession, picnic tables, grills/firepits, playground, parking lot.*

THE SOUTH SHORE

The South Shore's primary access road is Highway 520, a tree-lined, two-lane, windy road. As you drive along it, there's a sense of tunneling down a rabbit hole into another world, à la Alice. And the South Shore is certainly a wonderland. On average, it rains only 30 inches per year, so if you're looking for fun in the sun, this is a good place to start. The beaches with their powdery-fine sand are consistently good year-round, except during high surf, which, if it hits at all, will be in summer. If you want solitude, this isn't it; if you want excitement—well, as much excitement as quiet Kaua‘i offers—this is the place for you.

The beaches below are listed in order from Māhā‘ulepū west to Po‘ipū Beach Park. ■ TIP➔ **The best places to gear up for the beach are Nukumoi Surf Co. across from Po‘ipū Beach, and Seasport Divers at the junction to Spouting Horn on Po‘ipū Road.**

Māhā‘ulepū Beach. This 2-mi stretch of coast with its sand dunes, limestone hills, sinkholes, and caves is unlike any other on Kaua‘i. Remains of a large, ancient settlement, evidence of great battles, and the discovery of a now-underwater petroglyph field indicate that Hawaiians lived in this area as early as 700 AD. ■ TIP➔ **Māhā‘ulepū's coastline is unprotected and rocky, which makes venturing into the ocean hazardous.** There are three beach areas with bits of sandy-bottom swimming; however, we think the best way to experience Māhā‘ulepū is simply to roam, especially at sunrise. ■ TIP➔ **Access to this beach is via private property. The owner allows access during daylight hours, but be sure to depart before sunset or risk getting locked in for the night.** ⊠ *Continue on Po‘ipū Rd. past Hyatt Regency (it turns into dirt road) to T-intersection and turn makai; road ends at beach parking area.* ⌇ *Parking lot.*

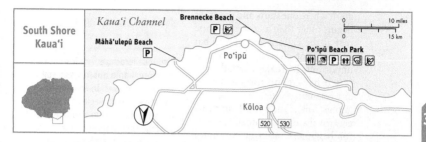

Keoniloa Beach. Few except the public relations specialists at the Hyatt Regency Kauai Resort and Spa—which backs the beach—refer to this beach by anything other than its common name: Shipwreck Beach. Its Hawaiian name means "long beach." Both give it meaning. It is a long stretch of crescent-shape beach punctuated by cliffs on both ends, and, yes, a ship was once wrecked here. With its onshore break, the waters off Shipwreck are best for body boarding and bodysurfing; however, the beach itself is plenty big for sunbathing, sand castle–building, Frisbee, and other beach-related fun. Fishermen pole fish from shore and off the cliff and sometimes pick opihi (limpets) off the rocks lining the foot of the cliffs. The eastern edge of the beach is the start of an interpretive dune walk (complimentary) held by the hotel staff every other Monday; check with the concierge for dates and times. ⊠ *Continue on Poʻipū Rd. past Hyatt Regency, turn makai on ʻAinako Rd.* ☞ *Parking lot.*

Brennecke Beach. There's little beach here on the eastern end of Poʻipū Beach Park, but Brennecke Beach is synonymous on the island with board and body surfing, thanks to its shallow sandbar and reliable shore break. Because the beach is small and often congested, surfboards are prohibited nearshore. The water on the rocky eastern edge of the beach is a good place to see the endangered green sea turtles noshing on plants growing on the rocks. ⊠ *Turn makai off Poʻipū Rd. onto Hoʻowili Rd., then left onto Hoʻōne Rd.; beach is at intersection with Kuai Rd.* ☞ *Food concession, parking lot.*

Poʻipū Beach Park. The most popular beach on the South Side, and perhaps on all of Kauaʻi, is Poʻipū Beach Park. The snorkeling's good, the body boarding's good, the surfing's good, the swimming's good, and the fact that the sun is almost always shining is good, too. The beach can be crowded at times, especially on weekends and holidays, but that just makes people-watching that much more fun. You'll see keiki experiencing the ocean for the first time, snorkelers trying to walk with their flippers on, ʻukulele players, birthday party revelers, young and old, visitors and locals. Even the endangered Hawaiian monk seal may make an appearance. ⊠ *From Poʻipū Rd., turn right on Hoʻōne Rd.* ☞ *Lifeguard, toilets, showers, food, picnic tables, grills/firepits, playground, parking lot.*

FodorsChoice
★

Waiʻohai Beach. The first hotel built in Poʻipū in 1962 overlooked this beach, adjacent to Poʻipū Beach Park. Actually, there's little to distinguish where one starts and the other begins other than a crescent-shape reef at the eastern end of Wai'hai Beach. That crescent, however, is important. It creates a small, protected bay—good for snorkeling and beginning surfers. If you're a beginner, this is the spot. Don't forget: we always recommend lessons for beginners. Stop in Nukumoi Surf Shop next to Brennecke's Restaurant if you don't see any instructors lurking around the beach. However, when a summer swell kicks up, the nearshore conditions become dangerous; offshore, there's a splendid surf break for experienced surfers. The beach itself is narrow and, like its neighbor, gets very crowded in summer. ⊠ *From Po'ipū Rd., turn right on Ho'ōne Rd.* ☞ *Parking lot.*

KAUA'I CAVE WOLF SPIDER

It sounds ferocious, but it's nothing more than a quarter-size spider—without eyes. In fact, it's on the endangered species list and known to live only in a couple of underground—dark—caves in the Kōloa region of south Kaua'i, and nowhere else in the world. In recent years, scientists reported spotting baby spiderlings of this unusual species, so there's hope for its survival; however, its habitat is under threat of development. Interestingly, the cave wolf spider's prey—the shrimplike Kaua'i cave amphipod—is also on the endangered species list and also eyeless.

Beach House Beach. Don't pack the beach umbrella, beach mats, and cooler for this one. Just your snorkel gear. The beach, named after its neighbor the Beach House restaurant and on the road to Spouting Horn, is a small slip of sand during low tide and a rocky shoreline during high; however, it is conveniently located by the road's edge, and its rocky coastline and somewhat rocky bottom make it great for snorkeling. (As a rule, sandy-bottom beaches are not great for snorkeling. The rocks create safe hiding places and grow the food that fish and other marine life like to eat.) A sidewalk along the coastline on the restaurant side of the beach makes a great vantage point from which to peer into the water and look for the Hawaiian green sea turtle. It's also a gathering spot to watch the sun set. ■ TIP➔ **Make reservations for dinner at the Beach House days in advance and time it around the sunset.** ⊠ *From Po'ipū Rd., turn onto Lāwa'i Rd; park on street near restaurant or in public parking lot across from beach.* ☞ *Toilets, showers, food, parking lot.*

☾ **Kukuiula Small Boat Harbor.** This is a great beach to sit and people-watch, as diving and fishing boats head out to sea, as well as kayakers and canoe paddlers. Shore and throw-net fishermen frequent this harbor as well. It's not a particularly large harbor, so it retains a quaint sense of charm, unlike Nāwiliwili Harbor or Port Allen. The bay is a nice, protected spot for swimming, but with all the boat traffic kicking up sand and clouding the water, probably not good for snorkeling. Outside the breakwater, there is a decent surf spot. ⊠ *From Po'ipū Rd., turn onto Lāwa'i Rd; watch for small green sign.* ☞ *Toilets, showers, picnic tables, grills/firepits, parking lot.*

Lawa'i Kai. One of the most spectacular beaches on the South Shore is inaccessible by land unless you tour the National Tropical Botanical Gar-

Seal-Spotting on the South Shore

WHEN STROLLING on one of Kaua'i's lovely beaches, don't be surprised if you find yourself in the rare company of Hawaiian monk seals. These are among the most endangered of all marine mammals, with perhaps fewer than 1,500 remaining. They primarily inhabit the Northwestern Hawaiian Islands, although more are showing their sweet faces on the main Hawaiian islands, especially on Kaua'i. They're fond of hauling out on the beach for a long snooze in the sun, especially after a night of gorging themselves on fish. They need this time to rest and digest, safe from predators.

During the past several summers, female seals have birthed young in the calm waters of Kaua'i's Po'ipū Beach, where they have stayed to nurse their pups for upward of six weeks. It seems the seals enjoy this particular beach for the same reasons we do: it's shallow and partially protected.

If you're lucky enough to see a monk seal, keep your distance and let it be. Although they may haul out near people, they still want and need their space. Stay several hundred feet away, and forget photos unless you've got a zoom lens. It's illegal to do anything that causes a monk seal to change its behavior, with penalties that include big fines and even jail time. In the water, seals may appear to want to play. It's their curious nature. Don't try to play with them. They are wild animals—mammals, in fact, with teeth. If you have concerns about the health or safety of a seal, or just want more information, contact the **Kaua'i Monk Seal Watch Program** (☎ 808/246-2860 ⊕ www.kauaimonkseal.com).

den's Allerton Garden—which we highly recommended—or trespass behind locked fences—which we don't recommend. On the tour, you'll see the beach, but you won't lounge on it or frolic in the calm water behind the promontory on the eastern point of the beach. One way to access the beach is by paddling a kayak 1 mi from Kukuiula Harbor. However, you have to rent the kayaks elsewhere and haul them on top of your car to the harbor. Also, the wind and waves usually run westward, making the in-trip a breeze but the return trip a workout against Mother Nature. Another way is to boulder-hop along the coast from Spouting Horn—a long trek over sharp lava rock that we do not recommend. ■ TIP→ Do not attempt this beach in any manner during a south swell. The shells are quite rare and more easily found at jewelry stores and crafts fairs around the island strung as pendants with Niihau shells. ⊠ *For kayakers, from Po'ipū Rd., turn onto Lāwa'i Rd and park at Kukui'ula small boat harbor.* ⚓ *No services.*

THE WEST SIDE

Whereas Kaua'i's North Shore is characterized by the color green, the West Side's coloring is red. When you look more closely, you'll see that the red is dirt, which happens to have a high iron content. With little vegetation on the West Side, the red dirt is everywhere—in the air, in a thin layer on the car, even in the river. In fact, the only river on the West Side is named Waimea, which means "reddish water." The West Side of the island receives hardly enough rainfall year-round to water a cactus, and because it's also the leeward side, there are hardly any tropical breezes. That translates to sunny and hot with long, languorous, and practically deserted beaches. You'd think the leeward waters—untouched by wind—would be calm, but there's no offshore reef system, so the waters are not as inviting as one would like. ■ TIP→ **The best place to gear up for the beaches on the West Side is on the South Shore or East Side.** Although there's some catering to visitors here, it's not much.

Salt Pond Beach Park. A great family spot, Salt Pond Beach Park features a naturally made, shallow swimming pond behind a curling finger of rock where keiki splash and snorkel. This pool is generally safe except during a large south swell, which usually occurs in summer, if at all. The center and western edge of the beach is popular with body boarders and bodysurfers. On a cultural note, the flat stretch of land to the east of the beach is the last spot in Hawai'i where ponds are used to harvest salt in the dry heat of summer. The beach park is popular with locals and can get crowded on weekends and holidays. ⊠ *From Rte. 50 in Hanapēpē, turn makai onto Lele Rd., Rte. 543.* ☞ *Lifeguard, toilets, showers, picnic tables, grills/firepits, parking lot, camping.*

Lucy Wright Beach Park. Named in honor of the first native Hawaiian schoolteacher, this beach is on the western banks of the Waimea River. It is also where Captain James Cook first came ashore in the Hawaiian Islands in 1778. If that's not interesting enough, the sand here is not the white, powdery kind you see along the South Shore. It's not even sandy like that on the East Side. It's a combination of pulverized, black lava rock and lighter-colored reef. In a way, it looks a bit like a mix of salt and pepper. Unfortunately, the intrigue of the beach doesn't extend to the waters, which are murky—thanks to river runoff—and choppy—thanks to an onshore break. So, it's not the best for water activities, but it is interesting. ■ TIP→ **If you want to talk-story about fishing with the locals, this would be a good spot.** ⊠ *From Rte. 50 in Waimea, turn makai on Moana Rd.* ☞ *Toilets, picnic tables, parking lot.*

Kekaha Beach Park. This is one of the premier spots on Kaua'i for sunset walks and the start of the state's longest beach; however, we don't recommend much water activity here without first talking to a lifeguard. The beach is exposed to open ocean and with an onshore break can be hazardous any time of year. However, there are some excellent

---

COUNTY & STATE BEACH PARKS

If restrooms, covered picnic areas, showers, and easy accessibility are important to you, stick to these county and state beach parks:

- Anahola Beach Park
- Haena State Park
- Hanalei Beach Park
- Kekaha Beach Park
- Kukuiula Landing
- Lydgate State Park
- Salt Pond Beach Park

surf breaks—for experienced surfers only. Or, if you would like to run on a beach, this is the one—hard-packed sand and several miles long. Although this beach runs all the way to Nā Pali Coast, you won't get past the Pacific Missile Range Facility and its post-9/11 restrictions. Another bonus for this beach is its relatively year-round dry weather. If it's raining where you are, try Kekeha Beach Park. ⊠ *From Rte. 50, drive to the west side of Kekaha.* ☞ *Lifeguard, toilets, showers, picnic tables, grills/firepits, parking lot.*

Fodor's Choice
★
Polihale State Park. The longest stretch of beach in Hawai'i starts in Kekeha and ends about 15 mi away at the start of Nā Pali Coast. At Nā Pali end of the beach is the 5-mi-long, 140-acre Polihale State Park. In addition to being long, this beach is 300 feet wide in places and backed by sand dunes 50 to 100 feet tall. Polihale is a remote beach accessed via a 5-mi haul cane road (four-wheel drive preferred but not required) at the end of Route 50 in Kekaha. ■ TIP➔ **Be sure to start the day with a full tank of gas and a cooler filled with food and drink.** Many locals wheel their four-wheel-drive vehicles up and over the sand dunes right onto the beach, but don't try this in a rental car. You're sure to get stuck and found in violation of your rental car agreement.

On weekends and holidays Polihale is a popular locals' camping location, but even on "busy" days this beach is never crowded. On days of high surf, only experts surf the waves. In general, the water here is extremely rough and not recommended for recreation; however, there's one small fringing reef, called Queen's Pond, where swimming is usually safe. Neighboring Polihale Beach is the Pacific Missile Range Facility (PMRF), operated by the U.S. Navy. Since September 11, 2001, access to the beaches fronting PMRF is restricted. ⊠ *Drive to end of Rte. 50 and continue on dirt road; several access points along the way.* ☞ *Toilets, showers, picnic tables, grills/firepits, parking lot, camping.*

HAWAI'I STATE SPORT: CANOE PADDLING

During summer, it's not unusual to see Hawai'i's state sport in action: outrigger canoe racing. These are the same styles of canoes ancient Hawaiians paddled in races that pitted one chief's warriors against another's. Summer is regatta season, and the half dozen or more canoe clubs around the island gather to race in ¼-mi, ½-mi, and longer races. You can catch the hundreds of paddlers lining the beaches and cheering on their clubs, oftentimes in Hanalei, Kalapaki, and Waimea Bay, as well as the Wailua River.

Water Sports & Tours

WORD OF MOUTH

"You have to do the Nā Pali kayak if you're an adventurous spirit."
—bluefan

"With the smaller boat, the captain was able to maneuver it into some awesome sea caves. Wow! I can't even begin to describe them. We saw spinner dolphins, turtles and yet another monk seal!"
—daydreamin

BOAT TOURS

Updated by
Kim
Steutermann
Rogers

DECIDING TO SEE NĀ PALI COAST BY BOAT IS THE EASY DECISION.
Choosing the outfitter to go with is the tough decision. There are numerous boat tour operators to choose from, and, quite frankly, they all do a good job. Before you even think about this company or that, answer these three questions: What kind of boat? Where am I staying? Morning or afternoon? Once you settle on these three, you can easily zero in on the tour outfitter.

Fodor'sChoice
★

First, the boat. The most important thing is to match you and your group's personality with the personality of the boat. If you like thrills and adventure, the rubber, inflatable rafts—often called Zodiacs, which Jacques Cousteau made famous and which the U.S. Coast Guard uses—will entice you. They're fast, sure to leave you drenched, and can get quite bouncy. If you prefer a smoother, more leisurely ride, then the large catamarans are the way to go. The next boat choice is size. Both the rafts and catamarans come in small and large. Again, think smaller: more adventurous; larger: more leisurely. ■ TIP➔ **Do not choose a smaller boat because you think there will be fewer people. There might be fewer people, but you'll be jammed together sitting atop strangers.** If you prefer privacy over socializing, go with a larger boat, so you'll have more room to spread out. One advantage to smaller boats, however, is that—depending on ocean conditions—some may slip into a sea cave or two. If that sounds interesting to you, call the outfitter and ask their policy on entering sea caves. Some won't, no matter the conditions, because they consider the caves sacred or because they don't want to cause any environmental damage.

There are three embarkation points around the island (Hanalei, Port Allen, and Waimea), and all head to the same spot: Nā Pali Coast. Here's the inside skinny on which is the best—because they'll all say they're the best. It's really pretty easy. If you're staying on the North Shore, choose to depart out of the North Shore. If you're staying anywhere else, depart out of the West Side. It's that easy. Sure, the North Shore is closer to Nā Pali Coast; however, you'll pay more for less overall time. The West Side boat operators may spend more time getting to Nā Pali Coast; however, they'll spend about the same amount of time along Nā Pali, plus you'll pay less. Finally, you'll also have to decide whether you want to go on the morning tour, which includes a deli lunch and a stop for snorkeling, or the afternoon tour, which does not stop to snorkel but does include a sunset over the ocean. The 5½-hour morning tour with snorkeling is more popular with families and those who love dolphins. You don't have

> **WORD OF MOUTH**
>
> "See Nā Pali Coast either by boat or by helicopter. By air the views are spectacular, but the ride is shorter than it is by boat, and the boat stops and lets you do some snorkeling. Another way to see it is a hike along the Kalalau Trail. Though long and sometimes strenuous, it's a fabulous day trip."   –Kealii

KAUA'I CATAMARAN TOURS

	Length	AM/PM	Departure Point	Adult/kid Price	Kid's Ages	Snack vs. meal	Alcoholic beverages included	Boat type	Total pax	Shore excursion	Snorkel	Sea caves	Shade
Snorkel Cruise													
Blue Dolphin	5 hours	AM & PM*	Port Allen	129/89	2 to 11	Meal	Yes	Sailing Cat	49	No	Yes	No	Yes
Capt. Andy's	5 hours	AM & PM*	Port Allen	139/99	2 to 12	Meal	Yes	Sailing Cat	49	No	Yes	No	Yes
Captain Sundown	6 hours	AM & PM*	Hanalei	162/138	7 to 12	Meal	BYOB	Sailing Cat	15	No	Yes	No	Yes
Catamaran Kahanu	5 hours	AM & PM*	Port Allen	125/85	4 to 11	Meal	No	Power Cat	18	No	Yes	Yes	Yes
Holo Holo	5 hours	AM & PM*	Port Allen	135/95	5 to 12	Meal	Yes	Sailing Cat	37	No	Yes	No	Yes
Kauai Sea Tours	5.5 hours	AM	Port Allen	129/99	3 to 12	Meal	Yes	Sailing Cat	49	Yes	Yes	No	Yes
Liko Kauai	4 hours	AM & PM*	Waimea	120/80	4 to 12	Meal	BYOB	Power Cat	30	No	Yes	Yes	Yes
Nā Pali Catamaran	4 hours	AM & PM*	Hanalei	140/120	5 to 11	Meal	No	Power Cat	16	No	Yes	Yes	Yes
Sightseeing Only													
Blue Dolphin	4 hours	PM	Port Allen	99/79	2 to 11	Meal	Yes	Sailing Cat	49	No	No	No	Yes
Capt. Andy's	4 hours	PM	Port Allen	105/80	2 to 12	Meal	Yes	Sailing Cat	49	No	No	No	Yes
Captain Sundown	3 hours	PM	Hanalei	138/120	7 to 12	Snacks	BYOB	Sailing Cat	15	No	No	No	Yes
Catamaran Kahanu	3.5 hours	PM	Port Allen	95/75	4 to 11	Snacks	No	Power Cat	18	No	No	Yes	Yes
Holo Holo	3.5 hours	PM	Port Allen	95/75	5 to 12	Snacks	Yes	Power Cat	49	No	No	No	Yes
Kauai Sea Tours	3.5 hours	PM	Port Allen	99/79	3 to 12	Meal	Yes	Sailing Cat	49	No	No	No	Yes

* In winter, only AM snorkel tours

to be an expert snorkeler or even have any prior experience, but if it is your first time, note that although there will be some snorkeling instruction, there might not be much. Hawaiian spinner dolphins are so prolific in the mornings that some tour companies guarantee you'll see them, although you can't get in the water and swim with them. The 3½-hour afternoon tour is more popular with nonsnorklers—obviously—and photographers interested in capturing the setting sunlight on the coast.

> ### WHAT TO BRING ON A BOAT TOUR
>
> - Swimsuit
> - Sunscreen
> - Hat
> - Sunglasses
> - Beach towel
> - Light jacket
> - Camera (in waterproof bag, just in case)
> - Motion sickness meds (take well before departure)
> - Change of clothes (post-cruise)

Catamaran Tours

Fodor'sChoice ★ **Blue Dolphin Charters.** This company operates 63-foot and 65-foot sailing (rarely raised and always motoring) catamarans designed with three decks of spacious seating with great visibility. ■ TIP→ **The lower deck is best for shade seekers.** Upgrades from snorkeling to scuba diving—no need for certification—are available and run $35, but the diving is really best for beginners or people who need a refresher course. On Tuesday and Friday a tour of Nā Pali Coast includes a detour across the channel to Ni'ihau for snorkeling and diving. Blue Dolphin likes to say they have the best mai tais "off the island," and truth is, they probably do. They recently upgraded their four-hour afternoon sightseeing tour to include a meal of kalua pork, teriyaki chicken, Caesar salad, and chocolate chip cookies. Prices range from $99 to $175. ⊠ *In Port Allen Marina Center. Turn makai onto Rte. 541 off Rte. 50, at 'Ele'ele.* ☎ *808/335–5553 or 877/511–1311* ⊕ *www.kauaiboats.com.*

Capt. Andy's. Departing from Port Allen and running two 55-foot sailing catamarans, Capt. Andy's runs the same five-hour snorkeling and four-hour sunset tours along Nā Pali Coast like everyone else, although we're not crazy about the boat's layout, which has most of the seating inside the cabin. What they do that no one else does is embark out of Kuku'ula Harbor in Po'ipū for a two-hour sunset sail—with live Hawaiian music—every Sunday evening, staying on the South Shore. ■ TIP→ **If the winds and swells are up on the North Shore, this is usually a good choice. Or, if you're susceptible to seasickness, this would be your best bet.** Note: If you have reservations for the shorter tour, you will check in at their Kukui'ula Harbor office. Prices range from $69 to $139. ⊠ *In Port Allen Marina Center. Turn makai onto Rte. 541 off Rte. 50 at 'Ele'ele.* ☎ *808/335–6833 or 800/535–0830* ⊕ *www.napali.com.*

Fodor'sChoice ★ **Captain Sundown.** If you're staying on the North Shore, it's really pretty simple. Captain Sundown is the choice. Get this: Captain Bob has been cruising Nā Pali Coast for 35 years—six days a week, sometimes twice a day. (And right alongside Captain Bob is his son Captain Larry.) To say he knows the area is a bit of an understatement. Here's the other

DOES RAIN MEAN CANCELLATION?

If it's raining where you're staying, that doesn't mean it's raining over the water, so don't shy away from a boat tour. Besides, it's not the rain that should concern you, it's the wind. The wind, especially from due north and south, creates surface chop and makes for rough riding. Larger craft are designed to handle winter's ocean swells, however, so unless monster waves are out there, your tour should depart without a hitch. If the water is too rough, your boat captain may reroute to calmer waters. It's always a tough call to make, but your comfort and safety is always the foremost factor.
■ TIP→ In winter months, North Shore departures are canceled much more often than those departing the West Side. This is because the boats are smaller and the waves are bigger on this side of the island. If you want the closest thing to a guarantee you'll get of seeing Nā Pali Coast in winter, choose a West Side outfitter. Oh, and even if your tour boat says they cruise the "entire Nā Pali," it's really ocean conditions permitting.

good thing about this tour: they take only 15 passengers. Now, you'll definitely pay more, but it's worth it. You don't check in too early—8:15—and there's no rushing down the coastline. The morning snorkeling cruise is a leisurely six hours. The views of the waterfall-laced mountains behind Hanalei and Haena start immediately—themselves breathtaking—but then it's around Keʻe Beach and the magic of Nā Pali Coast. All the while, the captains are trolling for fish, and if they catch any, guests get to reel 'em in. Afternoon sunset sails run three hours. BYOB. ■ TIP→ Healthy pregnant women are welcome aboard. Prices range from $138 to $162. There is no check-in office; check in on the beach in Hanalei where the river meets the sea. ⊠ *In Hanalei, turn makai at Aku Rd. and drive 1 block to Weli Weli Rd., turn right and drive to road's end and parking lot.* ☎ *808/826–5585* ⊕ *www.captainsundown.com.*

Catamaran Kahanu. This Hawaiian-owned-and-operated company has been in business since 1985 and runs a 40-foot power catamaran with 18-passenger seating. The boat is smaller than most and may feel a tad crowded, but the tour feels more personal, with a laid-back, ʻohana style. Salt water runs through the veins of this father-and-son team—Captains Lani and Kamua. Guests can learn the ancient cultural practice of weaving on board. There's no alcohol allowed. Prices range from $95 to $115. ⊠ *From Rte. 50, turn left on Rte. 541 at ʻEleʻele, proceed just past Port Allen Marina Center, turn right at sign; check-in booth on left* ☎ *808/ 645–6176 or 888/213–7711* ⊕ *www.catamarankahanu.com.*

HoloHolo Charters. Choose between a 50-foot sailing catamaran trip to Nā Pali Coast, and a 65-foot powered catamaran trip to the island of Niʻihau. Both boats have large cabins and little outside seating. Originators of the Niʻihau tour, HoloHolo Charters built their 65-foot powered catamaran with a wide beam to reduce side-to-side motion, and twin 425 HP turbo diesel engines specifically for the 17-mi channel crossing to Niʻihau. ■ TIP→ **They are the only outfitter running daily Niihau tours.** Prices range from $95 to $175. ⊠ *Check in at Port Allen Marina Center. Turn makai onto Rte. 541 off Rte. 50, at ʻEleʻele* ☎ *808/335–0815 or 800/848–6130* ⊕ *www.holoholocharters.com.*

Kauaʻi Sea Tours. This company operates a 61-foot sailing catamaran designed almost identically to that of Blue Dolphin Charters—hence, with all the same benefits. Snorkeling tours anchor at Nūalolo Kai (a great snorkeling spot), and in summer, guests can choose the "combo" tour, which includes a shuttle ride to shore on an inflatable raft and a tour of an ancient fishing village—a unique cultural experience. Prices range from $99 to $154. ⊠ *Turn makai off Rte. 50 onto Rte. 541 at ʻEleʻele and left at Aka Ula Rd. Office on right* ☎ *808/826–7254 or 800/733–7997* ⊕ *www.kauaiseatours.com.*

Liko Kauaʻi Cruises. There are many things to like about Liko Kauaʻi Cruises. The 49-foot powered cat will enter sea caves, ocean conditions permitting. Sometimes, even Captain Liko himself—a born-and-bred West Side boy—still takes the captain's helm. We particularly like the layout of his boat—most of the seating is in the bow, so there's good visibility. There's just one problem: even though they depart out of Kīkīaola Harbor in Waimea, at four hours in length, the snorkeling tour is altogether too short. The rate is $120. ⊠ *Mauka off Rte. 50 in Waimea just before Big Save, in Obsessions Café* ☎ *808/338—0333 or 800/732–5456* ⊕ *www.liko-kauai.com.*

Nā Pali Catamaran. One of the few tours departing Hanalei, this company has been around for a long time. Once on board, it takes only five minutes before you're witnessing the magnificence of Nā Pali Coast. Its 34-foot, powered catamaran is small enough—and with no mast, short enough—to dip into sea caves. In summer, they run two four-hour snorkeling tours per day, stopping at the best snorkeling site along Nā Pali—Nuʻalolo Kai. In winter, business slows as the surf picks up, and they run whale-watching tours, ocean conditions permitting. If it wasn't for the bench seating bisecting the boat—meaning one group of passengers enjoys unobstructed views of the open ocean instead of Nā Pali either on the way out or back—we'd really be happy. Rate is $140. ⊠ *In Ching Young Village in Hanalei* ☎ *808/826–6853 or 800/255–6853.*

Zodiac Tours

Captain Zodiac. Captain Zodiac first started running Nā Pali in 1974; however, the name has changed hands over the years, and currently, Capt. Andy's (as in the sailing catamaran Capt. Andy's) is operating the raft business known as Captain Zodiac. Departing out of Port

FODOR'S BEST BOATS

Best for snorkeling: Z-Tourz
Best for romance: Capt. Andy's Poʻipū Sail
Best for thrill seekers: Nā Pali Explorer (Zodiac 1)
Best for mai tais: Blue Dolphin Charters
Best for pregnant women: Captain Sundown or Capt. Andy's
Best for charters: Captain Sundown
Best price: Nā Pali Riders

Allen, this tour is much like the other raft tours—offering both snorkeling and beach landing excursions. Their rafts are on the smaller side—24 feet with a maximum of 15 passengers—and all seating is on the rubber hulls, so hang on. They operate three different rafts, so there's a good chance of availability. ⊠ *In Port Allen Marina Center. Turn makai onto Rte. 541 off Rte. 50 at 'Ele'ele.* ☎ *808/335–6833 or 800/535–0830* ⊕ *www. napali.com.*

FodorsChoice ★ **Nā Pali Explorer.** Owned by a couple of women, these tours operate out of two locations: Waimea, a tad closer to Nā Pali Coast than

> ## NI'IHAU
>
> That little island off Kaua'i's southwest shore is the privately owned Ni'ihau. It doesn't rain much there, so there's little runoff; plus, there's little boat traffic, so it all adds up to crystal-clear water. Perfect for snorkeling. Two companies—Blue Dolphin and Holo Holo—combine a Nā Pali sightseeing tour with snorkeling at Ni'ihau. If you're up for a full day on the water, you'll enjoy this. They run year-round, but during winter, the ocean crossing can get rough.

most of the West Side catamaran tours, and, after numerous years away, now back in Hanalei again. The company runs two different sizes of inflatable rubber rafts: a 48-foot, 35-passenger craft with an onboard toilet, freshwater shower, shade canopy, and seating in the stern (which is surprisingly smooth and comfortable) and bow (which is where the fun is); and a 26-foot, 16-passenger craft for the all-out fun and thrills of a white-knuckle ride in the bow. Both stop at Nūalolo Kai for snorkeling; in summer the smaller vessel ties up onshore for a tour of the ancient fishing village. Rates range from $79 to $125, and charters are available. ⊠ *Follow Rte. 50 west to Waimea; office mauka after crossing river. In Hanalei, meet at the river mouth, at the end of Weke Rd. Waimea and Hanalei* ☎ *808/338–9999 or 877/335–9909* ⊕ *www. napali-explorer.com.*

Nā Pali Riders. This tour boat outfitter distinguishes itself in two ways. First, they cruise the entire Nā Pali Coast, clear to Ke'e Beach and back. Second, they have an unbeatable price, because it's a no-frills tour—no lunch provided, just beverages and snacks. They run four-hour snorkeling trips out of Kīkīaola Harbor in Waimea on a 30-foot inflatable raft with a 32-passenger maximum—if it's full, you'll definitely feel like a sardine. ■ TIP➔ Rate is $99. To save up to $30, make reservations by calling direct—not online, not with an activities desk. ⊠ *In Waimea, makai, approximately 1 mi after crossing Waimea River* ☎ *808/742–6331* ⊕ *www. napaliriders.com.*

Kauai Sea Tours. This company also offers snorkeling and nonsnorkeling tours in an inflatable rubber raft. Check out the Combo Tour. ⇨ *See* Catamaran Tours.

Z-Tourz. What we like about Z-Tourz is that they are the only boat company to make snorkeling their priority. As such, they focus on the South Shore's abundant offshore reefs, stopping at two locations. If you want to see Nā Pali, this boat is not for you; if you want to snorkel with the myriad of Hawai'i's tropical reef fish and turtles (pretty much guaranteed), it is. They run two three-hour tours daily on a 26-foot rigid-hull inflatable (think Zodiac) with a maximum of 16 passengers. Rate is $94. Check in at Kukui'ula Harbor in Po'ipū. ⊠ *From Po'ipū Rd., turn onto Lawai Rd., drive 1 mi, turn left on Amio Rd. to harbor.* ☎ *808/742–7422 or 888/998–6879* ⊕ *www.ztourz.com.*

Riverboat Tours to Fern Grotto

This 2½-mi, upriver trip culminates at a yawning lava tube that is covered with enormous fishtail ferns. During the boat ride, guitar and 'ukulele players regale you with Hawaiian melodies and tell the history of the river. It's a kitschy bit of Hawaiiana, worth the little money ($20) and short time required. Flat-bottom, 150-passenger riverboats (that rarely fill up) depart from Wailua Marina at the mouth of the Wailua River. ■ TIP→ **It's extremely rare, but occasionally after heavy rains the tour does not disembark at the grotto, so if you're traveling in winter, you may want to ask beforehand.** Round-trip excursions take 1½ hours, including time to walk around the grotto and environs. Tours run every half hour from 9 to 3 daily. Reservations are not required. Contact **Smith's Motor Boat Services** (☎ 808/821–6892 ⊕ www.smithskauai.com) for more information.

> ## UP FOR A DINNER CRUISE?
>
> If you're thinking of a romantic dinner cruise—you know, getting dressed up, having a sit-down dinner, listening to some live music, watching hula dancers, the whole bit—well, you're on the wrong island. Kaua'i's waters are just not conducive to such. So, even though you'll see some boat companies advertising "dinner cruises," the only difference between their snorkeling cruise and this is that there is no snorkeling, of course, and instead of deli sandwiches, there might be kalua pig, teriyaki chicken, or something similar.

BOOGIE BOARDING & BODYSURFING

The most natural form of wave riding is bodysurfing, a popular sport on Kaua'i because there are many shore breaks around the island. Wave riders of this style stand waist deep in the water, facing shore, and swim madly as a wave picks them up and breaks. It's great fun and requires no special skills and absolutely no equipment other than a swimsuit. The next step up is Boogie boarding, also called body boarding. In this case, wave riders lie with their upper body on a foam board about half the length of a traditional surfboard and kick as the wave propels them toward shore. Again, this is easy to pick up, and there are many places around Kaua'i to practice. The locals wear short-finned flippers to help them catch waves, although they are not necessary for and even hamper beginners. It's worth spending a few minutes watching these experts as they spin, twirl, and flip—that's right—while they slip down the face of the wave. Of course, all beach safety precautions apply, and just because you see wave riders of any kind in the water doesn't mean it's safe. Any snorkeling gear outfitter also rents body boards.

Some of our favorite bodysurfing and body-boarding beaches are **Brennecke, Wailua, Keālia, Kalihi Wai,** and **Hanalei.**

DEEP-SEA FISHING

Simply step aboard and cast your line for mahimahi, 'ahi, ono, and marlin. That's about how quickly the fishing—mostly trolling with lures—begins on Kaua'i. The water gets deep here, so there's less cruising time to fishing grounds. Of course, your captain may elect to cruise to a hot location where he's had good luck lately.

There are oodles of charter fishermen around; most depart from Nāwiliwili Harbor in Līhu'e, and most use lures instead of live bait. Inquire about each boat's "fish policy," that is, what happens to the fish if any are caught. Some boats keep all; others will give you enough for a meal or two. On shared charters, ask about the maximum passenger count and about the fishing rotation; you'll want to make sure everyone gets a fair shot at reeling in the big one. Another option is to book a private charter. Shared and private charters run four, six, and eight hours in length.

Boats & Charters

Captain Don's Sport Fishing & Ocean Adventure. Captain Don is very flexible—he'll stop to snorkel or whale-watch if that's what the group (four to six) wants. Saltwater fly-fishermen (bring your own gear) are welcome. He'll even fish for bait and let you keep part of whatever you catch. The *June Louis* is a 34-foot twin diesel. Rates start at $125 for shared, $525 for private charters. ⊠ *Nāwiliwili Harbor* ☎ *808/639–3012* ⊕ *www.captaindonsfishing.com.*

Hana Pa'a. The advantage with Hana Pa'a is that they take fewer people (minimum two, maximum four), but you pay for it. Rates start at $200 for shared, $575 for private charters. Their fish policy is flexible and their boat is roomy. The *Maka Hou II* is a 38-foot Bertram. ⊠ *Nāwiliwili Harbor* ☎ *808/823–6031 or 866/776–3474* ⊕ *www.fishkauai.com.*

Kai Bear. The father of this father-and-son duo has it figured out: he lets the son run the business and do all the work. Or so he says. The two have a unique catch policy—you can keep coming by every couple of days for that day's fresh catch. Rates start at $149 for a four-hour, shared charter (six fishermen max) and run all the way to $2,000 for an eight-hour, keep-all-the-fish-you-

> ### THE ROLLING & REELING OCEAN
>
> As anyone who's been on a boat in Kaua'i's waters knows, the Pacific Ocean isn't always so pacific. Even lifelong Navy men have admitted to feeling queasy on a Nā Pali boat tour. Some people think the bigger the boat the better, but studies show that the lowest incidence of seasickness occurs on the rubber inflatable rafts. It may have something to do with being closer to the water and moving in a natural rhythm with the waves. If you think you're going to get sick, motion sickness tablets are probably a good idea.

want exclusive charter. What's particularly nice about this company are the boats: the 38-foot Bertram *Kai Bear* and the 42-foot Bertram *Grander.* Very roomy. ✉ *Nawiliwili Harbor* ☎ *808/652–4556 or 866/ 226–8340* ⊕ *www.kaibear.com.*

Nā Pali Explorer. If you're staying on the West Side, you'll be glad to know that Nā Pali Explorer of the longtime rafting tour business is now running fishing trips out of Port Allen. They offer shared and exclusive charters of four, six, and eight hours in a 41-foot Concord called *Happy Times.* Their shared tours max out at six fishermen, and a portion of the catch is shared with all. They also use this boat for specialty charters—that is, film crews, surveys, burials, and even Ni'ihau fishing. Rates start at $125 per person. ✉ *Check in at Port Allen Small Boat Harbor.* ☎ *808/ 338–9999 or 877/335–9909* ⊕ *www.napali-explorer.com.*

North Shore Charters. This is a great choice for anyone staying on the North Shore, although conditions may get iffy in the winter. The owner-operator—there are no hired hands running the boat—will fish for live bait or bottom fish if passengers are interested. You'll get to keep a share of whatever you catch. The boat carries four to six passengers and is also available for narrated tours of Nā Pali Coast, which is turning out to be a boon for business. Rates are $120 for shared, $675–$700 for private charters. ✉ *'Anini Beach Boat Ramp* ☎ *808/828–1379 or 877/ 728–1379.*

KAYAKING

★ Kaua'i is the only Hawaiian island with navigable rivers. As the oldest inhabited island in the chain, Kaua'i has had more time for wind and water erosion to deepen and widen cracks into streams and streams into rivers. Because this is a small island, the rivers aren't long, and there are no rapids; that makes them perfectly safe for kayakers of all levels, even beginners.

For more advanced paddlers, there aren't many places in the world more beautiful for sea kayaking than Nā Pali Coast. If this is your draw to Kaua'i, plan your vacation for the summer months, when the seas are at their calmest. ■ TIP➔ **Tour and kayak rental reservations are recommended at least a week in advance during peak summer and holiday seasons.** In general, tours and rentals are available year-round, Monday through Saturday. Pack a swimsuit, sunscreen, a hat, bug repellent, water shoes (sport sandals, aqua socks, old tennis shoes), and motion sickness medication if you're planning on sea kayaking.

River Kayaking

Tour outfitters operate on the Hule'ia, Wailua, and Hanalei rivers with guided tours that combine hiking to waterfalls, as in the case of the first two, and snorkeling, as in the case of the third. Another option is renting kayaks and heading out on your own. Each has its advantages and disadvantages, but it boils down as follows:

If you want to swim at the base of a remote 100-foot waterfall, sign up for a five-hour kayak (4-mi round-trip) and hiking (2-mi round-trip) tour of the **Wailua River.** It includes a dramatic waterfall that is best accessed with the aid of a guide, so you don't get lost. ■ TIP→ Remember that it's dangerous to swim directly under waterfalls no matter how good a water massage may sound. Rocks and logs are known to plunge down, especially after heavy rains.

If you want to kayak on your own, choose the **Hanalei River.** It's most scenic from the kayak itself—there are no trails to hike to hidden waterfalls. And better yet, a rental company (Kayak Kauai, ⇨ see Kayak Rentals & Tours) is right on the river—no hauling kayaks on top of your car.

WORD OF MOUTH

"The unforgettable kayak trip up the Nā Pali coast, surrounded by the electric turquoise water, immense green spires, and waterfalls plunging into the sea . . . me, out there, a little speck next to the grandeur of a part of the island that only those who truly seek it out can be intimate with."

—turn_it_on

If you're not sure of your kayaking abilities, head to the **Hulēʻia River;** 3½-hour tours include easy paddling upriver, a nature walk through a rain forest with a cascading waterfall, a rope swing for playing Tarzan and Jane, and a ride back downriver—into the wind—on a motorized, double-hull canoe.

As for the kayaks themselves, most companies use the two-person sit-on-top style that is quite buoyant—no Eskimo rolls required. The only possible danger comes in the form of communication. The kayaks seat two people, which means you'll share the work (good) with a spouse, child, parent, friend, or guide (the potential danger part). On the river, the two-person kayaks are known as "divorce boats." Counseling is not included in the tour price.

Sea Kayaking

In its second year and second issue, *National Geographic Adventure* ranked kayaking **Nā Pali Coast** second on its list of America's Best 100 Adventures, right behind rafting the Colorado River through the Grand Canyon. That pretty much says it all. It's the adventure of a lifetime in one day, involving eight hours of paddling. Although it's good to have some kayaking experience, feel comfortable on the water, and be reasonably fit, it doesn't require the preparation, stamina, or fortitude of, say, climbing Mt. Everest. Tours run May through September, ocean conditions permitting. In the winter months sea-kayaking tours operate on the **South Shore**—beautiful, but not Nā Pali.

Outfitters & Tours

Kayak Kauaʻi. Based in Hanalei, this company offers guided tours on the Hanalei and Wailua rivers, and along Nā Pali Coast. They have a great shop right on the Hanalei River for kayak rentals and camping gear. The guided Hanalei River Kayak and Snorkel Tour starts at the shop and heads downriver, so there's not much to see of the scenic river valley. (For that, rent a kayak on your own.) Instead, this three-hour tour paddles down to the river mouth, where the river meets the sea. Then, it's a short paddle around a point to snorkel at either Puʻu Poa

Beach or, ocean conditions permitting, a bit farther at Hideaways Beach. This is a great choice if you want to try your paddle at a bit of ocean kayaking.

A second location in Kapa'a is the base for Wailua River guided tours and kayak rentals. It's not right on the river, however, so shuttling is involved. For rentals, the company provides the hauling gear necessary for your rental car. Guided tours range from $60 to $200. Kayak rentals range from $28 to $75. ⊠ *Hanalei: 1 mi past Hanalei bridge, on makai side* ⊠ *Kapa'a: south end of Coconut Marketplace near movie theaters* ☎ *808/826–9844 or 800/437–3507.*

Kayak Wailua. We can't quite figure out how this family-run business offers pretty much the same Wailua River kayaking tour as everyone else—except for lunch and beverages, which are BYO—for half the price, but they do. They say it's because they don't discount and don't offer commission to activities and concierge desks. Their 4½-hour kayak, hike, and waterfall swim costs $39.95, and their 3-hour kayak-to-a-swimming-hole costs $34.95. We say fork over the extra $5 for the longer tour and hike to the beautiful 150-foot Secret Falls. ⊠ *In Wailua next to the Wailua Shell Food Mart* ☎ *808/822–3388* ⊕ *www.kayakwailua.com.*

Nā Pali Kayak. A couple of longtime guides for Kayak Kaua'i ventured out on their own a few years back to create this company that focuses solely on sea kayaking—Nā Pali Coast in summer, as the name implies, and the South Shore in winter (during peak times only). These guys are highly experienced and still highly enthusiastic about their livelihood. So much so, that REI Adventures recently hired them to run their multiday, multisport tours. Now, that's a feather in their cap, we'd say. Prices start at $180. You can also rent kayaks; prices range from $35 to $70. ⊠ *5-575 Kūhiō Hwy., next to Postcards Café* ☎ *808/826–6900 or 866/977–6900* ⊕ *www.napalikayak.com.*

☾ **Outfitters Kaua'i.** This well-established tour outfitter operates year-round river-kayak tours on the Hule'ia and Wailua rivers, as well as sea-kayaking tours along Nā Pali Coast in summer and the South Side in winter. Outfitters Kauai's specialty, however, is the **Kipu Safari.** This all-day adventure starts with kayaking up the Hule'ia River and includes a rope swing over a swimming hole, a wagon ride through a working cattle ranch, a picnic lunch by a private waterfall, hiking, and a "zip" across the river (strap on a harness, clip into a cable, and zip across the river). It ends with a ride on a motorized double-hull canoe. It's a great tour for the family, because no one ever gets bored. The Kipu Safari costs $155; other guided tours range from $94 to $185. ⊠ *2827-A Po'ipū Rd., Po'ipū 96756* ☎ *808/742–9667 or 888/742–9886* ⊕ *www.outfitterskauai.com.*

Wailua Kayak & Canoe. This is the only purveyor of kayak rentals on the Wailua River, which means no hauling your kayak on top of your car (a definite plus). Rates are $45 for a single; $75 for a double. ⊠ *Across from Wailua Beach, turn mauka at Kuamo'o Rd. and take first left, 169 Wailua Rd., Kapa'a* ☎ *808/821–1188.*

CLOSE UP

The Forbidden Isle

SEVENTEEN MILES from Kaua'i, across the Kaulakahi Channel, lies the privately owned island of Ni'ihau. It's known as the "Forbidden Isle" because access is limited to the Robinson family, which owns it, and the 200 or so Native Hawaiians who were born there.

Ni'ihau was bought from King Kamehameha in 1864 by a Scottish widow, Eliza Sinclair. Sinclair was introduced to the island after an unusually wet winter; she saw nothing but green pastures and thought it would be an ideal place to raise cattle. The cost was $10,000. It was a real deal, or so Sinclair thought.

Unfortunately, Ni'ihau's usual rainfall is about 12 inches a year, and the land soon returned to its normal desertlike state. Regardless, Sinclair did not abandon her venture and today the island and ranching operation are owned by Bruce Robinson, Eliza Sinclair's great-great-grandson.

Visits to the island are restricted to custom hunting expeditions and flightseeing tours through Ni'ihau Helicopter. Tours depart from Kaumakani and avoid the western coastline, especially the village of Pu'uwai. There's a four-passenger minimum for each flight, and reservations are essential. A picnic lunch on a secluded Ni'ihau beach is included, with time for swimming, beachcombing, and snorkeling. The half-day tour is $325 per person.

For more information contact **Ni'ihau Tours** (⌂ Box 690370, Makaweli 96769 ☎ 808/335–3500 or 877/441–3500 ⊕ www.niihau.us)

KITEBOARDING

Several years ago, the latest wave-riding craze to hit the islands was **kiteboarding** and the sport is still going strong. As the name implies, there's a kite and a board involved. The board you strap on your feet; the kite is attached to a harness around your waist. Steering is accomplished with a rod that's attached to the harness and the kite. Depending on conditions and the desires of the kiteboarder, the kite is played out some 30 to 100 feet in the air. The result is a cross between waterskiing—without the boat—and windsurfing. Speeds are fast and aerobatic maneuvers are involved. If you're a surfer of any kind, you might like to give this a try. (We highly recommend a lesson; besides, there's no rental gear available on the island.) Otherwise, you might find it more fun to watch. The most popular year-round spot for kiteboarding is **Kapa'a Beach Park** because of its reliable northeast trade winds.

■ TIP➜ Many visitors come to Kaua'i dreaming of parasailing. If that's you, make a stop at Maui or the Big Island. There's no parasailing on Kaua'i.

'Anini Beach Windsurfing. The certified kiteboarding instructors here give five-hour lessons for $400 for one person or $600 for two. Lessons are usually held at Hanalei Bay and are available only when conditions allow. Call for reservations. ✉ *Meet at beach, Hanalei* ☎ *808/826–9463.*

SCUBA DIVING

The majority of scuba diving on Kaua'i occurs on the South Side. Boat and shore dives are available, although boat sites surpass the shore sites for a couple of reasons. First, they're deeper and exhibit the complete symbiotic relationship of a reef system, and second, the visibility is better a little farther offshore.

The dive operators below offer a full range of services, including certification dives, referral dives, boat dives, shore dives, night dives, and drift dives. As for certification, ■ TIP➔ **we recommend completing your confined-water training and classroom testing before arriving on island.** That way, you'll spend less time training and more time diving.

Best Spots

The best and safest scuba-diving sites are accessed by boat on the South Side of the island, right off the shores of Po'ipū. The captain selects the actual site based on ocean conditions of the day; **Sheraton Caverns, General Store,** and **Brennecke's Ledge** are good picks. Beginners may prefer shore dives, which are best at **Kōloa Landing** on the South Side year-round and **Mākua (Tunnels) Beach** on the North Shore in the calm summer months. Keep in mind, though, that you'll have to haul your gear a ways down the beach.

For the advanced diver, the island of Ni'ihau—across an open ocean channel in deep and crystal-clear waters—beckons and rewards, usually with some big fish. Seasport Divers, Fathom Five, and Bubbles Below venture the 17 mi across the channel in summer when the crossing is smoothest. Divers can expect deep dives, walls, and strong currents at Ni'ihau, where conditions can change rapidly. To make the long journey worthwhile, three dives and Nitrox are included.

Outfitters & Tours

Bubbles Below. Marine ecology is the emphasis here aboard the 36-foot Kai Manu custom-built Radon. This company discovered some pristine dive sites on the West Side of the island where white-tip reef sharks are common—and other divers are not. Thanks to the addition of a 32-foot powered catamaran—the six-passenger *Dive Rocket*—they also run Ni'ihau, Nā Pali, and North Shore dives year-round (depending on ocean conditions, of course). A bonus on these tours is the Grinds pizza served between dives. Open-water certification dives, check-out dives, and intro shore dives are available upon request. There's a charge of $120 for a standard two-tank boat dive and up to $25 extra for rental gear. ✉ *Port Allen Small Boat Harbor; turn makai onto Rte. 541 from Rte. 50 in 'Ele'ele.* ☎ *808/332–7333 or 866/524–6268* ⊕ *www.bubblesbelowkauai.com.*

Fathom Five/Ocean Quest Watersports. A few years ago, Fathom Five, the South Shore boat-diving specialists, teamed up with Ocean Quest Watersports, a separate company specializing in shore dives at Tunnels on

SCUBA Q&A

Q: Do I have to be certified to go scuba diving?

A: Absolutely not. You can try Discover Scuba, which allows you to dive up to 40 feet after an introductory lesson in a pool. Most dive outfitters on Kaua'i offer this introductory program.

Q: Can I dive if I have asthma?

A: Only if your doctor signs a medical release—the original of which you must present to your dive outfitter.

Q: Can I get certified on Kaua'i?

A: Yes. Start to finish, it'll take three days. Or, you can complete your classroom and confined water training at home and just do your check-out dives on Kaua'i.

Q: How old do you have to be to learn how to dive?

A: Most certifying agencies require that you be at least 12 years old (with PADI it's 10) when you start your scuba-diving course. You will normally receive a junior certification, which can be upgraded to a full certification when you are 15 years old.

Q: Can I wear contact lenses or glasses while diving?

A: You can either wear contact lessons with a regular mask or opt for a prescription mask—just let your dive outfitter know in advance.

Q: What if I forget my certification card?

A: Let your dive outfitter know immediately; with advance notice, they can usually dig up your certification information online.

4

the North Shore. Today, they offer it all: boat dives, shore dives, night dives, certification dives. They're pretty much doing what everyone else is with a couple of twists. First, they offer a three-tank premium charter for those really serious about diving. Second, they operate a Nitrox continuous flow mixing system, so you can decide the mix rate. Third, they tag on a twilight dive to the standard, one-tank night dive, making the outing worth the effort. Fourth, their shore diving isn't an afterthought. Finally, we think their dive masters are pretty darn good, too. They even dive Ni'ihau in the summer aboard their 35-foot Force. Prices start at $65 for a one-tank shore dive and top out at $495 for full certification. The standard two-tank boat dive runs $115 plus $30 for gear rental, if needed. ■ TIP➔ **In summer, book way in advance.** ✉ *Just south of Kōloa on Po'ipū Rd. 3450 Po'ipū Rd.* ☎ *808/742–6991 or 800/ 972–3078* ⊕ *www.fathomfive.com.*

Sacred Seas Scuba. This company specializes in shore diving only, typically at Kōloa Landing (year-round) and Tunnels (summers). They're not only geared toward beginning divers—for whom they provide a very thorough and gentle certification program as well as the Discover Scuba program—but also offer night dives and scooter (think James Bond) dives. Certified divers can participate in turtle surveys for the National Marine

Fisheries. Their main emphasis is a detailed review of marine biology, such as pointing out rare dragon eel and harlequin shrimp tucked away in pockets of coral. ■ TIP➔ **Hands down, we recommend Sacred Seas Scuba for beginners, certification, and refresher dives.** One reason is that their instructor-to-student ratio never exeeds 1:4—that's true of all their dive groups. Rates range from $79 for a one-tank, certified dive to $450 for certification. ✉ ☎ 877/441–3483 or 808/635–7327 ⊕ www.sacredseasscuba.com.

Seasport Divers. Rated highly by readers of Rodale's *Scuba Diving* magazine, Seasport Divers' 48-foot *Anela Kai* tops the chart for dive boat luxury. But owner Marvin Otsuji didn't stop with that. In 2006, he added a second boat—a 32-foot catamaran—that's outfitted for diving, but we like it as an all-around charter. The company does a brisk business, which means they won't cancel at the last minute because of a lack of reservations, like some other companies, and although they may book up to 12 people per boat, they provide two dive masters per group of six divers. ■ TIP➔ **They offer advanced-only trips in the morning and beginner/refresher groups in the afternoon.** They also run a good-size dive shop for purchase and rentals, as well as a classroom for certification. Ni'ihau trips are available in summer. All trips leave from Kukuiula Harbor in Po'ipū. Rates start at $115 for a two-tank boat dive; rental gear is $20 extra. ✉ *Check-in office on Po'ipū Rd. just north of Lāwa'i Rd. turnoff to Spouting Horn. Look for yellow submarine in parking lot, 2827 Po'ipū Rd., Po'ipū* ☎ 808/742–9303 or 800/685–5889 ⊕ www.seasportdivers.com.

> ### SNUBA
>
> If you're not quite up for scuba—even the introductory lessons—you might consider snuba. (Personally, we think if you're ready to advance beyond snorkeling, you might as well go for Discover Scuba, but we realize that some people will feel more comfortable tethered to something.) With snuba, up to eight divers are attached to a floating scuba tank by way of a 20-foot air line, so that feeling of security is never far away. You can float on the surface or dive below. No certification is required. For reservations, call Snuba Kauai at 808/823-8912.

SNORKELING

Generally speaking, the calmest water and best snorkeling can be found on Kaua'i's North Shore in summer and South Shore in winter. The East Side, known as the windward side, has year-round, prevalent northeast trade winds that make snorkeling unpredictable, although there are some good pockets. The best snorkeling on the West Side is accessible only by boat.

A word on feeding fish: don't. As Captain Ted with HoloHolo Charters says, fish have survived and populated reefs for much longer than we have been donning goggles and staring at them. They will continue to do so without our intervention. Besides, fish food messes up the reef and—one thing always leads to another—can eliminate a once-pristine reef environment. As for gear, if you're snorkeling with one of Nā Pali boat tour outfitters, they'll provide it. However, depending on the company, it might not be the latest or greatest. If you have your own, bring it. On the other hand, if you're going out with SeaFun or Z-Tourz, not to worry. Their gear is top-notch. If you need to rent, hit one of the "snorkel-and-surf" shops such as Snorkel Bob's in Kōloa and Kapaʻa, Play Dirty in Kapaʻa, Nukumoi in Poʻipū and Waimea, or Seasport in Pōipū and Kapaʻ, or shop Wal-Mart or Kmart if you want to drag it home. Typically, though, rental gear will be better quality than that found at Wal-Mart or Kmart. ■ TIP→ **If you wear glasses, you can rent prescription masks at the rental shops—just don't expect them to match your prescription exactly.**

Best Spots

Just because we say these are good places to snorkel doesn't mean that the exact moment you arrive, the fish will flock—they are wild, after

TIPS ON SAFE SNORKELING

Mike Hopkins with SeaFun Kauaʻi, a guided walk-in snorkeling tour operator, suggests these tips for safe snorkeling:

■ Snorkel with a buddy and stay together.

■ Choose a location where lifeguards are present.

■ Ask the lifeguard about conditions, especially currents, before getting in the water.

■ Plan your entry and exit points before getting in the water.

■ Swim into the current on entering and then ride the current back to your exit point.

■ Look up periodically to gauge your location with a reference point on land.

■ When in doubt, try a guided tour.

all. The beaches here are listed in clockwise fashion starting on the North Shore.

Although it can get quite crowded, **Keʻe Beach** (⊠ At the end of Rte. 560) is quite often a good snorkeling destination. Just be sure to come during the off-hours, say early in the morning or later in the afternoon. ■ TIP→ **Snorkeling here in winter can be hazardous—summer is the best and safest time for snorkeling—although you should never swim beyond the reef.**

The search for **Tunnels (Mākua)** (⊠ At Hāʻena Beach Park, near end of Rte. 560, across from lava-tube sea caves, after stream crossing) is as tricky as the snorkeling. Park at Hāʻena Beach Park and walk east—away from Nā Pali Coast—until you see a sand channel entrance in the water, almost at the point. Once you get here, the reward is fantastic. The name of this beach comes from the many underwater lava tubes, which always attract marine life. The shore is mostly beach rock interrupted by three sand channels. You'll want to enter and exit at one of these channels (or risk stepping on a sea urchin or scraping your stomach on the reef). Follow the sand channel to a drop-off; the snorkeling along here is always full of nice surprises. Expect a current running east to west. ■ TIP→ **Snorkeling here in winter can be hazardous; summer is the best and safest time for snorkeling.**

Continued on page 98

SNORKELING IN HAWAI'I

The waters surrounding the Hawaiian Islands are filled with life—from giant manta rays cruising off the Big Island's Kona Coast to humpback whales giving birth in Maui's Māʻalaea Bay. Dip your head beneath the surface to experience a spectacularly colorful world: pairs of milletseed butterflyfish dart back and forth, red-lipped parrotfish snack on coral algae, and spotted eagle rays flap past like silent spaceships. Sea turtles bask at the surface while tiny wrasses give them the equivalent of a shave and a haircut. The water quality is typically outstanding; many sites afford 30 foot-plus visibility. On snorkel cruises, you can often stare from the boat rail right down to the bottom.

Certainly few destinations are as accommodating to every level of snorkeler as Hawai'i. Beginners can tromp in from sandy beaches while more advanced divers descend to shipwrecks, reefs, craters, and sea arches just offshore. Because of Hawai'i's extreme isolation, the island chain has fewer fish species than Fiji or the Caribbean—but many of the fish that are here exist nowhere else. The Hawaiian waters are home to the highest percentage of endemic fish in the world.

The key to enjoying the underwater world is slowing down. Look carefully. Listen. You might hear the strange crackling sound of shrimp tunneling through coral, or you may hear whales singing to one another during winter. A shy octopus may drift along the ocean's floor beneath you. If you're hooked, pick up a waterproof fish key from Long's Drugs. You can brag later that you've looked the Hawaiian turkeyfish in the eye.

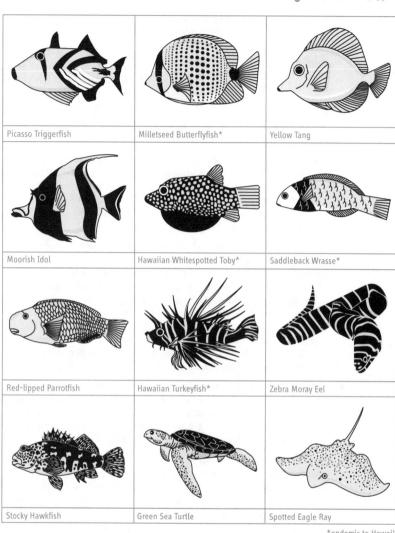

Picasso Triggerfish	Milletseed Butterflyfish*	Yellow Tang
Moorish Idol	Hawaiian Whitespotted Toby*	Saddleback Wrasse*
Red-lipped Parrotfish	Hawaiian Turkeyfish*	Zebra Moray Eel
Stocky Hawkfish	Green Sea Turtle	Spotted Eagle Ray

*endemic to Hawai'i

4

SNORKELING IN HAWAI'I

POLYNESIA'S FIRST CELESTIAL NAVIGATORS: HONU

Honu is the Hawaiian name for two native sea turtles, the hawksbill and the green sea turtle. Little is known about these dinosaur-age marine reptiles, though snorkelers regularly see them foraging for *limu* (seaweed) and the occasional jellyfish in Hawaiian waters. Most female honu nest in the uninhabited Northwestern Hawaiian Islands, but a few sociable ladies nest on Maui beaches. Scientists suspect that they navigate the seas via magnetism—sensing the earth's poles. Amazingly, they will journey up to 800 mi to nest—it's believed that they return to their own birth sites. After about 60 days of incubation, nestlings emerge from the sand at night and find their way back to the sea by the light of the stars.

☺ **Lydgate Beach Park** (✉ Just south of Wailua River, turn makai off Rte. 56 onto Lehu Dr. and left onto Nalu Rd.) is the absolute safest place to snorkel on Kaua'i. With its lava-rock wall creating a protected swimming pool, this is the perfect spot for beginners, young and old. The fish are so tame here it's almost like swimming in a saltwater aquarium.

You'll generally find good year-round snorkeling at **Po'ipū Beach Park** (✉ From Po'ipū Rd., turn right on Ho'ōne Rd.), except during summer's south swells (which are not nearly as frequent as winter's north swells). The best snorkeling fronts the Marriott Waiohai Beach Club. Stay inside the crescent shape created by the sandbar and rocky point. The current runs east to west.

Don't pack the beach umbrella, beach mats, or cooler for snorkeling at **Beach House (Lāwa'i Beach)** (✉ Makai side of Lāwa'i Rd.; park on road in front of Lāwa'i Beach Resort). Just bring your snorkeling gear. The beach—named after its neighbor the Beach House restaurant (yum)—is on the road to Spouting Horn. It's a small slip of sand during low tide and a rocky shoreline during high tide. However, it's right by the road's edge, and its rocky coastline and somewhat rocky bottom make it great for snorkeling. Enter and exit in the sand channel (not over the rocky reef) that lines up with the Lāwa'i Beach Resort's center atrium. Stay within the rocky points anchoring each end of the beach. The current runs east to west.

★ **Nu'alolo Kai** was once an ancient Hawaiian fishpond and is now home to the best snorkeling along Nā Pali Coast (and perhaps on all of Kaua'i). The only way to access it is by boat, and only a few Nā Pali snorkeling tour operators are permitted to do so. We recommend Nā Pali Explorer and Kaua'i Sea Tours (⇨ *see* Boat Tours).

Fodor's Choice With little river runoff and hardly any boat traffic, the waters off the
★ island of **Ni'ihau** are some of the clearest in all Hawai'i, and that's good for snorkeling. Like Nu'alolo Kai, the only way to snorkel here is to sign on with one of the two tour boats venturing across a sometimes rough open ocean channel: Blue Dolphin Charters and HoloHolo (⇨ *see* Boat Tours). Sammy the monk seal likes to hang out behind Lehua Rock off the north end of Ni'ihau and swim with the snorkelers.

Guided Tours

☺ **SeaFun Kaua'i.** This guided snorkeling tour, for beginners and intermediates alike, is led by a marine expert, so not only is there excellent "how-to" instruction, but the guide actually gets in the water with you and identifies marine life. You're guaranteed to spot tons of critters you'd never see on your own. This is a land-based operation and the only one of its kind on Kaua'i. (Don't think those snorkeling cruises are guided snorkeling tours—they rarely are. A member of the boat's crew serves as lifeguard, not a marine life *guide*.) A half-day tour includes all your snorkeling gear—and a wet suit to keep you warm—and stops at two snorkeling locations, chosen based on ocean conditions. The cost is $80. ⊠ *Check in at Kilohana Plantation in Puhi, next to Kaua'i Community College.* ☎ *808/245–6400 or 800/452–1113* ⊕ *www.alohakauaitours.com.*

SURFING

Good old stand-up surfing is alive and well on Kaua'i, especially in winter's high surf season on the North Shore. If you're new to the sport, we highly recommend taking a lesson. Not only will this ensure you're up and riding waves in no time, but instructors will provide the right board for your experience and size, help you time a wave, and give you a push to get your momentum going. ■ TIP➡ **You don't really need to be in top physical shape to take a lesson. Because your instructor helps push you into the wave, you won't wear yourself out paddling. However, it's always a good idea to know how to swim!** If you're experienced and want to hit the waves on your own, most surf shops rent boards for all levels, from beginners to advanced.

Best Spots

Perennial-favorite beginning surf spots include **Po'ipū Beach** (the area fronting the Marriott Waiohai Beach Club); **Hanalei Bay** (the area next to the Hanalei Pier); and the stream end of **Kalapakī Beach.** More advanced surfers move down the beach in Hanalei to an area fronting a grove of pine trees known as **Pine Trees.** When the trade winds die, the north ends of **Wailua** and **Keālia** beaches are teeming with surfers. Breaks off **Po'ipū** and **Beach House/Lāwa'i Beach** attract intermediates year-round. During high surf, the break on the cliff side of **Kalihi Wai** is for experts only. ⇨ *See* Chapter 3, "Beaches," *for complete beach information and directions.*

Surfing Lessons

✆ **Blue Seas Surf School.** Surfer and instructor Charlie Smith specializes in beginners (especially children) and will go anywhere on the island to find just the right surf. His soft-top, long boards are very stable, making it easier to stand up. Rates start at $65 for a 1½-hour lesson. ⊠ *Meet at beach; location varies depending on surf conditions.* ☎ *808/634–6979* ⊕ *www.blueseassurfingschool.com.*

Margo Oberg Surfing School. Seven-time world surfing champion Margo Oberg runs a surf school that meets on the beach in front of the Sheraton Kaua'i in Po'ipū. Lessons are $60 for 1½ hours, though she herself rarely teaches anymore. ⊠ *Po'ipū Beach* ☎ *808/332–6100* ⊕ *www.surfonkauai.com.*

Nukumoi Surf Co. The parents of Kaua'i-grown and world-famous Rochelle Ballard own this surf shop. Not that the instructors who teach

> **THE NEXT WAVE IN SURFING**
>
> A few years ago, it was kiteboarding. Today, the latest in surfing is called "stand-up paddle surfing." It's really a heftier surfboard and a longer-than-normal canoe paddle. Just like the name implies, stand-up paddle surfers (we're sure a shorter, hipper name will eventually emerge) do not start on their bellies. If they're on top of their game, they stand throughout the entire process. They tend to catch a wave earlier and ride it longer than even long-board surfers.

WANT TO GO SURFING?

Thinking about taking surf lessons? These are a few good questions to ask your potential surf instructor:

■ What equipment do you provide? (If you're a beginner, you'll want to hear about their soft-top beginner boards. You'll also want to know if they'll provide rash guards and aqua socks.)

■ Who will be my instructor? (It's not always the name on the company logo. Ask about your instructor's qualifications.)

■ How do you select the location? (Ideally, you'll be assured that they pick the location because of its gentle waves, sandy beach bottom, and good year-round conditions.)

■ What if the waves are too big? (Under the best circumstances, they'll select another location or reschedule for another day.)

■ How many students do you take at a time? (Don't book if it's more than four students per instructor. You'll definitely want some personal attention.)

■ Are you CPR- and lifeguard-certified? (It's good to know your instructor will be able to help if you get into trouble.)

surfing there these days taught Rochelle, but if they're working with the family, we figure they know a thing or two about surfing. Actually, the three surf instructors operating out of Nukumoi Surf Co. are themselves die-hard surfers, even if they never made the international scene. Lessons run $75 for a two-hour lesson with no more than four students per instructor. Their primary surf spot is the beach fronting the Sheraton. ⊠ *On Hoʻone Rd. across from Poʻipū Beach Park* ☎ *808/742–8019* ⊕ *www. nukumoisurf.com.*

Titus Kinimaka Hawaiian School of Surfing. Famed as a pioneer of big-wave surfing, this Hawaiian believes in giving back to his sport. Beginning, intermediate, and "extreme" lessons, including tow-in, are available. If you want to learn to surf from a living legend, this is the man. ■ TIP➔ **He does employ some other instructors, so if you want Titus, be sure to ask for him.** Rates are $65 for a 90-minute group lesson; $100 to $120 per hour for a private lesson; $150 for a one-hour, tow-in lesson. A surf DVD is included with each lesson. ⊠ *Meets at various beaches* ☎ *808/652–1116.*

Outfitters

Kai Kane. ⊠ *Makai as you enter Hanalei* ☎ *808/826–5594.*
Nukumoi Surf Co. ⊠ *On Hoʻone Rd. across from Poʻipū Beach Park* ☎ *808/ 742–8019.*
Nukumoi Surf Co. West Side. ⊠ *In Waimea, makai on Rte. 50* ☎ *808/ 338–1617.*
Progressive Expressions. ⊠ *On Kōloa Rd. in Old Kōloa Town* ☎ *808/ 742–6041.*

Tamba Surf Company. ⊠ *Mauka on north end of Hwy. 56 in Kapa'a; across from Scotty's Beachside BBQ; 4-1543 Kūhiō Hwy., Kapa'a* ☎ *808/ 823–6942.*

Hanalei Surf Company. ⊠ *Mauka at Hanalei Center, 5-5161 Kūhiō Hwy., Hanalei* ☎ *808/826–9000.*

WHALE-WATCHING

Every winter North Pacific humpback whales swim some 3,000 mi over 30 days, give or take a few, from Alaska to Hawai'i. Whales arrive as early as November and sometimes stay through April, though they seem to be most populous in February and March. They come to Hawai'i to breed, calve, and nurse their young.

Although humpbacks spend more than 90% of their lives underwater, they can be very active above water while they're in Hawai'i. Here are a few maneuvers you may see:

- Blow: the expulsion of air that looks like a geyser of water.

- Spy hop: the raising of just the whale's head out of the water, as if to take a look around.

- Tail slap: the repetitive slap of the tail, or fluke, on the surface of the water.

- Pec slap: the repetitive slap of one or both fins on the surface of the water.

- Fluke up dive: the waving of the tail above water as the whale slowly rolls under water to dive.

- Breach: the launching of the entire whale's body out of the water.

Tours

Of course, nothing beats seeing a whale up close. During the season, any boat on the water is looking for whales; they're hard to avoid, whether the tour is labeled "whale-watching" or not. Several boat operators will add two-hour, afternoon whale-watching tours during the season that run on the South Shore (not Nā Pali). Operators include **Blue Dolphin, Catamaran Kahanu, HoloHolo,** and **Nā Pali Explorer** (⇨ *see* Boat Tours). There are a few lookout spots around the island with good land-based viewing: Kīlauea Lighthouse on the North Shore, the Kapa'a Scenic Overlook just north of Kapa'a town on the East Side, and the cliffs to the east of Keoneloa (Shipwreck) Beach on the South Shore.

WINDSURFING

Windsurfing on Kaua'i isn't nearly as popular as it is on Maui but 'Anini Beach Park is the place if you're going to windsurf or play the spectator. Rentals and lessons are available from **Windsurf Kaua'i** (☎ 808/ 828–6838). Lessons run $85 for three hours; rentals run $25 for one hour, and up to $75 for the day. The instructor will meet you on 'Anini Beach.

Golf, Hiking & Outdoor Activities

WORD OF MOUTH

"If you like to do lots of outdoor activities (hiking, snorkeling, sight-seeing), then I think you'll love Kaua`i. We've been to O`ahu, Maui, and Kaua`i, and Kaua`i is our favorite."   —Samsaf

"The views of the valley and surrounding cliffs from along the Nu`alolo cliff trail are incredible; the sight made me joyfully stretch out my arms at the cliff's edge only to scream out "this is why I spend all those hours keying things into a computer at work . . . to afford moments like this!"   —bluefan

Updated by
Pamela
Woolway

FOR THOSE OF US WHO LOVE ocean sports but need a little break from all that sun, sand, and salt, there are plenty of options. Stay grounded and hike the island's many trails, or consider taking your vacation into flight with a tree-top zipline. Have a backcountry adventure in a four-wheel drive, or relax in an inner tube floating down the cane-field irrigation canals.

It's a good idea to do some planning while still at home. Before booking tours, check with your concierge to find out what the forecast has been for water and weather conditions. If you happen to arrive during a North Shore lull in the surf, you'll want to plan to be on the ocean in a kayak or snorkeling

> **TIP ON TIPPING**
>
> It's common knowledge that the average Kaua'i resident works more than one job, and usually one of those jobs is in the tourist industry. The folks who are entertaining you while swinging through the trees on a zipline tour and serving you lunch by a waterfall are working for just a dollar or two above minimum wage. They rely heavily on gratuities. The recommended tipping procedure for a guide is 10 percent of the cost per person of the activity. Factor this into your budget when planning your vacation.

on the reef. If it's been raining, ATV tours are the activity of choice.

For the golfer in the family, Kaua'i's spectacular courses have been rated among the most scenic as well as the most technical. Princeville Golf Course has garnered accolades from three national publications, and Poipu Bay Golf Course has been home to the prestigious season-end PGA Grand Slam of Golf since 1994.

One of the most popular Kaua'i experiences is to see the island from the air. In an hour you can see waterfalls, craters, and other places that are inaccessible even by hiking trails (some say that 70% or more of the island is inaccessible). The majority of flights depart from the Līhu'e airport and follow a clockwise pattern around the island. ■ **TIP→ If you plan to take an aerial tour, it's a good idea to fly when you first arrive, rather than saving it for the end of your trip.** It will help you visualize what's where on the island, and it may help you decide what you want to see from a closer vantage point during your stay. Many companies advertise a low-price 30- or 40-minute tour, which they rarely fly, so don't expect to book a flight at the advertised rate. The most popular flight is 60 minutes long, and some companies offer DVDs for an additional charge, so there's no need to spend your time in the air snapping pictures.

AIRPLANE TOURS

Kaua'i Aero Tours. This tour is really a flying lesson in a Citabria tail dragger that was designed specifically for aerobatics. You can take the stick or let your pilot handle the controls. The aerobatics roll on until you say stop. The plane can take only one passenger at a time. Tours last 30 to 60 minutes; prices range from $129 to $179. ⊠ *Līhu'e Airport* ☎ *808/639–9893.*

Tropical Biplanes. This company flies a bright red Waco biplane, built in 2002 based on a 1936 design. An open cockpit and staggered wing design means there's nothing between you and the sights. The plane can carry two passengers in front and flies at an altitude of 1,000 feet, at about 85 mph. The price for a couple is $356. ✉ *Līhu'e Airport Commuter Terminal* ☎ *808/246–9123* ⊕ *www.tropicalbiplanes.com.*

Lessons

Birds in Paradise. This company declares itself the number-one ultralight flying school in Kaua'i. A serene cruise over the island, skimming clouds with the breeze in your hair, is a meditative and magical way to take in the sights. Although many tours are available, the most popular package is the 50–60-minute tour for $190. ✉ *Salt Pond Beach Park/Port Allen Airport* ☎ *888/359–3656* ⊕ *birdsinparadise.com.*

Fodor'sChoice ★ **Ultralight Adventures Kauai.** Have you ever had a flying dream and woken up deliciously hungry for wings? Here's an opportunity to leave this earthbound existence and realize your potential for flight. Those delicate contraptions you see buzzing the island offer a breezy and liberated option for seeing Kaua'i from the air. Take a lesson from instructors with more than 20 years of experience and U.S. Ultralight Association certification. The cost is $190 for the one-hour lesson. ✉ *Salt Pond Beach Park, Port Allen Airport* ☎ *808/645–6444.*

ATV TOURS

Kaua'i ATV Tours. This is *the* thing to do when it rains on Kaua'i. Consider it an extreme mud bath. Kaua'i ATV in Kōloa is the originator of the island's all-terrain-vehicle tours. Their $99 three-hour jaunt takes you through a private sugar plantation and historic cane-haul tunnel. The $145 four-hour tour visits secluded waterfalls and includes a picnic lunch. The more popular longer excursion includes a hike through a bamboo forest and a swim in a freshwater pool at the base of the falls—to rinse off all that mud. You must be 16 or older to operate your own ATV, but Kaua'i ATV also offers its four-passenger and two-passenger "Mud Bugs" to accommodate families with kids ages five and older. ✉ *5330 Kōloa Rd., Kōloa* ☎ *808/742–2734 or 877/707–7088* ⊕ *www.kauaiatv.com.*

> **WORD OF MOUTH**
>
> "Kipu Ranch Adventures was recommended by our guidebook, and they didn't disappoint. This was by far the best money spent on my trip to Kauai."   –annahead

Kipu Ranch Adventures. This 3,000-acre property extends from the Huleia River to the top of Mt. Haupu. *Jurassic Park, Indiana Jones,* and *Mighty Joe Young* were filmed here, and you'll see the locations for all of them on the $105 three-hour Ranch Tour. The $140 four-hour Waterfall Tour includes a visit to two waterfalls and a picnic lunch. Kipu Ranch was once a sugar plantation, but today it is a working cattle ranch, so you'll be in the company of bovines as well as pheasants, wild boars, and peacocks. ☎ *808/246–9288* ⊕ *www.kiputours.com.*

5

Robinson Family Adventures. Gay & Robinson, one of the last two sugar plantations in the state of Hawaii, has raised cattle and grown sugarcane on the west side of Kaua'i for more than a century. It's been only in the last few years that the family has allowed visitors to tour Makaweli Ranch, the family's 18,000-acre working cattle ranch. This is not a fun-in-the-mud, thrill seeker's ride. Landscape, horticulture, and island history are the focus of this tour. You'll be introduced to edible plants on the property, glean insight into Robinson family history, and hear plenty of talk about the island's past. For $145, the four-hour Mountain Pool tour meanders 13 mi of winding red dirt trails that offer ocean views over Port Allen Harbor and include a barbecue lunch and a cool dip in the Hanapepe River. As is the rule for all ATV tours, you must be 16 or older to operate an ATV. For the four-passenger vehicle, the cutoff age is eight years old. ⊠ *Kaumakani Ave, past mile marker 19 Kaumakani* ☏ *808/335–2824* ⊕ *www.gandrtours-kauai.com.*

BIKING

Kaua'i is a labyrinth of cane-haul roads, which are fun for exploring on two wheels. The challenge is to find the roads where biking is allowed and then to not get lost in the maze. Maybe that explains why Kaua'i is not a hub for the sport . . . yet. Still, there are some epic rides for those who are interested—both the adrenaline-rushing and the mellower beach cruiser kinds. If you want to grind out some mileage, the main highway that skirts the coastal areas is perfectly safe, though there are only a few designated bike lanes. It's hilly, but you'll find that keeping your eyes on the road and not the scenery is the biggest challenge. You can rent bikes (with helmets) from the activities desks of certain hotels, but these are not the best quality. You're better off renting from either Kaua'i Cycle in Kapa'a or Outfitters Kaua'i in Po'ipū. ■ **TIP→ If you're headed for the dirt tracks, be sure your bike is in top condition, take plenty of water and energy bars, and let someone know when and where you're going. If you're venturing into the unknown, explain what you've got in mind to someone who knows the area and heed any advice offered. And be sure to get explicit directions; don't expect signs.**

Keālia Coastal Road. For the cruiser, this dirt-haul cane road is easy to follow along the coastline to Donkey Beach. From here, the trail splinters into numerous, narrower trails through fallow sugarcane fields where dirt bikers now roam, especially on weekends. It's easy to get lost here, but eventually all trails lead to Anahola Beach Park, some 4 mi from Keālia. If you're not sure you'll find your way back the way you came, follow Anahola Road inland to Route 56 and return to Keālia via the highway. ⊠ *Trailhead: 1 mi north of Kapa'a; park at north end of Keālia Beach.*

> ### DOWN IN THE DIRT
>
> Unless you love the juxtaposition of red dirt against say, baby blue or white, wear only dark colors and thrashed clothing for outdoor adventuring. There's good reason businesses fare well dyeing T-shirts red with the dirt here.

Moalepe Trail. This trail is perfect for intermediate to advanced riders. The first 2 mi of this 5-mi, double-track road wind through pasture-land. The real challenge begins when you reach the steep and rutted switchbacks, which during a rainy spell can be hazardous to attempt. Moalepe intersects Kuilau Trail at the U-turn. If you choose to continue down the trail, it will end at the Keāhua Arboretum stream. From Kuhio Highway in Kapaa drive mauka on Kuamo'o Road for 3 mi and turn right on Kamalu Road. It dead-ends at Olohena Road. Turn left and follow until the road veers sharply to the right. The trailhead will be right in front of you.

> ## PRACTICALLY FREE BIKING/HIKING TOURS
>
> For five bucks, nonmembers of Kaua'i's Sierra Club can participate in guided hikes and bike outings all over the island. In fact, Sierra Club occasionally has access to private land you'd not be able to see otherwise. Visit their group outing Web page at www.hi.sierraclub.org/kauai/kauai-hikes for a current listing of organized hikes.

5

Powerline Trail. Advanced riders should try this trail. It's actually a service road for the electric company that splits the island. It's 13 mi in length; the first 5 mi goes from 620 feet in elevation to almost 2,000. The remaining 8 mi is a gradual descent over a variety of terrain, some technical. Some sections will require carrying your bike. The views will stay with you forever. Trailhead is mauka just past the stream crossing at Keāhua Arboretum.

Spalding Monument Loop. For the novice rider, this loop offers a good workout and a summit ocean view that is not overly strenuous to reach. If you pick up a bike at Kaua'i Cycle in Kapa'a, you can literally ride a mile up the bike path to reach the head of the loop, and even make a snack-stop at the Kealia Store without a detour. From Kealia Store, ride up a gradual incline 2 mi through horse pastures to Spalding Monument, named for a former plantation owner. Palms circle the lava rock wall where you can picnic while enjoying a 180-degree ocean view. Behind you is a glorious backdrop of Kalalea. Follow the paved road north toward Kalalea for 2 more mi. Turn right at the highway, and it's another 2 mi south to a parking lot on the ocean side. The lot is not far from mile marker 12 and sits on the top of a hill. Follow the dirt path down to the beach. The bike path is an old cane-haul road that heads right back into Kapaa Town. ⊠ *The loop begins at the Kealia Store, past mile marker 10 on the mauka side of the Rd.*

Wailua Forest Management Road. For the novice mountain biker, this is an easy ride and is easy to find. From Route 56 in Wailua, turn mauka on Kuamo'o Road and continue 6 mi to the picnic area, known as Keāhua Arboretum; park here. The potholed four-wheel-drive road includes some stream crossings—■ TIP→ stay away during heavy rains, because the streams flood—and continues for 2 mi to a T-stop, where you should turn right. Stay on the road for about 3 mi until you reach a gate; this is the spot where the gates in the movie *Jurassic Park* were filmed, though it looks nothing like the movie. Go around the gate and down the road for another mile to a confluence of streams at the base of Mt. Wai'ale'ale. Be sure to bring your camera.

Waimea Canyon Road. For those wanting a road workout, climb this road, also known as Route 550. After a 3,000-foot climb, the road tops out at mile 12 adjacent to Waimea Canyon, which will pop in and out of view on your right as you ascend. From here it continues several miles (mostly level) past the Kōke'e Museum and ends at the Kalalau Lookout. It's paved the entire way, uphill 100%, and curvy. ■ TIP→ **There's not much of a shoulder—sometimes none—so be extra cautious.** The road gets busier as the day wears on, so you may want to consider a sunrise ride. ⊠ *Road turns mauka off Rte. 50 just after grocery store in downtown Waimea.*

Outfitters & Tours

Kaua'i Cycle. This reliable, full-service bike shop rents, sells, and repairs bikes. Mountain bikes and road bikes are available for $15 to $40 per day and $75 to $125 per week with directions to trails. Their new location is on the ocean, so no more fighting that Kapaa traffic to reach the beach. The Kealia bike path is right out their back door and can be ridden 10 uninterrupted mi up to Anahola. ⊠ *Across from Taco Bell, 934 Kūhiō Hwy., Kapa'a* ☎ *808/821–2115* ⊕ *www.bikehawaii.com/kauaicycle.*

Outfitters Kaua'i. Beach cruisers and mountain bikes are available at this shop in Po'ipū. You can ride right out the door to tour Po'ipū, or get information on how to do a self-guided tour of Kōe'e State Park and Waimea Canyon. The company also leads sunrise coasting tours (under the name **Bicycle Downhill**) from Waimea Canyon to the island's West Side beaches. Rentals cost $20 to $45 per day. Tours cost $94. ⊠ *2827-A Po'ipū Rd., Po'ipū, Follow Po'ipū Rd. south from Kōloa town; shop is on right before turnoff to Spouting Horn* ☎ *808/742–9667 or 888/742–9887* ⊕ *www.outfitterskauai.com.*

Pedal 'n' Paddle. This company rents beach cruisers, tandems, and mountain bikes for $10 to $20 per day; $30 to $80 per week. Tandem bicycles have a $10 hourly rate. In the heart of Hanalei, this is a great way to cruise the town; the more ambitious cyclist can head to the end of the road. Be careful, though, because there are no bike lanes on the twisting and turning road to Ke'e. ⊠ *Ching Young Village, Rte. 560, Hanalei* ☎ *808/826–9069* ⊕ *www.pedalnpaddle.com.*

GOLF

For golfers, the Garden Isle might as well be known as the Robert Trent Jones Jr. Isle. Four of the island's nine courses, including Po'ipū Bay—home of the PGA Grand Slam of Golf—are the work of Jones, who maintains a home at Princeville. Combine these four courses with those from Jack Nicklaus, Robin Nelson, and local legend Toyo Shirai, and you'll see that golf sets Kaua'i apart from the other islands as much as the Pacific Ocean does.

FodorśChoice **Kauaʻi Lagoons Golf Club.** When Jack
★ Nicklaus opened the Kiele (pro-
nounced kee-*el*-ay) Course here in
1989, it was immediately compared
to Mauna Kea, Robert Trent Jones
Sr.'s Big Island masterpiece. Depending on the rater, Kiele continues to be considered among the top
three or four courses in the state.
Nicklaus's design is like a sym-
phony, starting nice and easy and
finishing with a rousing par-4 that
plays deceptively uphill—into the

trade winds—to an island green. The adjacent Mokihana Course (Nicklaus, 1990) is flatter and doesn't have Kiele's oceanfront. According to
handicap ratings it's supposed to play easier, but Nicklaus makes par a
challenge with creative mounding, large waste areas, and false fronts
for greens. The boomerang-shape par-5 18th is among the state's finest
finales. ☒ *3351 Hoʻolaulea Way, Līhuʻe* ☎ *808/241–6000* ⊕ *www.
golfbc.com* ⛳ *Kiele Course: 18 holes. 6,674 yds. Par 72. Greens fee:
$195. Mokihana Course: 18 holes. 6,578 yds. Par 72. Greens fee: $130
☞ Facilities: Driving range, putting green, golf carts, rental clubs, lessons, restaurant, bar.*

Kiahuna Plantation Golf Course. A meandering creek, lava outcrops, and
thickets of trees give Kiahuna its character. Robert Trent Jones Jr. (1983)
was given a smallish piece of land just inland at Poʻipū, and defends par
with smaller targets, awkward stances, and optical illusions. In 2003 a
group of homeowners bought the club and brought Jones back to ren-
ovate the course, adding tees and revamping bunkers. ☒ *2545 Kiahuna
Plantation Dr., Kōloa* ☎ *808/742–9595* ⊕ *www.kiahunagolf.com* ⛳ *18
holes. 6,183 yds. Par 70. Greens fee: $110 ☞ Facilities: Driving range,
putting green, rental clubs, lessons, pro shop, restaurant, bar.*

Kukuiolono Golf Course. Local legend Toyo Shirai designed this fun,
funky 9-holer where holes play across rolling, forested hills that afford
views of the distant Pacific. Though Shirai has an eye for a good golf
hole, Kukuiolono is out of the way and a bit rough, and probably not
for everyone. But at $8 for the day, it's a deal. ☒ *854 Puʻu Rd., Kalāheo*
☎ *808/332–9151* ⛳ *9 holes. 3,173 yds. Par 36. Greens fee: $8 ☞ Fa-
cilities: Driving range, putting green, golf carts, pull carts, rental clubs.*

FodorśChoice **Poʻipū Bay Golf Course.** Poʻipū Bay has been called the Pebble Beach of
★ Hawaiʻi, and comparisons are apt. Like Pebble Beach, Poʻipū is a links
course built on headlands, not true links land. And as at Monterey Bay,
there's wildlife galore. It's not unusual for golfers to see monk seals sun-
ning on the beach below, sea turtles bobbing outside the shore break,
and humpback whales leaping offshore. ☒ *2250 Ainako St., Kōloa*
☎ *808/742–8711* ⊕ *www.poipubay.com* ⛳ *18 holes. 6,612 yds. Par
72. Greens fee: $130 ☞ Facilities: Driving range, putting green, rental
clubs, golf carts, golf academy/lessons, restaurant, bar.*

5

Fodor's Choice
★

Princeville Resort. Robert Trent Jones Jr. built two memorable courses overlooking Hanalei Bay, the 27-hole Princeville Makai Course (1971) and the Prince Course (1990). The three Makai nines—Woods, Lake, Ocean—offering varying degrees of each element, plus lush mountain views above. Three quick snapshots: the par-3 seventh on the Ocean nine drops 100 feet from tee to green, with blue Hanalei Bay just beyond. The Ocean's par-3 eighth plays across a small bay where dolphins often leap. On the Woods's par-3 eighth,

> ### GOLFING GEAR
>
> In theory you can play golf in Hawai'i 365 days a year. But there's a reason the Hawaiian Islands are so green. Better to bring an umbrella and light jacket and not use them than to not bring them and get soaked. When it's not raining, afternoons can get hot and windy; this will benefit your wallet. Greens fees drop considerably in the afternoon.

two large lava rocks in Jones's infamous Zen Bunker really are quite blissful, until you plant a tee shot behind one of them. The Prince was ranked by *Golf Digest* as Hawai'i's number-one golf course on their 2006 list of America's Top 100 Greatest Courses. It's certifiably rated Hawai'i's second toughest (behind O'ahu's Ko'olau). This is jungle golf, with holes running through dense forest and over tangled ravines, out onto headlands for breathtaking ocean views, then back into the jungle. **Makai Golf Course:** ⊠ *4080 Lei O Papa Rd., Princeville* ☎ *808/826–3580* ⊕ *www.princeville.com* ⅃ *27 holes. 6,886 yds. Par 72. Greens fee: $110* ☞ *Facilities: Driving range, putting green, rental clubs, golf carts, pro shop, golf academy/lessons, snack bar.* **Prince Golf Course:** ⊠ *5-3900 Kūhiō Hwy., Princeville* ☎ *808/826–5001* ⊕ *www.princeville. com* ⅃ *18 holes. 6,960 yds. Par 72. Greens fee: $150* ☞ *Facilities: Driving range, putting green, rental clubs, golf carts, pro shop, golf academy/lessons, restaurant, bar.*

Wailua Municipal Golf Course. Voted by *Golf Digest* as one of Hawai'i's 15-best golf courses, this seaside course was first built as a 9-hole golf course in the 1930s. The second 9 holes were added in 1961. Course designer Toyo Shirai created a course that is fun but not punishing. Not only is this an affordable game with minimal water hazards, but it is challenging enough to have been chosen to host three USGA Amateur Public Links Championships. The trade winds blow steadily on the east side of the island and make the game all the more challenging. An ocean view and affordability make this one of the most popular courses on the island. ⅃ *18 holes. Par 72. Greens fee: $32 weekdays, $44 weekends. Half price after 2 PM.* ☞ *Facilities: Driving range, rental clubs, golf carts, pro shop, lessons, snack bar* ⊠ *5350 Kūhiō Hwy. Five mins north of airport, Lihue* ☎ *808/241–6666.*

> ### RENTAL CLUBS
>
> All resort courses and most daily fee courses provide rental clubs. In many cases they're the latest lines from Titleist, Ping, Callaway, and the like. This is true for men and women, as well as left-handers, which means you don't have to schlepp clubs across the Pacific.

HELICOPTER TOURS

Blue Hawaiian Helicopters. The newest helicopter company to the island is not new to Hawai'i, having flown for 20 years on Maui and the Big Island. They are the only company on Kaua'i flying the latest in helicopter technology, the Eco-Star, costing $1.8 million. It has 23% more interior space for its six passengers, has unparalleled

viewing, and offers a few extra safety features none of the other helicopters on the island has. As the name implies, the helicopter is a bit more environmentally friendly, with a 50% noise-reduction rate. Their flights run a tad shorter than others (approximately 50 minutes instead of the 55 to 65 minutes that others tout), although the flight feels very complete. The rate is $232. A DVD of your actual tour is available for an additional $25. ⊠ *Harbor Mall in Nawiliwili, Līhu'e* ☎ *808/245–5800 or 800/745-2583* ⊕ *www.bluehawaiian.com.*

Fodor$Choice ★ **Inter-Island Helicopters.** This company flies four-seater Hughes 500 helicopters *with the doors off.* It can get chilly at higher elevations, so bring a sweater and wear long pants. They offer a spectacular tour that includes landing by a waterfall for a picnic and swim. Tours depart from Hanapēpē's Port Allen Airport. Prices range from $189 to $280 per person. ⊠ *From Rte. 50, turn makai onto Rte. 543 in Hanapēpē* ☎ *808/335-5009 or 800/656-5009* ⊕ *www.interislandhelicopters.com.*

Safari Helicopters. This company flies the "Super" ASTAR helicopter, which offers floor-to-ceiling windows on its doors, four roof windows, and Bose X-Generation headphones. Two-way microphones allow passengers to converse with the pilot. The price is $213; a DVD is $28 extra. ⊠ *3225 Akahi St., Līhu'e* ☎ *808/246–0136 or 800/326-3356* ⊕ *www.safariair.com.*

Will Squyres Helicopter Tours. The majority of this company's pilots were born and raised in Hawai'i, making them excellent tour guides. Will Squyres removed its two-way microphones, eliminating the possibility of one passenger hogging the airwaves. Prices start at $189. ⊠ *3222 Kūhiō Hwy., Līhu'e* ☎ *808/245-8881 or 888/245-4354* ⊕ *www.helicopters-hawaii.com.*

HIKING

The best way to experience the '*aina*—the land—on Kaua'i is to step off the beach and hike into the remote interior. You'll find waterfalls so tall you'll strain your neck looking, pools of crystal-cool water for swimming, tropical forests teeming with plant life, and ocean vistas that will make you wish you could stay forever.

Continued on page 114

HAWAI'I'S PLANTS 101

Hawai'i is a bounty of rainbow-colored flowers and plants. The evening air is scented with their fragrance. Just look at the front yard of almost any home, travel any road, or visit any local park and you'll see a spectacular array of colored blossoms and leaves. What most visitors don't know is that the plants they are seeing are not native to Hawai'i; rather, they were introduced during the last two centuries as ornamental plants, or for timber, shade, or fruit.

Hawai'i boasts every climate on the planet, excluding the two most extreme: arctic tundra and arid desert. The Islands have wine-growing regions, cactus-speckled ranchlands, icy mountaintops, and the rainiest forests on earth.

Plants introduced from around the world thrive here. The lush lowland valleys along the windward coasts are predominantly populated by nonnative trees including yellow- and red-fruited **guava**, silvery leafed **kukui**, and orange flowered **tulip trees.**

The colorful **plumeria flower**, very fragrant and commonly used in lei making, and the giant multicolored **hibiscus flower** are both used by many women as hair adornments, and are two of the most common plants found around homes and hotels. The umbrellalike **monkeypod tree** from Central America provides shade in many of Hawai'i's parks including Kapiolani Park in Honolulu. Hawai'i's largest tree, found in Lahaina, Maui, is a giant **banyan tree.** Its canopy and massive support roots cover several acres. The native **o'hia tree**, with its brilliant red brushlike flowers, and the **hapu'u**, a giant tree fern, are common in Hawai'i's forests and are also used ornamentally in gardens and around homes.

Bougainvillea	Guava	Monkeypod Tree
Banyan Tree	O'hia Lehua*	Tulip Tree
Plumeria	Pandanus	Hibiscus
Anthurium	Kukui Tree	Hapu'u*

*endemic to Hawai'i

5

HAWAII'S PLANTS 101

DID YOU KNOW?

Over 2,200 plant species are found in the Hawaiian Islands, but only about 1,000 are native. Of these, 282 are so rare, they are endangered. Hawai'i's endemic plants evolved from ancestral seeds arriving on the islands over thousands of years as baggage on birds, floating on ocean currents, or drifting on winds from continents thousands of miles away. Once here, these plants evolved in isolation creating many new species known nowhere else in the world.

LEPTOSPIROSIS

The sparkling waters of those babbling brooks trickling around the island can be life threatening, and we're not talking about the dangers of drowning, although they, too, exist. Leptospirosis is a bacterial disease that is transmitted from animals to humans. It can survive for long periods of time in fresh water and mud contaminated by the urine of infected animals, such as mice, rats, and goats. The bacteria enter the body through the eyes, ears, nose, mouth, and broken skin. To avoid infection, do not drink untreated water from the island's streams; do not wade in waters above the chest or submerge skin with cuts and abrasions in island streams or rivers. Symptoms are often mild and resemble the flu—fever, diarrhea, chills, nausea, headache, vomiting, and body pains. Symptoms may occur 2 to 20 days after exposure. If you think you have these symptoms, see a doctor right away.

■ **TIP**→ For your safety wear sturdy shoes—preferably water-resistant ones for the many stream crossings you will most likely encounter—bring plenty of water, never hike alone, stay on the trail, and avoid hiking when it's wet and slippery. All hiking trails on Kaua'i are free, so far. There's a rumor that the Waimea Canyon and Kōke'e state parks will someday charge an admission fee. Whatever it may be, it will be worth it.

Hanalei-Okolehao Trail. *Okolehao* means "moonshine" in Hawaiian. This trail follows the Hihimanu Ridge, which was established in the days of Prohibition, when kolehao was being distilled from the roots of ti plants. This 2-mi hike climbs 1,200 feet and offers a 360-degree view of Hanalei Bay and Wai'oli Valley. Were it not for Kaua'i Sierra Club volunteers, this trail would have perished after Hurricane Iniki. It took eight years of hauling chain saws and weed whackers up the ridge to clear the trail. Your ascent begins at the China Ditch off the Hanalei River. Follow the trail through a lightly forested grove, at the Y take the first right, and then take the next left up a steep embankment. From here the trail is well marked. Most of the climb is lined with hala, ti, wild orchid, and eucalyptus. You'll get your first of many ocean views at the 1-mile marker. ⊠ *Follow Ohiki Road (north of the Hanalei Bridge) .7 mi to the U.S. Fish and Wildlife Service parking area. Directly across the street is a small bridge that marks the trailhead.*

Ho opi'i Falls. Tucked among the winding roads and grassy pastures of Kapahi, 3 mi inland from Kapa'a town, is an easy hike to two waterfalls. A 10-minute walk will deliver you to the creek. Follow the creek around to see the first set of falls. The more impressive second falls are a mere 25 minutes away. The swimming hole alone is worth the journey. Just climb the rooted path next to the first falls and turn left on the trail above. Turn left on the very next trail to descend back into the canyon and follow the leafy trail that zigzags along the creek. The falls and the swimming hole will lie below. Now is your chance to live that Indiana

Jones fantasy of swinging from tree limb to tree limb. Okay, it's not that bad, but you will be grateful for all the trees on the descent that will help you brace yourself on the steep decline. Once you step into that cool, clear water, you'll be glad you made the extra effort. ⊠ *On the north end of Kapaa, ¼ mi past the last lookout, is a small side road called Kawaihau. Follow the road up 3 mi, then turn right on Kapahi Road into a residential neighborhood. Kapahi Road dead-ends near the trailhead. Look for the yellow gate on your left.*

Kalalau Trail. Of all the hikes on the island, Kalalau Trail is by far the most famous and in many regards the most strenuous. A recreational hiker can easily make the 2-mi trek to Hanakapi'ai Beach, and for the seasoned outdoorsman, the additional 2 mi up to the falls is manageable. But be prepared to rock-hop along a creek and ford waters that can get waist high during the rain. Round-trip to Hanakapi'ai Falls is 8 mi. This steep and often muddy trail is best approached with a walking stick. The narrow trail will deliver one startling ocean view after another along a path that is alternately shady and sunny. Wear tennis shoes or hiking sandals, and bring drinking water since the creeks on the trail are not potable. Snacks are always encouraged on a strenuous hike such as this one. If your plan is to venture the full 11 mi into Kalalau, you need to acquire a camping permit. ⊠ *Drive north past Hanalei to the end of the road. Trailhead is directly across from Ke'e Beach.*

Shipwreck Shoreline Trail. This trail offers the novice hiker an accessible way to appreciate the rugged southern coast of Kaua'i. A cross-country course wends its way along the water, high above the ocean, through a lava field and past a sacred *heiau* (stone structure). Usually you can walk all the way to Maha'ulepu, just 2 mi north, but at the time of this writing it was closed a mile in because of a landslide. Regardless of this shortened version, it is well worth the one-hour round-trip walk. ⊠ *Drive north on Poi Pu Road, turn right at the Poi Pu Bay Golf Course sign. The street name is Ainako but is*

GOT GPS?

Geocaching is the modern pirate's treasure hunt where GPS coordinates are given for the buried treasure. The general rule is that if you take an item, you leave an item, and sign the logbook. Some caches are themed, so read the description before going on a hunt. Go to geocaching.com and type in a Kaua'i zip code and Hawaii as your destination to discover the coordinates for the cache. In Kapa'a alone, more than 70 treasures are hidden on hikes varying in length from 1 to 17 mi. The booty is usually well hidden and requires some digging around once you are on the exact spot.

WORD OF MOUTH

"We did the Nu'lolo/Cliffs/Awa'awapuhi Loop and agree that it is the most spectacular hike we have ever done. There is an absolutely amazing view from Lolo Vista—be sure to go beyond the Cliffs trail crossing at the end of the Nu'alolo to get to Lolo Vista."
        —LindainOhio

hard to see. Drive down to the beach and park in the lot.

Sleeping Giant Trail. An easy and easily accessible trail practically in the heart of Kapaʻa, the Sleeping Giant Trail—or simply "Sleeping Giant"—gains 1,000 feet over 2 mi. We prefer an early-morning—say, sunrise—hike, with sparkling blue-water vistas, up the east-side trailhead. At the top you can see a grassy grove with a picnic table; don't stop here. Continue carefully along the narrow trail toward the Giant's nose and chin. From here there are 360-degree views of the island. ☒ *In Wailua, turn mauka off Rte. 56 onto Haleilio Rd.; proceed 1 mi to small parking area on right.*

Waimea Canyon and Kōkeʻe State Parks. This park contains a 50-mi network of hiking trails of varying difficulty that take you through acres of native forests, across the highest-elevation swamp in the world, to the river at the base of the canyon, and onto pinnacles of land sticking their necks out over Nā Pali Coast. All hikers should register at Kōkeʻe Natural History Museum, where you'll find trail maps, current trail information, and specific directions. All mileage mentioned here is one-way.

> **LILLIKOI ALERT**
>
> In May and June you'll see what appear to be yellow eggs scattered among the ferns along the trail. This leathery fruit survives a 30-foot fall from vines above because of the cushion of its rind. Lillikoi, often referred to as passion fruit, tastes as sweet and floral as it smells. Bite the tip of the rind off and you'll see a speckled jelly with tiny black seeds. Slurp it right out of the skin. If you miss lillikoi season, be sure to scout out some of the delicious lillikoi mustards and jams that are sold by local grocers. Lillikoi pie is also served at a few Hawaiian eateries.

The **Kukui Trail** descends 2½ mi and 2,200 feet into Waimea Canyon to the edge of the Waimea River—it's a steep climb. The **Awaʻawapuhi Trail,** with 1,600 feet of elevation gains and losses over 3¼ mi, feels more gentle than the Kukui Trail, but it offers its own huffing-and-puffing sections in its descent along a spiny ridge to a perch overlooking the ocean.

The 3½-mi **Alakaʻi Swamp Trail** is accessed via the **Pihea Trail** or a four-wheel-drive road. There's one strenuous valley section, but otherwise it's a pretty level trail—once you access it. This trail is a birder's delight and includes a painterly view of Wainiha and Hanalei valleys at the trail's end. The trail traverses the purported highest-elevation swamp in the world on a boardwalk so as not to disturb the fragile plant- and wildlife.

The **Canyon Trail** offers much in its short trek: spectacular vistas of the canyon and the only dependable waterfall in Waimea Canyon. The easy, 2-mi hike can be cut in half if you have a four-wheel-drive vehicle. If you were outfitted with a headlamp, this would be a great hike at sunset as the sun's light sets the canyon walls awash in color. ☒ *Kōkeʻe Natural History Museum: Kōkeʻe Rd., Rte. 550* ☏ *808/335–9975 for trail conditions.*

HORSEBACK RIDING

Most of the horseback riding tours on Kaua'i are primarily walking tours with very little trotting and no cantering or galloping, so no experience is required. Zip. Zilch. Nada. If you're interested, most of the stables offer private lessons. The most popular tours are the ones including a picnic lunch by the water. Your only dilemma may be deciding what kind of water you want—waterfalls or ocean. You may want to make your decision based on where you're staying. The "waterfall picnic" tours are on the wetter North Shore, and the "beach picnic" tours take place on the South Shore.

CJM Country Stables. Just past the Hyatt in Po'ipū, CJM Stables offers breakfast and lunch rides with noshing on the beach. Shorter rides are available. The landscapes here are rugged and beautiful, featuring sand dunes and limestone bluffs. CJM sponsors seasonal rodeo events that are free and open to the public. Prices range from $90 to $115. ⊠ *1½ mi from Hyatt Regency Kaua'i off Po'ipū Rd., Kōloa* ☎ *808/742–6096* ⊕ *www.cjmstables.com.*

Esprit de Corps. If you ride, this is the company for you. Esprit de Corps has three- to eight-hour rides and allows some trotting and cantering based on the rider's experience and comfort with the horse. There are also pony parties and half-day horse camps for kids (usually summers). Weddings on horseback can be arranged, and custom rides for less experienced and younger riders (as young as two) are available, as well as private lessons. Rates range from $120 to $375. ⊠ *End of Kualapa Pl., Kapa'a* ☎ *808/822–4688* ⊕ *www.kauaihorses.com.*

Fodor'sChoice ★ **Princeville Ranch Stables.** A longtime *kama'āina* (resident) family operates Princeville Ranch. They originated the waterfall picnic tours, which run three or four hours and include a short but steep hike down to Kalihi Wai Falls, a dramatic three-tier waterfall, for swimming and picnicking. Princeville also has shorter, straight riding tours and private rides, and if they're moving cattle while you're visiting, you can sign up for a cattle drive. Prices range from $80 to $135. ⊠ *West of Princeville Airport mauka between mile markers 27 and 28, Princeville* ☎ *808/826–6777* ⊕ *www.princevilleranch.com.*

MOUNTAIN TUBING

Kaua'i Backcountry Adventures. Very popular with all ages, this laid-back adventure can book up two weeks in advance in busy summer months. Here's how it works: you recline in an inner tube and float down fern-lined irrigation ditches that were built more than a century ago—the engineering is impressive—to divert water from Mt. Wai'ale'ale to sugar and pineapple fields around the island. Simple as that. They'll even give you a headlamp so you can see as you float through a couple of stretches of covered tunnels. The scenery from the island's interior at the base of Mt. Wai'ale'ale on Līhu'e Plantation land is superb. Ages five and up are welcome. The tour takes about three hours and includes a picnic lunch and a swim in a swimming hole. ■ TIP➔ In winter or after the rain, the water can be chilly; some people wear a surfer's rash guard over their swimsuit. You'll definitely want to pack water-friendly shoes (or rent some from the outfitter), sunscreen, a hat, bug repellent, and a beach towel. Tours cost $99 per person and are offered morning and afternoon, daily. ✉ *3–4131 Kūhiō Hwy., across from gas station, Hanamā'ulu* ☎ *808/245–2506 or 888/270–0555* ⊕ *www.kauaibackcountry.com.*

SKYDIVING

Skydive Kauai. Ten thousand feet over Kaua'i and falling at a rate of 120 miles per hour is probably as thrilling as it gets while airborne. First, there's the 25-minute plane ride to altitude in a Cessna 182, then the exhilaration of the first step into sky, the sensation of sailing weightless in the air over Kaua'i, and finally the peaceful buoyancy beneath the canopy of your parachute. A tandem free fall rates among the most unforgettable experiences of a lifetime. Wed that to the aerial view over Kaua'i and you've got a winning combination. ✉ *Salt Pond Beach Park, Port Allen Airport* ☎ *808/335–5859 or 808/652–2044* ⊕ *skydivekauai.com.*

TENNIS

If you're interested in booking some court time on Kaua'i, there are public tennis courts in Waimea, Kekaha, Kōloa, Kalaheo, Līhu'e, Wailua Homesteads, Wailua Houselots, and Kapa'a New Park. For specific directions or more information, call the **County of Kaua'i Parks and Recreation Office** (☎808/241–4463). Many hotels and resorts have tennis courts on property; even if you're not staying there, you can still rent court time. Rates range from $10 to $30 per person per hour. On the South Shore, try the **Hyatt Regency Kaua'i Resort and Spa** (☎ 808/742–1234) and **Kiahuna Swim and Tennis Club** (☎ 808/742–9533). On the North Shore try the **Princeville Tennis Center** (☎ 808/826–1230).

ZIPLINE TOURS

The latest adventure on Kaua'i is "zipping" or "ziplining." It's so new that the vernacular is still catching up with it, but regardless of what you call it, chances are you'll scream like a rock star fan while trying it. Strap on a harness, clip onto a cable running from one side of a river or valley to the other, and zip across. The step off is the scariest part. ■ TIP➔ Pack knee-length shorts or pants, athletic shoes, and courage for this adventure.

Fodor'sChoice   **Just Live.** When Nichol Baier and Julie Lester started Just Live in 2003,
★   their market was exclusively school-age children, but now they've added visitor tours. Experiential education through adventure is how they describe it. Whatever you call it, sailing 70 feet above the ground for 3½ hours will take your vacation to another level. This is the only treetop zipline in the state where your feet never touch ground once you're in the air: six zips and two swinging bridges make the Tree Top Tour their most popular one. For the heroic at heart, there's the Ex-

treme Adventure ropes course that includes two ziplines, a climbing wall, and a free fall from 40 feet. They still incorporate team building in the visitor tours, although their primary focus remains on community programming. Enjoy knowing that money spent here serves Kaua'i's children. ⊠ *Koloa* ☎ *808/482–1295* ⊕ *justlive.org.*

WORD OF MOUTH

"We did the Princeville zipline tour/day trip a few months ago, and I highly recommend it. This was our third visit to Kaua'i, and we wanted something different."
                                    –StephCar

Outfitters Kaua'i. This company offers a half-day adventure of multiple zips, along with rope swinging off a cliff adjacent to Kīpū Falls. Only one zipline is involved, so you'll be making the same crossing several times, but it's a Swiss Family Robinson–like setting with a tree-house launching pad and a swinging bridge. Plus, you'll trek over to Kīpū Falls to enjoy the rope swing. The price is $115. Outfitters Kaua'i also has a zipline stream crossing as part of their Kipu Safari tour (⇨ *see* Kayaking *earlier in this chapter*). ⊠ *2827-A Po'ipū Rd., Po'ipū* ☎ *808/742–9667 or 888/742–9887* ⊕ *www.outfitterskauai.com.*

Princeville Ranch Adventures. The North Shore's answer to ziplining is an eight-zipline course with a bit of hiking, waterfall crossing, and swimming thrown in for a half-day adventure. This is as close as it gets to flying; just watch out for the albatross. Prices start at $110 for the Zip Express and $125 for the Zip and Dip. ⊠ *West of Princeville Airport on Rte. 56, between mile markers 27 and 28, Princeville* ☎ *808/826–7669* ⊕ *www.adventureskauai.com.*

Shops & Spas

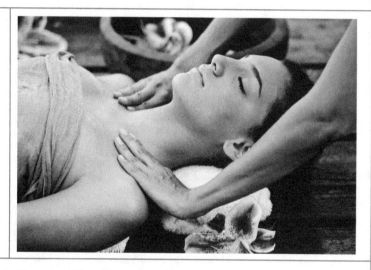

WORD OF MOUTH

"The Anara Spa at the Grand Hyatt in Poipu is wonderful. It's not cheap, but you're on vacation and by gosh, you deserve it!"

—daydreamin

"I always point folks toward Hanalei's assorted (and ever-changing) little shops—especially for locally made items."

—auntiemaria

SHOPS

Updated by
Joan Conrow

ALONG WITH ONE MAJOR SHOPPING MALL, a few shopping centers, and a growing number of big-box retailers, Kaua'i has some delightful mom-and-pop shops and specialty boutiques with lots of character.

The Garden Isle also has a large and talented community of artisans and fine artists, with galleries all around the island showcasing their creations. You can find many island-made arts and crafts in the small shops, and it's worthwhile to stop in at crafts fairs and outdoor markets to look for bargains and mingle with island residents.

If you're looking for a special memento of your trip that is unique to Kaua'i County, check out the distinctive Ni'ihau shell leis. The tiny shells are collected from beaches on Kaua'i and Ni'ihau, pierced, and strung into beautiful necklaces, chokers, and earrings. It's a time-consuming and exacting craft, and these items are much in demand, so don't be taken aback by the high price tags. Those made by Ni'ihau residents will have certificates of authenticity and are worth collecting. You often can find cheaper versions made by non-Hawaiians at crafts fairs.

Stores are typically open daily from 9 or 10 AM to 5 PM, although some stay open until 9 PM, especially those near resorts. Don't be surprised if the posted hours don't match the actual hours of operation at the smaller shops, where owners may be fairly casual about keeping to a regular schedule.

The North Shore

Shopping Centers

Ching Young Village. Despite a face-lift, this popular shopping center looks a bit worn, but that doesn't deter business. The town's only grocery store, **Big Save,** is here along with a number of other shops useful to locals and visitors. These include **Aloha Juice Bar,** with its supply of fresh organic produce; **Hanalei Music and Video,** where you can buy Hawaiian sheet music, compact discs, and handmade instruments; **Village Variety,** which has a bit of everything; **Savage Pearls,** a fine-jewelry store that specializes in Tahitian pearls and gifts; a teen-oriented surf-wear shop called **Hot Rocket; Essence of Hanalei,** a bath-and-body boutique, and **Hula Moon Gifts of Kaua'i,** with an assortment of island-themed treasures. **Village Snack & Bakery,** with excellent chocolate cake and coconut-cream pie and several restaurants. A few steps away are **Evolve Love Artists Gallery,** a good place to find high-quality work by local artisans, and **On the Road to Hanalei,** a neat boutique with gifts, clothing, jewelry, housewares, and collectibles from Indonesia. ✉ *Makai, after mile marker 2, 5-1590 Kūhiō Hwy., Hanalei* ☎ *808/826–7222.*
Hanalei Center. Listed on the Historic Register, the old Hanalei school has been refurbished and rented out to boutiques and restaurants. You can dig through '40s and '50s vintage memorabilia in the **Yellow Fish Trading Company,** search for that unusual gift at **Sand People,** or buy beach gear at the classic **Hanalei Surf Company,** casual island wear at **Hula Beach Clothing,** or women's clothing at **Tropical Tantrum.** You

can pick up something for the kids at **Rainbow Ducks Toys & Clothing.** You can even catch a class at the **Hanalei Yoga studio** in the two-story modern addition to the center, which also houses **Papaya's,** a well-stocked health-food store. ⊠ *Mauka, after mile marker 2, 5-5161 Kūhiō Hwy., Hanalei* ☎ *808/826–7677.*

Princeville Shopping Center. Foodland, a full-service grocery store, and **Island Ace Hardware** are the big draws at this small center. This is the last stop for gas and banking on the North Shore. You'll also find two restaurants, a mail service center, a post office, an ice-cream shop. **Magic Dragon Toy & Art Supply Co.,** a tiny but interesting toy-and-hobby shop, as well as **Paradise Music,** a kiosk with a good collection of Hawaiian and contemporary island artists. ⊠ *Makai, mile marker 28, 5-4280 Kūhiō Hwy., Princeville* ☎ *808/826–7513.*

Shops & Stores

Kong Lung Co. Sometimes called the Gump's of Kaua'i, this gift store sells elegant clothing, exotic glassware, ethnic books, gifts, and artwork—all very lovely and expensive. The shop is housed in a beautiful 1892 stone structure right in the heart of Kīlauea. It's the showpiece of the pretty little Kong Lung Center, whose shops feature distinctive jewelry, handmade soaps and candles, hammocks, plants, excellent pizza and baked goods, artwork, and consignment clothing, among other items. Next door is Kīlauea'i farmers' market, a good place to buy natural and gourmet foods, wines, and sandwiches. ⊠ *2490 Keneke St., Kīlauea* ☎ *808/828–1822.*

Village Variety Store. How about a fun beach towel for the folks back home? That's just one of the gifts you can find here, along with shell leis, Kaua'i T-shirts, macadamia nuts, and other great souvenirs at low prices. The store also has many small, useful items such as envelopes, housewares, and toiletries. ⊠ *Ching Young Village, Kūhiō Hwy., Hanalei* ☎ *808/826–6077.*

Crystal & Gems Gallery. Sparkling crystals of every shape, size, type, and color are sold in this small, amply stocked boutique. The knowledgeable staff can help you choose crystals for specific healing purposes. ⊠ *4489 Aku Rd., Hanalei* ☎ *808/826–9304.*

The East Side: Kapa'a & Wailua

Shopping Centers

Coconut Marketplace. This visitor-oriented complex is on the busy Coconut Coast near resort hotels and condominiums. Sixty shops sell everything from snacks and slippers (as locals call flip-flop sandals) to scrimshaw. There are also two movie theaters with first-run features, restaurants open from breakfast to evening, and a free Wednesday evening Polynesian show at 5. ⊠ *4-484 Kūhiō Hwy., Kapa'a* ☎ *808/ 822–3641.*

Kaua'i Village Shopping Center. The buildings of this Kapa'a shopping village are in the style of a 19th-century plantation town. **ABC Discount Store** sells sundries; **Safeway** carries groceries and alcoholic beverages; **Longs Drugs** has a pharmacy, health and beauty products, and a good

KAUA'I: THE HEALING ISLAND

If you look at a globe, you'll notice that Hawai'i is in the middle of the ocean, yes, and then you'll realize that it's also a connecting point between East and West. Over the centuries, as people migrated, the islands have become a melting pot not only of cultures but of healing practices as well. You'll find healing modalities from around the world on Kaua'i. Some practitioners have offices; many work out of their homes. ■ TIP→ **Virtually all will require a reservation—no walk-ins—except in yoga studios.** Here is a sampling of the healing arts offered on Kaua'i. You can also visit www.kauaihealing.org and www.kauaihwa.org. **Acupuncture & Natural Healing Center.** Acupuncture and complimentary medicine by Latifa Amdur. ☎ 808/828-1155.

Amorosa Therapes. Massage on an out-call basis. ☎ 808/652-6818.

Bikram Yoga Kaua'i. A wide selection of daily classes. ✉ 4504 Kukui St., Ste. 10 ☎ 808/822-5053. ⊕ www.bikramyogaretreats.com.

Deborah Burnham, PT. AquaCranial and CranialSacral therapies. ☎ 808/651-4534.

Dr. Leia Melead. Naturopathic physician and acupuncturist in Kapa'a. ☎ 808/822-2087.

Kaua'i Center for Holistic Medicine and Research. A range of holistic therapies and modalities in Kapa'a. ☎ 808/823-0994 ⊕ www.hawaiiholisticmedicine.com.

Kaua'i Osteopathic, Inc. Lisa Chun, doctor of osteopathy, in Kōloa. ☎ 808/742-1200 ⊕ www.health-from-within.com.

Mana Massage. Various locations and out-call. ☎ 808/822-4746 ⊕ www.manamassage.com.

Pilates Kaua'i. Full studio offering private and semiprivate lessons in secluded setting. Mauka Ki'lauea. ☎ 808/639-3074.

Rex Holt. Certified advanced Rolfer in Kīlauea. ☎ 808/828-0567.

Shalandra Abbey. Reiki in Lāwa'i. ☎ 808/332-5396 ⊕ www.reikikauai.com.

Tai Chi by the Sea. Free tai chi at the Hanalei Pavilion, overlooking the beach, on Saturday mornings at 8:15. Led by Skip Rush, doctor of traditional Chinese medicine.

Yoga Hanalei. Wide variety of daily classes at the Hanalei Center. ☎ 808/826-9642 ⊕ www.yogahanalei.com.

selection of Hawaiian merchandise; **Papaya's** has health foods; and other shops sell jewelry, gift items, children's clothes and toys, and art. In addition to interactive exhibits, the **Kaua'i Children's Discovery Museum** offers children's day-camp programs. ✉ 4-831 Kūhiō Hwy., Po'ipū Beach ☎ 808/822-3900.

Kinipopo Shopping Village. Kinipopo is a tiny little center on Kūhiō Highway. **Korean Barbeque** fronts the highway, as does **Goldsmith's Kaua'i Gallery**, which sells handcrafted Hawaiian-style gold jewelry. Worth a stop is **Tin Can Mailman,** with its eclectic collection of used books, stamps and coins, rare prints, vintage maps, and collectibles. ⊠ *4-356 Kūhiō Hwy., Kapaʻa* ☎ *No phone.*

Marta's Boat. This boutique sells some of the most fashionable clothes on the island for mom and child. ⊠ *4-770 Kuhio Hwy.* ☎ *808/822–3926* ☉ *Mon.–Sat. 10–6.*

Waipouli Town Center. **Foodland** is the focus of this small retail plaza, one of three shopping centers anchored by grocery stores in Kapaʻa. You can also find a **Blockbuster** video outlet, **McDonald's, Pizza Hut,** and **Fun Factory** video arcade, along with a local-style restaurant and a bar. ⊠ *4-901 Kūhiō Hwy., Kapaʻa* ☎ *808/524–2023.*

Shops & Galleries

★ **Bambulei.** Two 1930s-style plantation homes have been transformed into a boutique featuring vintage and contemporary clothing, antiques, jewelry, and accessories. ⊠ *4-369 Kūhiō Hwy., Wailua* ☎ *808/823–8641.*

Fodor'sChoice **Davison Arts.** This utterly charming gallery is owned and staffed by a
★ talented couple, John and Hayley Davison, whose fine art and custom furniture handcrafted from native woods comprise the bulk of the offerings. Original creations by select Kauaʻi artists and imported handmade rugs are also offered, and the pet dog Pia is often on hand to greet customers. ⊠ *4-1322 Kūhiō Hwy., Kapaʻa* ☎ *808/821–8022.*

Divine Planet. This friendly, hip boutique sells unusual merchandise from India and other Asian locales. Dangly earrings, loose clothing, beads, campy home furnishings, and other eclectic offerings make this fun shop worth a stop. If you miss it here, you can check out the Līhuʻe location. ⊠ *4-1351 Kūhiō Hwy., Kapaʻa* ☎ *808/821–1835* ⊠ *Kukui Grove Shopping Center, 3-2600 Kaumualiʻi Hwy., Līhuʻ* ☎ *808/245–3535.*

Jim Saylor Jewelers. Jim Saylor has been designing beautiful keepsakes for more than two decades on Kauaʻi. Gems from around the world, including black pearls and diamonds, appear in his unusual settings. ⊠ *1318 Kūhiō Hwy., Kapaʻa* ☎ *808/822–3591.*

Kahn Galleries. You can purchase the works of many local artists—including seascapes by George Sumner and Roy Tabora—at this gallery's many locations. ⊠ *Coconut Marketplace, 4-484 Kūhiō Hwy., Kapaʻa* ☎ *808/822–3636* ⊠ *Kōloa Rd., Old Kōloa Town* ☎ *808/742–2277* ⊠ *Hanalei Center, 5-5161 Kūhiō Hwy., Hanalei* ☎ *808/826–6677* ⊠ *Poʻipū Shopping Village, 2360 Kiahuna Plantation Dr., Poʻipū* ☎ *808/742–5004.*

Kauaʻi Gold. A wonderful selection of rare Niʻihau shell leis ranges in price from $20 to $200. To appreciate the craftsmanship, understand the sometimes-high prices, and learn to care for and preserve these remarkable necklaces, ask how they are made. The store also sells a selection of 14-karat gold jewelry. ⊠ *Coconut Marketplace, 4-484 Kūhiō Hwy., Kapaʻa* ☎ *808/822–9361.*

Kaua'i Products Fair. Open weekends, this outdoor market features fresh produce, tropical plants and flowers, aloha wear, and collectibles along with craftspeople, artisans, and wellness practitioners who will give you a massage right on the spot. ⊠ *Outside on north side of Kapa'a, next to Shack restaurant* ☎ *808/246–0988.*

Kela's Glass Gallery. The colorful vases, bowls, and other fragile items sold in this distinctive gallery are definitely worth viewing if you appreciate quality handmade glass art. It's expensive, but if something catches your eye, it can be packed safely for transport home. ⊠ *4-1354 Kūhiō Hwy., Kapa'a* ☎ *808/822–4527.*

M. Miura Store. This mom-and-pop operation has a great assortment of surfwear and clothes for outdoor fanatics, including tank tops, visors, swimwear, and Kaua'i-style T-shirts at low prices. ⊠ *4-1419 Kūhiō Hwy., Kapa'a* ☎ *808/822–4401.*

Otsuka's Furniture & Appliances. This family-owned furniture store has a surprisingly large clientele of visitors, who appreciate the large selection of artwork, candles, tropical-print pillows, accessories, and knickknacks, all of which can be packed and shipped to the customer's home. ⊠ *4-1624 Kūhiō Hwy., Kapa'a* ☎ *808/822–7766.*

Tin Can Mailman Books and Antiques. Both new and used books can be found here, along with an extensive collection of Hawaiian and South Pacific literature. The shop also sells maps, tapa cloth from Fiji, and specialty gift items. ⊠ *Kinipopo Shopping Village, 4-356 Kūhiō Hwy., Kapa'a* ☎ *808/822–3009.*

Vicky's Fabric Shop. This small shop is packed with tropical prints, silks, slinky rayons, soft cottons, and other fine fabrics, making it a must-stop for any seamstress. If you're seeking something that's truly one of a kind, check out the selection of purses, aloha wear, and other quality handsewn items. ⊠ *4-1326 Kūhiō Hwy., Kapa'a* ☎ *808/822–1746.*

The East Side: Līhu'e

Shopping Centers

Kilohana Plantation. This 16,000-square-foot Tudor mansion contains art galleries, a jewelry store, and Gaylord's restaurant. The restored outbuildings house a craft shop and a Hawaiian-style clothing shop. The house itself is filled with antiques from its original owner and is worth a look. Horse-drawn carriage rides are available, with knowledgeable guides reciting the history of sugar on Kaua'i. ⊠ *3-2087 Kaumuali'i Hwy., 1 mi west of Līhu'e* ☎ *808/245–5608.*

Kukui Grove Center. This is Kaua'i's only true mall. Besides **Sears Roebuck** and **Kmart,** anchor tenants are **Longs Drugs, Macy's,** and **Star Market. Borders Books & Music,** and its coffee shop, is one of the island's most popular stores. The mall's stores offer women's clothing, surf wear, art, toys, athletic shoes, jewelry, and locally made crafts. Restaurants range from fast food and sandwiches to Mexican and Chinese. The center stage often has entertainment. ⊠ *3-2600 Kaumuali'i Hwy., west of Līhu'e* ☎ *808/245–7784.*

Shops & Galleries

Art Shop. This intimate gallery in Līhu'e sells original oils, photos, and sculptures, many by local artists. ⊠ *3196 'Akahi St., Līhu'e* ☎ *808/245–3810.*

Hilo Hattie, The Hore of Hawai'i, Fashion Factory. This is the big name in aloha wear for tourists throughout the islands. You can visit the only store on Kaua'i, a mile from Līhu'e Airport, to pick up cool, comfortable aloha shirts and mu'umu'us in bright floral prints, as well as other souvenirs. While here, check out the line of Hawaiian-inspired home furnishings. ⊠ *3252 Kūhiō Hwy., Līhu'e* ☎ *808/245–3404.*

Fodor'sChoice ★ **Kapaia Stitchery.** Hawaiian quilts made by hand and machine, a beautiful selection of fabrics, quilting kits, and fabric arts fill this cute little red plantation-style structure. The staff is friendly and helpful, even though a steady stream of customers keeps them busy. ⊠ *Kūhiō Hwy., ½ mi north of Līhu'e* ☎ *808/245–2281.*

> ### BUY LOCAL
>
> It's not easy to make a living on Kaua'i, especially for artists, craftspeople, and shopkeepers. With such a small resident population, most merchants depend on visitor traffic to survive.
>
> Although it may be tempting to shop at a big-box discount outlet or chain store, where there's always the promise of a bargain, don't overlook the small shops. That's where you'll typically find distinctive items and original creations from island artists. You'll also be helping to support the local economy, which is heavily based on small businesses.

6

Kaua'i Fruit and Flower Company. At this shop near Līhu'e you can buy tropical cut flowers, fresh sugarloaf pineapple, sugarcane, ginger, coconuts, local jams, jellies, and honey, plus Kaua'i-grown papayas, bananas, and mangos in season. Stop by on your way to the airport (although it's hard to make a left turn back onto Kūhiō Highway) to buy fruit that's been inspected and approved for shipment to the mainland. ⊠ *3-4684 Kūhiō Hwy., Kapa'a* ☎ *808/245–1814 or 800/943–3108.*

★ **Kaua'i Museum.** The gift shop at the museum sells some fascinating books, maps, and prints, as well as lovely feather lei hatbands, Ni'ihau shell jewelry, handwoven *lau hala* hats, and other good-quality local crafts at reasonable prices. ⊠ *4428 Rice St., Līhu'e* ☎ *808/246–2470.*

Kaua'i Products Store. Every seed lei, every finely crafted koa-wood box, every pair of tropical-flower earrings, indeed every item in this boutique is handcrafted on Kaua'i. Other gift options include koa-oil lamps, pottery, hand-painted silk clothing, sculpture, and homemade fudge. Although some of the merchandise isn't all that appealing, it's nice to support local talent when you can. ⊠ *Kukui Grove Center, 3-2600 Kaumuali'i Hwy., Līhu'e* ☎ *808/246–6753.*

Kilohana Clothing Company. This store in the guest cottage by Gaylord's restaurant offers vintage Hawaiian clothing as well as contemporary styles using traditional Hawaiian designs. The store also features a wide selection of home products in vintage fabrics. ⊠ *Kilohana Plantation, 3-2087 Kaumuali'i Hwy., Līhu'e* ☎ *808/246–6911.*

★ **Piece of Paradise Gallery.** Fine art, koa-wood clocks and sushi platters, handblown glass, sculptures, and unusual jewelry—all designed by talented Kaua'i-based artisans—are available here. ⊠ *Kaua'i Beach Resort, 4331 Kaua'i Beach Dr., Līhu'e* ☎ *808/246–2834.*

Two Frogs Hugging. This spacious store has lots of interesting housewares, accessories, knickknacks and hand-carved collectibles, as well as baskets and furniture, with a primarily Indonesian influence. ⊠ *3215 Kūhiō Hwy., Līhu'e* ☎ *808/246–8777.*

The South Shore & West Side

Shopping Centers

'Ele'ele Shopping Center. Kaua'i's West Side has a scattering of stores, including those at this no-frills strip-mall shopping center. It's a good place to rub elbows with local folk or to grab a quick bite to eat at the casual **Grinds Cafe** or **Tois Thai Kitchen.** ⊠ *Rte. 50 near Hanapēpē, 'Ele'ele* ☎ *808/246–0634.*

Po'ipū Shopping Village. Convenient to nearby hotels and condos on the South Shore, the two dozen shops here sell resort wear, gifts, souvenirs, and art. The upscale **Black Pearl Kaua'i** and **Na Hoku** shops are particularly appealing jewelry stores. There's a couple of art galleries and several fun clothing stores, including **Making Waves** and **Blue Ginger.** Also worth a visit are **Hale Mana Gifts for the Spirited** and **Whaler's General Store.** Restaurants include **Keoki's Paradise, Roy's, Po'ipū Tropical Burgers,** and **Pattaya Asian Cafe.** A Tahitian dance troupe performs in the open-air courtyard Tuesday and Thursday at 5 PM. ⊠ *2360 Kiahuna Plantation Dr., Po'ipū Beach* ☎ *808/742–2831.*

Waimea Canyon Plaza. As Kekaha's retail hub and the last stop for supplies before heading up to Waimea Canyon, this tiny, tidy complex of shops is surprisingly busy. Look for local foods, souvenirs, and island-made gifts for all ages. ⊠ *Kōke'e Rd. at Rte. 50, Kekaha* ☎ *No phone.*

Shops & Galleries

Kaua'i Coffee Visitor Center and Museum. Kaua'i produces more coffee than any other island in the state. The local product can be purchased from grocery stores or here at the source, where a sampling of the nearly one dozen coffees is available. Be sure to try some of the estate-roasted varieties. ⊠ *870 Halawili Rd., off Rte. 50, west of Kalāheo* ☎ *808/ 335–0813 or 800/545–8605.*

Kaua'i Tropicals. You can have this company ship heliconia, anthuriums, ginger, and other tropicals in 5-foot-long boxes directly from its flower farm in Kalāheo. It accepts phone-in orders only. ⊠ *Kalāheo* ☎ *808/ 742–9989 or 800/303–4385.*

Fodor'sChoice **Kebanu Gallery.** A stunning collection of original wood sculptures, ★ whimsical ceramics, beaded jewelry, colorful glassware, and other creations—many of them by Hawai'i artists—makes this contemporary shop a pleasure to visit. ⊠ *Old Kōloa Town, 3440 Po'ipū Rd., Kōloa* ☎ *808/ 742–2727.*

Paradise Sportswear. This is the retail outlet of the folks who invented Kauaʻi's popular "red dirt" shirts, which are dyed and printed with the characteristic local soil. Ask the salesperson to tell you the charming story behind these shirts. Sizes from infants up to 5X are available. ☒ *4350 Waialo Rd., Port Allen* ☎ *808/335–5670.*

SPAS

Updated by
Kim
Steutermann
Rogers

Kauaʻi is often touted as the healing island, and local spas try hard to fill that role. With the exception of the Hyatt's ANARA Spa, the facilities aren't as posh as some might want. But it's in the human element that Kauaʻi excels. Island residents are known for their warmth, kindness, and humility, and you can find all these attributes in the massage therapists and technicians who work long hours at the resort spas. These professionals take their therapeutic mission seriously; they genuinely want you to experience the island's relaxing, restorative qualities. Private massage services abound on the island—your spa therapist may offer the same services at a much lower price outside the resort—but if you're looking for a variety of health-and-beauty treatments, an exercise workout, or a full day of pampering, a spa will prove most convenient. Though most spas on Kauaʻi are associated with resorts, none is restricted to guests only. There is much by way of healing and wellness to be found on Kauaʻi beyond the traditional spa—or even the day spa. More and more retreat facilities are opening what some would call alternative healing therapies. Others would say there's nothing alternative about them.

6

Alexander Day Spa & Salon at the Kauaʻi Marriott. This sister spa of Alexander Simson's Beverly Hills spa focuses on body care rather than exercise, so don't expect any fitness equipment or exercise classes. Tucked away in the back corner of the Marriott, the spa has the same ambience of stilted formality as the rest of the resort, but it is otherwise a sunny, pleasant facility. Massages are available in treatment rooms and on the beach, although the beach locale isn't as private as you might imagine. The spa offers a couple of unusual treatments not found elsewhere: oxygen inhalation therapy and Thai massage. Wedding-day and custom spa packages can be arranged. The spa's therapists also offer massages in poolside cabanas at Marriott's Waiohai Beach Club in Poʻipū, but there are no facilities (showers, steam, and so forth). ☒ *Kauaʻi Marriott Resort & Beach Club, 3610 Rice St., Lihuʻe* ☎ *808/246–4918* ⊕ *www.alexanderspa.com* ☞ *$60–$195 massage. Facilities: Hair salon, steam room. Services: Body treatments—including masks, scrubs, and wraps—facials, hair styling, makeup, manicures, massages, pedicures, waxing.*

Fodor'sChoice **ANARA Spa.** This luxurious facility is far and away the best on Kauaʻi, ★ setting a standard that no other spa has been able to meet. It has all the equipment and services you expect from a top resort spa, along with a pleasant, professional staff. Best of all, it has indoor and outdoor areas that capitalize on the tropical locale and balmy weather, further distinguishing it from the Marriott and Princeville spas. Its 46,500 square feet

Continued on page 132

ALL ABOUT LEIS

Leis brighten every occasion in Hawai'i, from birthdays to bar mitzvahs to baptisms. Creative artisans weave nature's bounty—flowers, ferns, vines, and seeds—into gorgeous creations that convey an array of heartfelt messages: "Welcome," "Congratulations," "Good luck," "Farewell," "Thank you," "I love you." When it's difficult to find the right words, a lei expresses exactly the right sentiments.

WHERE TO BUY THE BEST LEIS

The best leis on Kauai can be found—believe it or not—in the major chain stores, including **Foodland** (✉ 5-4290 Kūhiū Hwy., Princeville, ☎ 808/862-7513), in the Princeville Shopping Center, and **Safeway** (✉ 4-831 Kūhiū Hwy., Po'ipū Beach), in the Kaua'i Village Shopping Center. Also fabulous leis can be found at the various roadside vendors you'll see as you drive around the island.

LEI ETIQUETTE

■ To wear a closed lei, drape it over your shoulders, half in front and half in back. Open leis are worn around the neck, with the ends draped over the front in equal lengths.

■ Pīkake, ginger, and other sweet, delicate blossoms are "feminine" leis. Men opt for cigar, crown flower, and carnation, which are sturdier and don't emit as much fragrance.

■ Leis are always presented with a kiss, a custom that supposedly dates back to World War II when a hula dancer fancied an officer at a U.S.O. show. Taking a dare from members of her troupe, she took off her lei, placed it around his neck, and kissed him on the cheek.

■ You shouldn't wear a lei before you give it to someone else. Hawaiians believe the lei absorbs your *mana* (spirit); if you give your lei away, you'll be giving away part of your essence.

ORCHID

Growing wild on every continent except Antarctica, orchids—which range in color from yellow to green to purple—comprise the largest family of plants in the world. There are more than 20,000 species of orchids, but only three are native to Hawai'i—and they are very rare. The pretty lavender vanda you see hanging by the dozens at local lei stands has probably been imported from Thailand.

MAILE

Maile, an endemic twining vine with a heady aroma, is sacred to Laka, goddess of the hula. In ancient times, dancers wore maile and decorated hula altars with it to honor Laka. Today, "open" maile leis usually are given to men. Instead of ribbon, interwoven lengths of maile are used at dedications of new businesses. The maile is untied, never snipped, for doing so would symbolically "cut" the company's success.

'ILIMA

Designated by Hawai'i's Territorial Legislature in 1923 as the official flower of the island of O'ahu, the golden 'ilima is so delicate it lasts for just a day. Five to seven hundred blossoms are needed to make one garland. Queen Emma, wife of King Kamehameha IV, preferred 'ilima over all other leis, which may have led to the incorrect belief that they were reserved only for royalty.

PLUMERIA

This ubiquitous flower is named after Charles Plumier, the noted French botanist who discovered it in Central America in the late 1600s. Plumeria ranks among the most popular leis in Hawai'i because it's fragrant, hardy, plentiful, inexpensive, and requires very little care. Although yellow is the most common color, you'll also find plumeria leis in shades of pink, red, orange, and "rainbow" blends.

PĪKAKE

Favored for its fragile beauty and sweet scent, pīkake was introduced from India. In lieu of pearls, many brides in Hawai'i adorn themselves with long, multiple strands of white pīkake. Princess Kaiulani enjoyed showing guests her beloved pīkake and peacocks at Āinahau, her Waikīkī home. Interestingly, pīkake is the Hawaiian word for both the bird and the blossom.

KUKUI

The kukui (candlenut) is Hawai'i's state tree. Early Hawaiians strung kukui nuts (which are quite oily) together and burned them for light; mixed burned nuts with oil to make an indelible dye; and mashed roasted nuts to consume as a laxative. Kukui nut leis may not have been made until after Western contact, when the Hawaiians saw black beads from Europe and wanted to imitate them.

of space includes the new Garden Treatment Village (opening in 2007), an open-air courtyard with private thatched-roof huts, each featuring a relaxation area, misters, and open-air shower in a tropical setting. At the Kupono Café, you can relax and enjoy a healthful breakfast, lunch, or smoothie. Ancient Hawaiian remedies and local ingredients are featured in many of the treatments, such as a red-dirt clay wrap, coconut-mango facial, and a body brush scrub that polishes your skin with a mix of ground coffee, orange peel, and vanilla bean. The open-air lava-rock showers are wonderful, introducing many guests to the delightful island practice of showering outdoors. The spa, which includes a full-service salon, adjoins the Hyatt's legendary swimming pool. ⊠ *Hyatt Regency Kaua'i Resort and Spa, 1571 Po'ipū Rd., Po'ipū* ☎ *808/240–6440* ⊕ *www.anaraspa.com* ☞ *$85–$370 massage. Facilities: Hair salon, outdoor hot tubs, sauna, steam room. Gym with cardiovascular machines, free weights, weight-training equipment. Services: Body scrubs and wraps, facials, manicures, massage, pedicures. Classes and programs: Aerobics, aquaerobics, body sculpting, fitness analysis, flexibility training, personal training, Pilates, step aerobics, weight training, yoga.*

Angeline's Mu'olaulani Wellness Center. It doesn't get more authentic than this. In the mid-'80s Aunty Angeline Locey opened her Anahola home to offer traditional Hawaiian healing practices. Now her son and granddaughter carry on the tradition. There's a two-hour treatment ($140) that starts with a steam, followed by a sea-salt-and- clay body scrub and a two-person massage. The real treat, however, is relaxing on Aunty's open-air garden deck. Hot-stone lomi is also available. Aunty's mission is to promote a healthy body image; as such, au naturel is the accepted way here, so if you're nudity-shy, this may not be the place for you. On second thought, Aunty would say it most definitely is. *Mu'olaulani* translates to "a place for young buds to bloom." ⊠ *Directions provided upon reservation* ☎ *808/ 822–3235* ⊕ *www.auntyangelines. com* ☞ *Facilities: Steam room. Services: Body scrubs and massage.*

Hanalei Day Spa. As you travel beyond tony Princeville, life slows down. The single-lane bridges may be one reason. Another is the Hanalei Day Spa (opened in 2004), an open-air, thatched-roof, Hawaiian-style hut nestled just off the beach on the grounds of Hanalei Colony Resort in Hā'ena. With a location like this, the spa itself can be no frills—and it is. Though the unassuming day spa offers facials, waxing, wraps, scrubs, and the like,

---

WHEN IN LOMI

Living in ancient Hawai'i wasn't all sunbathing and lounging at the beach. Surfing was hard work, you know. So, too, canoe building, fishing for dinner, and pounding tapa for clothing, sails, and blankets. Enter *lomilomi*–Hawaiian-style massage. It's often described as being more vigorous, more rhythmical, and faster than Swedish massage, and it incorporates more elbow and forearm work. It might even involve chanting, music, and four hands (in other words, two people). However, styles varied from one island to the next, even from one family to the next.

its specialty is massage: Ayurveda, Zen shiatsu, Swedish, and even a baby massage (and lesson for mom, to boot). On Tuesdays and Thursdays, owner Darci Frankel teaches yoga, a discipline she started as a young child living in south Florida. That practice led her to start the Ayurveda Center of Hawaii, operating out of the spa and offering an ancient Indian cleansing and rejuvenation program known as Pancha Karma. Think multiday wellness retreat. ⊠ *Hanalei Colony Resort, Rte. 560, 6 mi past Hanalei* ☎ *808/826–6621* ⊕ *www.hanaleidayspa.com* ☞ *$85–$165 massage. Services: Body scrubs and wraps, facials, massage, waxing. Classes and programs: Pancha Karma, yoga.*

★ **Hart-Felt Massage & Day Spa.** This is the only full-service day spa on the laid-back West Side. It's in one of the restored plantation cottages that make up the guest quarters at Waimea Plantation Cottages, creating a cozy and comfortable setting you won't find elsewhere. The overall feel is relaxed, casual, and friendly, as you'd expect in this quiet country town. The staff is informal, yet thoroughly professional. Try the kava kava ginger wrap followed by the lomi *'ili'ili*—hot stone massage. Ooh la la. ⊠ *Waimea Plantation Cottages, 9400 Kaumuali'i Hwy., Waimea* ☎ *808/ 338–2240* ⊕ *www.waimea-plantation.com* ☞ *$46–$155 massage. Facilities: Outdoor hot tub, steam room. Services: Acupuncture, body scrubs and wraps, facials, hydrotherapy, massage. Classes and programs: Yoga.*

Kahuna Valley. Tucked at the foot of the mountains known as Makaleha, this retreat center also offers regular qigong workshops and *watsu*—a warm-water-based healing treatment that incorporates elements of shiatsu massage. On the property are an octagonal, off-the-grid classroom; meditation gazebos; and a bodywork treatment studio along with a two-bedroom bed-and-breakfast-type suite. Having built their dream property side by side, owners Francesco and Daisy Garripoli are actively engaged in many health, wellness, and peace programs with the island's children, and they run Kahuna Valley as a nonprofit to support their charitable efforts. ⊠ *Directions provided upon reservation* ☎ *808/ 822–4268* ⊕ *www.kahunavalley.com.*

Princeville Health Club & Spa. Inspiring views of mountains, sea, and sky provide a lovely distraction in the gym area of this spa, which is well equipped but small and often overly air-conditioned. The treatment area is functional but lacks charm and personality. Luckily the gorgeous setting helps make up for it. This is the only facility of this kind on the North Shore, so it's well used, and the generally well-heeled clientele pays attention to their gym attire. It's in the clubhouse at the Prince Golf Course, several miles from the Princeville Hotel. A room in the hotel or round of golf at a Princeville course entitles you to reduced admission to the spa; otherwise it's $20 for a day pass. ⊠ *Prince Golf Course clubhouse, 53-900 Kūhiō Hwy., Princeville* ☎ *808/826–5030* ⊕ *www. princeville.com* ☞ *$105–$150 massage. Gym with cardiovascular machines, free weights, weight-training equipment. Services: Body scrubs and wraps, facials, massage. Classes and programs: Aerobics, aquaerobics, personal training, Pilates, step aerobics, tai chi, yoga.*

Qi Center. Technically, the Qi Center of Kaua'i is not a spa. It does, however, concern itself with healing, and because its technique is so gentle, it is, in a sense, pampering. More than that, it can be life changing—even life saving. Hong Liu, a qigong grand master of the highest degree opened the center in 2005 as part of his lifelong goal to share qigong with the West. The essence of qigong centers on building, increasing, and directing energy: physical, mental, and spiritual. Master Liu does not suggest qigong as an alternative to Western medicine but as an adjunct. The center in Līhu'e conducts all levels of qigong training as well as "humanitarian" (i.e., free) events for the community on such topics as asthma, allergies, and heart and senior health. ⊠ *3343 Kanakolu St.* ☎ *808/639–4300* ⊕ *www.qimaster.com.*

Tri Health Ayurveda Spa. The goal of this spa isn't a onetime massage for relaxation bliss, although relaxation is a key ingredient. Rather, this spa's focus is a multiweek, multitreatment, intensive program designed to eliminate toxins stored in the body and increase the flow and energy of all systems. Treatments are designed around the ancient Ayurvedic tradition of heat to open the pores, oil to deliver nutrients to tissues and nerve endings, and massage (by two therapists working in synchronized movement) to accelerate circulation. Note: Because the massage strokes are long and can run the length of the body, there is no draping involved. Ayurvedic doctors, food, and treatments are available, as is lodging in the 10-bedroom retreat facility, on 25 acres hidden by design for the privacy of its clients—hence, no glaring signs. Single sessions are available. ⊠ *Directions provided upon reservation* ☎ *808/828–2104* ⊕ *www. trihealthayurveda.com* ☞ *$105–$295 massage. Facilities: Steam room. Services: Herbal body scrubs, massage. Classes and programs: Pancha Karma.*

Entertainment & Nightlife

WORD OF MOUTH

"We like Keoki's Paradise in the Po'ipū Shopping Center. It has a very nice tropical setting, and you won't think you are in a shopping center. They often have happy-hour local musicians and a nice bar/pupu menu."

—BrendaM

"For cocktails I recommend the Bali Hai Restaurant at the Hanalei Bay Resort. Definitely try the Lava Flow."

—annahead

Updated by
Pamela
Woolway

KAUA'I HAS NEVER BEEN KNOWN for its nightlife. It's a rural island, where folks tend to retire early, and the streets are dark and deserted well before midnight. The island does have its nightspots, though, and the after-dark entertainment scene may not be expanding, but it is consistently present in areas frequented by tourists.

Most of the island's dinner and lū'au shows are held at hotels and resorts. Hotel lounges are a good source of live music, often with no cover charge, as are a few bars and restaurants around the island.

Check the local newspaper, *The Garden Island,* for listings of weekly happenings, or tune in to community radio station KKCR—found at 90.9 and 91.9 on the FM dial—at 5:30 PM for the arts and entertainment calendar. Free publications such as *Kaua'i Gold, This Week on Kaua'i,* and *Kaua'i Beach Press* also list entertainment events. You can pick them up at Līhu'e Airport near the baggage claim area, as well as at numerous retail areas on the island.

ENTERTAINMENT

Although lū'aus remain a primary source of evening fun for families on vacation, there are a handful of other possibilities. There are no traditional dinner cruises, but some boat tours do offer an evening buffet with music along Nā Pali coast. A few times a year, Women in Theater (WIT), a local women's theater group, performs dinner shows at the Hukilau Lānai in Wailua. You can always count on a performance of *South Pacific* at the Hilton, and the Kaua'i Community College Performing Arts Center draws well-known artists.

Kaua'i Community College Performing Arts Center. This is the main venue for island entertainment, hosting a concert music series, visiting musicians, dramatic productions, and special events such as the International Film Festival. ⊠ *3-1901 Kaumuali'i Hwy., Līhu'e* ☎ *808/245–8270.*

Dinner Show

South Pacific Dinner Show. It seems a fitting tribute to see the play that put Kaua'i on the map. Rodgers and Hammerstein's *South Pacific* has been playing at the Hilton Kaua'i Beach Resort to rave reviews since 2002. The full musical production, accompanied by a cocktail reception and buffet, features local Kaua'i talent. ⊠ *Grand Ballroom, Hilton Kaua'i Beach Resort, Kaua'i Beach Dr., Līhu'e* ☎ *808/246–0111* 🍴 *$75* ⊙ *Mon. and Wed. dinner and cocktails at 5, show at 6:45.*

Festival

Bon Festival. Traditional Japanese celebrations in honor of loved ones who have died are held from late June through August at various Buddhist temples all over the island. It sounds somber, but it's really a community festival of dance. To top it off, you're welcome to participate. Dance, eat, play carnival games, and hear Japanese *taiko* drumming by Kaua'i youth at one of the Bon folk dances, which take place on temple lawns every Friday and Saturday night from dusk to midnight. Some dancers wear the traditional kimono; others wear board shorts and a tank top. The moves are easy to follow, the event is lively and wholesome, and it's free. A different temple hosts a dance each weekend. Watch the local paper for that week's locale.

Lūʻau

Although the commercial lūʻau experience is a far cry from the backyard lūʻau thrown by local residents to celebrate a wedding, graduation, or baby's first birthday, they're nonetheless entertaining and a good introduction to the Hawaiian food that isn't widely sold in restaurants. Besides the feast, there's often an exciting dinner show with Polynesianstyle music and dancing. It all makes for a fun evening that's suitable for couples, families, and groups, and the informal setting is conducive to meeting other people. Every lūʻau is different, reflecting the cuisine and tenor of the host facility, so compare prices, menus, and entertainment before making your reservation. Most lūʻau on Kauaʻi are offered only on a limited number of nights each week, so plan ahead to get the lūʻau you want. We tend to prefer those *not* held on resort properties, because they feel a bit more authentic. The lūʻau shows listed below are our favorites.

Grand Hyatt Kauaʻi Lūʻau. What used to be called Drums of Paradise has a new name and a new dance troupe but still offers a traditional lūʻau buffet and an exceptional performance. This oceanfront lūʻau comes with a view of the majestic Keoneloa Bay. ⊠ *Grand Hyatt Kauaʻi Resort & Spa, 1571 Poʻipū Rd., Poʻipū* ☎ *808/240–6456* 💲 *$75* ⊗ *Thurs. and Sun. at 5:15.*

Lūʻau Kilohana. This lūʻau—on a former sugar plantation manager's estate—has a twist: all guests arrive at the feast by horse-drawn carriage (reservations are staggered to prevent lines). Families especially seem to enjoy the food and fun here. Even though sugar plantations are a decidedly Western affair, this lūʻau feels more authentic than those on a portable stage on resort grounds. The evening's theme is the history of sugar on the islands. ⊠ *3-2087 Kaumualiʻi St., Līhuʻe* ☎ *808/245–9593* 💲 *$65* ⊗ *Tues. and Thurs. carriage rides begin at 5, dinner at 6, show at 7.*

Paʻina o Hanalei. A conch shell is blown in the traditional way to signal the start of this gourmet lūʻau feast held on the shore of Hanalei Bay. It's lavish, as one might expect from the Princeville Hotel, with a buffet line that's heavy on upscale, Pacific Rim cuisine and light on traditional lūʻau fare. The event includes entertainment that celebrates the songs and dances of the South Pacific. ⊠ *Princeville Resort, 5520 Ka Haku Rd., Princeville* ☎ *808/ 826–2788* 💲 *$69* ⊗ *Mon. and Thurs. at 6.*

> ### WORD OF MOUTH
>
> "If you decide to attend Smith's lūʻau make sure you go early so you have time to tour the grounds . . . many beautiful birds and plants. They had about 200 male peacocks (one albino) on the property, and when we were there in June it was mating season and the peacocks were all 'strutting their stuff,' so to speak. It was a nice way to spend a couple of hours."   —okieinkauai

Continued on page 141

MORE THAN A FOLK DANCE

Hula has been called "the heartbeat of the Hawaiian people." Also, "the world's best-known, most misunderstood dance." Both true. Hula isn't just dance. It is storytelling. No words, no hula.

Chanter Edith McKinzie calls it "an extension of a piece of poetry." In its adornments, implements, and customs, hula integrates every important Hawaiian cultural practice: poetry, history, genealogy, craft, plant cultivation, martial arts, religion, protocol. So when 19th century Christian missionaries sought to eradicate a practice they considered depraved, they threatened more than just a folk dance.

With public performance outlawed and private hula practice discouraged, hula went underground for a generation, to rural villages. The fragile verbal link by which culture was transmitted from teacher to student hung by a thread. Even increasing literacy did not help because hula's practitioners were—and, to a degree, still are—a secretive and protected circle.

As if that weren't bad enough, vaudeville, Broadway, and Hollywood got hold of the hula, giving it the glitz treatment in an unbroken line from "Oh, How She Could Wicky Wacky Woo" to "Rock-A-Hula Baby." Hula became shorthand for paradise: fragrant flowers, lazy hours. Ironically, this development assured that hundreds of Hawaiians could make a living performing and teaching hula. Many danced 'auana (modern form) in performance; but taught kahiko (traditional), quietly, at home or in hula schools.

Today, 30 years after the cultural revival known as the Hawaiian Renaissance, language immersion programs have assured a new generation of proficient–and even eloquent–chanters, songwriters, and translators. Visitors can see more, and more authentic, hula than anytime in the last 200 years.

Like the culture of which it is the beating heart, hula has survived.

Lei *po'o*. Head lei. In kahiko, greenery only. In 'auana, flowers.

Face emotes appropriate expression. Dancer should not be a smiling automaton.

Shoulders remain relaxed and still, never hunched, even with arms raised. No bouncing.

Eyes always follow leading hand.

Lei. Hula is rarely performed without a shoulder lei.

Arms and hands remain loose, relaxed, below shoulder level—except as required by interpretive movements.

Traditional hula skirt is loose fabric, smocked and gathered at the waist.

Hip is canted over weight-bearing foot.

Knees are always slightly bent, accentuating hip sway.

In kahiko, feet are flat. In 'auana, may be more arched, but not tiptoes or bouncing.

Kupe'e. Ankle bracelet of flowers, shells, or—traditionally—noise-making dog teeth.

MORE THAN A FOLK DANCE

7

BASIC MOTIONS

Speak or Sing

Moon or Sun

Grass Shack or House

Mountains or Heights

Love or Caress

At backyard parties, hula is performed in bare feet and street clothes, but in performance, adornments play a key role, as do rhythm-keeping implements.

In hula kahiko (traditional style), the usual dress is multiple layers of stiff fabric (often with a pellom lining, which most closely resembles *kapa*, the paperlike bark cloth of the Hawaiians). These wrap tightly around the bosom but flare below the waist to form a skirt. In pre-contact times, dancers wore only kapa skirts. Monarchy-period hula is performed in voluminous Mother Hubbard muʻumuʻu or high-necked muslin blouses and gathered skirts. Men wear loincloths or, for monarchy period, white or gingham shirts and black pants—sometimes with red sashes.

In hula ʻauana (modern), dress for women can range from grass skirts and strapless tops to contemporary tea-length dresses. Men generally wear aloha shirts, but sometimes grass skirts over pants or even everyday gear. (One group at a recent competition wore wetsuits to do a surfing song!)

SURPRISING HULA FACTS

■ Grass skirts are not traditional; workers from Kiribati (the Gilbert Islands) brought this custom to Hawaiʻi.

■ In olden-day Hawaiʻi, *mele* (songs) for hula were composed for every occasion—name songs for babies, dirges for funerals, welcome songs for visitors, celebrations of favorite pursuits.

■ Hula *maʻi* is a traditional hula form in praise of a noble's genitals; the power of the *aliʻ* (royalty) to procreate gave *mana* (spiritual power) to the entire culture.

■ Hula students in old Hawaiʻi adhered to high standards: scrupulous cleanliness, no sex, daily cleansing rituals, certain food prohibitions, and no contact with the dead. They were fined if they broke the rules.

WHERE TO WATCH

■ Coconut Marketplace, ✉ 4-484 Kūhiō Hwy., Kapaʻa, ☎ 808/ 822-3900, ⊙ Wed. 5 PM. Dinner included.

■ Poʻipū Shopping Village, ✉ 2360 Kiahuna Plantation Dr., Poʻipū Beach, ⊙ Tues. and Thurs. 5 pm. Dinner included.

■ Smith's Tropical Paradise, ✉ 174 Wailua Rd., Kapaʻa, ☎ 808/ 821-6895, ⊙ Mon., Wed., and Fri. 5–9:15.

■ Festivals: There are many festivals on the island year-round where you can see hula performed. For more information visit *www.kauaifestivals.com*.

Fodor'sChoice ★ **Smith's Tropical Paradise Lū'au.** A 30-acre tropical garden provides the lovely setting for this popular lū'au, which begins with the traditional blowing of the conch shell and *imu* (pig roast) ceremony, followed by cocktails, an island feast, and an international show in the amphitheater overlooking a torchlighted lagoon. It's fairly authentic and a better deal than the pricier resort events. ✉ *174 Wailua Rd., Kapa'a* ☎ *808/821–6895* *$58* ⏲ *Mon., Wed., and Fri. 5–9:15.*

Music

Check the local papers for outdoor reggae and Hawaiian-music shows, or one of the numbers listed below for more formal performances.

Hanalei Slack Key Concerts. Relax to the instrumental musical art form created by Hawaiian *paniolo* (cowboys) in the early 1800s. Shows are held at the Hanalei Family Community Center, which is mauka down a dirt access road across from St. Williams Catholic Church (Malolo Road) and then left down another dirt road. Look for a thatched-roof *hale,* or house, several little green plantation-style buildings, and the brown double-yurt community center around the gravel parking lot. ✉ *Hanalei Family Community Center, Hanalei* ☎ *808/826–1469* 🌐 *www.hawaiianslackkeyguitar.com* *$10* ⏲ *Fri. at 4, Sun. at 3.*

Kaua'i Concert Association. This group offers a seasonal program at the Kaua'i Community College Performing Arts Center. A range of big-name artists, from Ricky Lee Jones to Taj Mahal, have been known to show up on Kaua'i for planned or impromptu performances. ✉ *3-1901 Kaumuali'i Hwy., Līhu'e* ☎ *808/245–7464.*

Theater

Kaua'i Community Players. This talented local group presents plays throughout the year. ✉ *Līhu'e Parish Hall, 4340 Nāwiliwili Rd., Līhu'e* ☎ *808/245–7700* 🌐 *www.kauaicommunityplayers.org.*

NIGHTLIFE

For every new venue that opens on Kaua'i, another one closes. Perhaps it's simply the result of the island's ubiquitous but little-known epidemic: paradise paralysis. Symptoms include a slight fragrance of coconut wafting from the pores, pink cheeks, and nose; a relaxed gait; and a slight smile curving on the lips. Let's face it: Kaua'i lulls people into a stupor that puts them to bed before 10 PM. But if you are one of those immune to the disease, Kaua'i may have a place or two for you to while away your spare hours.

Bars & Clubs

Nightclubs that stay open until the wee hours are rare on Kaua'i, and the bar scene is pretty limited. The major resorts generally host their own live entertainment and happy hours. All bars and clubs that serve alcohol must close at 2 AM, except those with a cabaret license, which allows them to close at 4 AM.

7

Kaua'i: Undercover Movie Star

THOUGH KAUA'I HAS PLAYED itself in the movies (you may remember Nicolas Cage frantically shouting "Is it Kapa'a or Kapa'a-a?" into a pay phone in *Honeymoon in Vegas* [1992]), most of its screen time has been as a stunt double for a number of tropical paradises. The island's remote valleys and waterfalls portrayed Venezuelan jungle in Kevin Costner's *Dragonfly* (2002) and a Costa Rican dinosaur preserve in Steven Spielberg's *Jurassic Park* (1993). Spielberg was no stranger to Kaua'i, having filmed Harrison Ford's escape via seaplane from Menehune Fishpond in *Raiders of the Lost Ark* (1981). The fluted cliffs and gorges of Kaua'i's rugged Nā Pali Coast play the misunderstood beast's island home in *King Kong* (1976), and a jungle dweller of another sort, in *George of the Jungle* (1997), frolicked on Kaua'i. Harrison Ford returned to the island for 10 weeks during the filming of *Six Days, Seven Nights* (1998), a romantic adventure set in French Polynesia.

But these are all relatively recent movies. What's truly remarkable is that Hollywood discovered Kaua'i in 1933 with the making of *White Heat*, which was set on a sugar plantation and—like another more memorable movie filmed on Kaua'i—dealt with interracial love stories. In 1950, Esther Williams and Rita Moreno arrived to film *Pagan Love Song*, a forgettable musical. Then, it was off to the races, as Kaua'i saw no fewer than a dozen movies filmed on the island in the 1950s, not all of them Oscar contenders. Rita Hayworth starred in *Miss Sadie Thompson* (1953) and no one you'd recognize starred in the tantalizing *She Gods of Shark Reef* (1956).

The movie that is still immortalized on the island in the names of restaurants, real estate offices, a hotel, and even a sushi item is *South Pacific* (1957). (You guessed it, right?) That mythical place called Bali Hai is never far away on Kaua'i. There's even an off-off-off-Broadway musical version performed today—some 50 years after the movie was released—at the Kaua'i Beach Resort in Līhu'e.

In the 1960s Elvis Presley filmed *Blue Hawaii* (1961) and *Girls! Girls! Girls!* (1962) on the island. A local movie tour likes to point out the stain on a hotel carpet where Elvis's jelly doughnut fell.

Kaua'i has welcomed a long list of Hollywood's A-List: John Wayne in *Donovan's Reef* (1963); Jack Lemmon in *The Wackiest Ship in the Army* (1961); Richard Chamberlain in *The Thorn Birds* (1983); Gene Hackman in *Uncommon Valor* (1983); Danny DeVito and Billy Crystal in *Throw Momma From the Train* (1987); and Dustin Hoffman, Morgan Freeman, Renee Russo, and Cuba Gooding Jr. in *Outbreak* (1995).

Yet the movie scene isn't the only screen on which Kaua'i has starred. A long list of TV shows, TV pilots, and made-for-TV movies make the list as well, including *Gilligan's Island*, *Fantasy Island*, *Starsky & Hutch*, *Baywatch-Hawai'i*—even reality TV shows *The Bachelor* and *The Amazing Race 3*.

For the record, just because a movie was filmed here, doesn't mean the entire movie was filmed on Kaua'i. Take *Honeymoon in Vegas*: one scene.

The North Shore

Hanalei Gourmet. The sleepy North Shore stays awake—until 9:30, that is—each evening in this small, convivial setting inside Hanalei's restored old school building. The emphasis here is on local live jazz, rock, and folk music. ⊠ *5-5161 Kūhiō Hwy., Hanalei Center, Hanalei* ☎ *808/826-2524.*

★ **Happy Talk Lounge.** Hawaiian entertainment takes center stage Monday through Friday evenings (6:30–9:30) in this lounge at the Hanalei Bay Resort. Come Saturday (6:30–9:30) and Sunday (4–7), the joint is swinging to the sounds of jazz in jam sessions. Tuesday evenings at 7, there's a hula show. ⊠ *5380 Honoiki Rd., Princeville* ☎ *808/826-6522.*

Princeville Resort Living Room Lounge. Every night from 7:30 to 10:30 this spacious lounge overlooking Hanalei Bay offers music with an ocean view. Musical selections range from contemporary to jazz to traditional Hawaiian. ⊠ *Princeville Resort, 5520 Ka Haku Rd., Princeville* ☎ *808/826-9644.*

Tahiti Nui. This venerable and decidedly funky institution in sleepy Hanalei no longer offers its famous lūʻau, ever since owner and founder Auntie Louise Marston died. Its fun-loving new owner, a Kiwi from New Zealand, is doing his best to keep the place hopping with nightly entertainment: Hawaiian music Tuesday, Thursday, and Friday; karaoke on Monday and Thursday; and rock and roll Sunday, Wednesday, and Saturday. ⊠ *Kūhiō Hwy., Hanalei* ☎ *808/826-6277.*

The East Side

Duke's Barefoot Bar. This is one of the liveliest bars on Kalapakī Beach. Contemporary Hawaiian music is performed in the beachside bar on Friday, and upstairs a traditional Hawaiian trio plays nightly for diners. The bar closes at 11 most nights. ⊠ *Kalapakī Beach, Līhuʻe* ☎ *808/246-9599.*

Hukilau Lānai. This open-air bar and restaurant is on the property of the Kauaʻi Coast Resort but operates independently. Trade winds trickle through the modest little bar, which looks out into a coconut grove. If the mood takes you, go on a short walk to the sea, or recline in big, comfortable chairs while listening to mellow jazz or Hawaiian slack key guitar. Live music plays Sunday, Tuesday, and Friday, though the bar is open every day but Monday. Freshly infused tropical martinis—perhaps locally grown lychee and pineapple or a Big Island vanilla bean infusion—are house favorites. ⊠ *520 Aleka Loop Kūhiō Hwy., Wailua* ☎ *808/822-0600.*

Rob's Good Times Grill. Let loose at this sports bar, which also houses Kauaʻi's hottest DJs spinning Thursday through Saturday from 9 PM to 2 AM. Wednesday you can kick up your heels with country line dancing from 7:30 PM to 11. Sunday, Monday, and Tuesday evenings are open mike for karaoke enthusiasts. ⊠ *4303 Rice St., Līhuʻe* ☎ *808/246-0311.*

Tradewinds—A South Seas Bar. This salty mariner's den is surprisingly located within the cliché confines of a cheesy mall. Tradewinds has a tattered palm-frond roof and a tropical theme reminiscent of Jimmy Buffett, but you aren't likely to hear Buffett tunes here. In fact, you're more likely to meet Ernest Hemingway types. From karaoke to dart league competitions to live music, this little bar busts at the seams with local flavor. It's open daily from 10 AM to 2 AM. ⊠ *Coconut Marketplace, Kūhiō Hwy., Kapa'a* ☎ *808/822–1621.*

WORD OF MOUTH

"We saw a free music/hula show at the Po'ipū Shopping Village. We had a seat and watched a very fun show with excellent dancing . . ."

–iamq

The South Shore & West Side

Keoki's Paradise. A young, energetic crowd makes this a lively spot on Thursday, Friday, and Saturday nights, with live music from 7 to 9. After 9 PM, when the dining room clears out, there's a bit of a bar scene for singles. The bar closes at midnight. ⊠ *Po'ipū Shopping Village, 2360 Kiahuna Plantation Dr., Po'ipū* ☎ *808/742–7354.*

The Point at Sheraton Kaua'i. This is *the* place to be on the South Shore to celebrate sunset with a drink; the ocean view is unsurpassed. Starting at 8 PM on Friday, Saturday, and Monday, there's live entertainment until 12:30 AM, with a live band on Friday, salsa dancing and a DJ on Saturday, and swing dancing on Monday. ⊠ *Sheraton Kaua'i Resort, 2440 Ho'onani Rd., Po'ipū* ☎ *808/742–1661.*

Waimea Brewing Company. Sip one of the award-winning beers in an airy plantation-style house in a 100-year-old coconut grove on the property of the Waimea Plantation Cottages. Home-brewed beer, outdoor seating, and a wraparound lānai make this brewery/eatery an authentic West Side experience. No promises, but there is usually live music on Tuesday, Wednesday, and Thursday. ⊠ *9400 Kaumuali'i Hwy., Waimea* ☎ *808/338–9733.*

Coffeehouses

Fodor'sChoice ★ **Caffé Cocoa.** Nestled in a bamboo forest draped in bougainvillea and flowering vines and hidden from view off the Kūhiō Highway is a charming little venue where local musicians perform nightly. Café Cocoa offers pūpūs (appetizers), entrées, and desserts. It may not have a liquor license, but don't let that stop you from enjoying the local talent; just bring your own wine or beer. The outdoor setting—twinkle lights and tiki torches beneath a thatched hut—is what the Kaua'i of old must have been like. There's hula every Friday, and a belly-dancing group performs on Tuesday. It's open until 9 Tuesday through Sunday. ⊠ *4-369 Kūhiō Hwy., Wailua* ☎ *808/822–7990.*

Fodor'sChoice ★ **Small Town Coffee.** This funky little coffeehouse is the best thing to happen to the East Side in years. Owner Annie Caporuscio had a vision for a venue that supports music, community, and art. Poetry slams, improv jazz, open mike nights, comedy and writing groups—you'll find them all on this tiny lot across the street from the beach in Kapa'a. You can't miss the bright blue façade of this two-story house or the crowd hanging out beneath umbrellas on the front stoop. Open daily with nightly entertainment, this café is abuzz with local talent and soulful conversation. And it hasn't hurt business to offer free Wi-Fi either. ⊠ *4-1495 Kūhiō Hwy., Kapaʻa* ☎ *808/821–1604.*

Where to Eat

WORD OF MOUTH

"My overall recommendation is to be sure to try the local foods. Hawai'i has some awesome fish, including no and opakapaka. They are so fresh and delicious—don't miss them. Anything pineapple-, coconut-, or macadamia-nut-flavored is good to try."

—Erin74

"Hanalei Bay Resort had live music . . . excellent views and great drinks."

—salgal

Updated by
Joan Conrow

FOOD IS A BIG PART OF LOCAL CULTURE, PLAYING A PROMINENT role at parties, celebrations, events, and even casual gatherings. The best grinds (food) are homemade, so if you're lucky enough to win an invitation to a potluck, baby lū'au, or beach party, accept. Folks are urged to eat until they're full, then rest, eat some more, and make a plate to take home, too. Small, neighborhood eateries are a good place to try local-style food, which bears little resemblance to the fancy Pacific Rim cuisine served in upscale restaurants. Expect plenty of meat—usually deep-fried or marinated in a teriyaki sauce and grilled *pulehu*-style—over an open fire— and starches. Rice is ubiquitous, even for breakfast, and often served alongside potato-macaroni salad, another island specialty. Another local favorite is *poke,* made from chunks of raw tuna or octopus seasoned with sesame oil, soy sauce, onions, and pickled seaweed. It's a great *pūpū* (appetizer) when paired with a cold beer.

Kaua'i's cultural diversity is apparent in its restaurants, which offer authentic Vietnamese, Chinese, Korean, Japanese, Thai, Filipino, Mexican, Italian, and Hawaiian specialties. Less specialized restaurants cater to the tourist crowd, serving standard American fare—burgers, pizza, sandwiches, surf-and-turf combos, and so on. Kapa'a offers the best selection of restaurants, with options for a variety of tastes and budgets; most fast-food joints are in Lihū'e.

Parents will be relieved to encounter a tolerant attitude toward children, even if they're noisy. Men can leave their jackets and ties at home; attire tends toward informal, but if you want to dress up, you can. Reservations are accepted in most places and required at some of the top restaurants. ■ TIP➜ One cautionary note: most restaurants stop serving dinner at 8 or 9 PM, so plan to eat early.

WHAT IT COSTS				
$$$$	**$$$**	**$$**	**$**	**¢**
RESTAURANTS over $35	$27–$35	$18–$26	$10–$17	under $10

Prices are for one main course at dinner.

THE NORTH SHORE

Because of the North Shore's isolation, restaurants have enjoyed a captive audience of visitors who don't want to make the long dark trek into town for dinner. As a result, dining in this region has been characterized by expensive fare that isn't especially tasty. Fortunately, the situation is slowly improving as new restaurants open and others change hands or menus.

Still, dining on the North Shore tends to be pricey and not especially conducive to families. Most of the restaurants are found either in Hanalei town or the Princeville resorts. Consequently, you'll encounter delightful mountain and ocean views but just one restaurant with oceanfront dining.

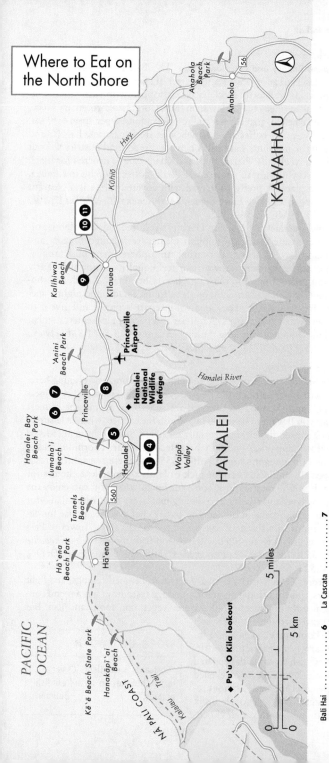

Where to Eat on the North Shore

PACIFIC OCEAN

KAWAIHAU

HANALEI

American–Casual

¢–$$$ ✕ **Kīlauea Bakery and Pau Hana Pizza.** This bakery has garnered tons of well-deserved good press for its starter of Hawaiian sourdough made with guava as well as its specialty pizzas topped with such yummy ingredients as smoked ono (a Hawaiian fish), Gorgonzola-rosemary sauce, barbecued chicken, goat cheese, and roasted onions. Open from 6:30 AM, the bakery serves coffee drinks, delicious fresh pastries, bagels, and breads in the morning. Late risers beware: breads and pastries sell out quickly on weekends. Pizza, soup, and salads can be ordered for lunch or dinner. If you want to hang out or do the coffee shop bit in Kīlauea, this is the place. A pretty courtyard with covered tables is a pleasant place to linger. ⊠ *Kong Lung Center, 2490 Keneke St., Kīlauea* ☎ *808/ 828–2020* ▤ *MC, V. $6–$30.*

¢–$$ ✕ **Hanalei Gourmet.** This spot in Hanalei's restored old schoolhouse offers dolphin-safe tuna, low-sodium meats, fresh-baked breads, and homemade desserts as well as a casual atmosphere where both families and the sports-watching crowds can feel equally comfortable. Early birds can order coffee and toast or a hearty breakfast. Lunch and dinner menus feature sandwiches, burgers, filling salads, and nightly specials of fresh local fish. They also will prepare a picnic and give it to you in an insulated backpack. A full bar and frequent live entertainment keep things hopping even after the kitchen closes. ⊠ *5-5161 Kūhiō Hwy., Hanalei* ☎ *808/826–2524* ▤ *D, DC, MC, V. $9–$25.*

Contemporary

★ $$–$$$ ✕ **Café Hanalei and Terrace.** You're in for a very romantic evening here: the view from the Princeville Resort overlooking Hanalei Bay is mesmerizing, and the food and service are superb. In all but the rainiest weather you'll want to be seated outside on the terrace, where a leisurely lunch or sunset dinner are especially nice. The Sunday brunch ($48 or $55 with champagne) and daily breakfast buffet are enormous feasts, as is the Friday night seafood buffet ($55). Japanese specialties, fresh-fish specials, and Kaua'i coffee rack of lamb are excellent choices for dinner. If you're on a budget, come for lunch when you can enjoy the fabulous views and a leisurely, relaxing meal—try the Cobb salad—for less than you'd spend at dinner. The pastry chef deserves praise for delicious, innovative desserts. Save room for the decadent Tower of Passion, a chocolate tower filled with passion-fruit mousse. ⊠ *Princeville Resort, 5520 Ka Haku Rd., Princeville* ☎ *808/826–2760* ▤ *AE, D, DC, MC, V. $21–$35.*

★ $$–$$$ ✕ **Postcards Café.** With its postcard artwork, beamed ceilings, and light interiors, this traditional plantation-cottage restaurant has a menu consisting mostly of organic, additive-free vegetarian foods and fish. But don't get the wrong idea—this isn't simple cooking: choices might include carrot-ginger soup, taro fritters, fresh fish served with peppered pineapple-sage sauce, or blackened ahi. Desserts are made without refined sugar. Try the chocolate silk pie made with barley malt choco-

> **WORD OF MOUTH**
>
> "Postcards is excellent. It's vegetarian, but they do serve fresh fish entrées."   –Budman

BUDGET-FRIENDLY EATS: NORTH SHORE

It's not easy to find cheap food on the North Shore, but these little eateries serve dinner for two for under $20.

Foodland. In a pinch, you can pick up pretty good packaged sushi and ready-to-eat hot entrées and sandwiches at the Foodland grocery store. ✉ Princeville Shopping Center, Kūhio Hwy., Princeville ☎ 808/826-9880.

Hanalei Mixed Plate. Hearty portions, decent food, and low prices make this take-out restaurant in Ching Young Village worth a stop in pricey Hanalei. ✉ 5-5190 Kūhio Hwy., Hanalei ☎ 808/826-7888.

Neide's Salsa & Samba. One of the best low-cost eateries, with unusual and tasty Brazilian food to take out or eat in a casual garden setting at the Hanalei Center. ✉ 5-5161 Kūhio Hwy., Hanalei ☎ 808/826-1851.

Papaya's. Health foods, such as rice dishes, soups and salads, are served in the back of a natural foods store at the Hanalei Center; takeout only. ✉ 5-5161 Kūhio Hwy., Hanalei ☎ 808/826-0089.

Pizza Hanalei. Excellent pizza (the pesto with whole wheat crust is a winner), salads and a few pasta dishes can be taken out or enjoyed at inside and outside tables at Ching Young Village. ✉ 5-5190 Kūhio Hwy., Hanalei ☎ 808/826-9494.

Tropical Taco. This a good choice for a quick take-out meal of basic, simple Mexican food. ✉ 5-5088 Kūhio Hwy., Hanalei ☎ 808/827-8226.

late, pure vanilla, and creamy tofu with a crust of graham crackers, sun-dried cherries, and crushed cashews. This is probably your best bet for dinner in Hanalei town. ✉ *5-5075A Kūhiō Hwy., Hanalei* ☎ *808/ 826-1191* ▭ *AE, MC, V* ☺ *No lunch. $18–$24.*

Eclectic

$–$$ ✕ **Zelo's Beach House.** When you're traveling with a family or group and everyone wants to eat something different, a restaurant such as Zelo's comes in handy. The menu offers burgers, pasta, hearty salads, seafood fajitas, and several combination meals. The portions are huge and the prices moderate. The tropical decor, relaxed family atmosphere, and outdoor seating add to its appeal, as does its prime location on Hanalei's main drag. New owners have improved the quality of the food and added excellent breads and desserts. ✉ *5-5156 Kūhiō Hwy., Hanalei* ☎ *808/ 826-9700* ▭ *MC, V. $10–$24.*

Italian

★ **$$–$$$$** ✕ **La Cascata.** Terra-cotta floors, hand-painted murals, and trompe-l'oeil paintings give La Cascata a Tuscan-villa flair that makes it ideal for cozy, romantic dining. Picture windows offer dazzling views of Hanalei Bay, though you'll have to come before sunset to enjoy them. Local ingredients figure prominently on a fairly standard menu of pasta, fresh seafood, and meats prepared with competence and creativity.

Savor *Brodetto di Pesce* (prawns, snapper, scallops, and clams with a lobster bourdelaise sauce served over linguine) or black-pepper-crusted duck breast with a sweet-potato mash and griotte cherry gastrique. The traditional tiramisu is exquisite, and the signature baby cake is a very adult chocolate confection. The service is professional and efficient. This is one of two excellent—though pricey—restaurants at the luxurious Princeville Resort. ⊠ *Princeville Resort, 5520 Ka Haku Rd., Princeville* ☎ *808/826–2761* ⚄ *Reservations essential* ☰ *AE, D, DC, MC, V* ⊘ *No lunch. $27–$41.*

$–$$$$ ✕ **Sabellas at Princeville.** The old Beamreach restaurant has been given a happy new life by the family that made Sabellas a dining star in California's Marin County. The menu here has a similar emphasis on Italian-seafood cuisine, with an understated Pacific Rim influence added by chef Gillie Ainoa. The produce is locally grown, and they serve fresh island fish. The result is good food and hearty portions. We enjoyed the deceptively simple steamed opakapaka (a local snapper), chicken saltimbocca and scallops with bacon and bleu cheese. The food is complemented by the competent service and friendly atmosphere. You can eat at the lively bar or in a snug dining room, or get anything to go. ⊠ *Pali Ke Kua, 5300 Kahaku Rd., Princeville* ☎ *808/826–6225* ☰ *AE, D, DC, MC, V* ⊘ *No lunch. Closed Mon.*

Mediterranean

¢–$$$ ✕ **Bar Acuda.** This tapas bar is a very welcome addition to the Hanalei
Fodor'sChoice   dining scene, rocketing right to top place in the categories of tastiness,
★   creativity and pizzazz. Owner/chef Jim Moffat's brief menu changes weekly: you might find sea bass, polenta, fried fish cakes, grilled veggies, a fresh mozzarella salad and sausages with onions, all served with fresh bread. The small servings are intended to be shared, tapas-style. The food is consistently remarkable, with subtly intense sauces that further elevate the outstanding cuisine. It's super casual, but chic, with a nice porch for outdoor dining and the service is discreet, but thorough. ⊠ *Hanalei Center, 5-5161 Kuhio Hwy., Hanalei* ☎ *808/826–7081* ☰ *MC, V* ⊘ *Closed Sun. and Mon.*

Steak & Seafood

$$–$$$$ ✕ **Bali Hai.** Sweeping views of Hanalei Bay and Nā Pali Coast are the highlight at this open-air restaurant, though it can be a bit too exposed to winter winds and rain (bring a jacket). When it comes to surf and turf, this restaurant's selection is hard to beat: Black Angus tenderloin, lamb chops, New York strip, shrimp, scallops, lobster, and island fish served five ways. One of the best choices is the Pele Goddess of Fire selection—fresh catch blackened and glazed with a peppered pineapple-mango chutney—and numerous seafood medleys and combination plates. Breakfast includes poi pancakes, fried taro, and eggs; lunch is a mix of salads and sandwiches. The menu descriptions sound good, but the food lacks refinement, making it hard to justify prices that are among the highest on the island. If you arrive before sunset, however, the view makes it worth it. (Or come for a drink and pūpū—especially the sashimi.) ⊠ *Hanalei Bay Resort, 5380 Honoiki Rd., Princeville* ☎ *808/826–6522* ☰ *AE, D, DC, MC, V. $22–$46.*

SHAVE ICE

Nothing goes down quite so nice as shave ice on a hot day. This favorite island treat has been likened to a sno-cone, but that description doesn't do a good shave ice justice. Yes, it is ice served up in a cone-shaped cup and drenched with sweet syrup, but the similarities end there. As its name implies, the ice should be feathery, light—the texture of snowflakes, not frozen slush. And alongside the standard cherry and grape, you'll find all sorts of exotic island flavorings, such as passion fruit, pineapple, coconut, mango and of course, a rainbow mix.

Not all shave ice meets these high standards, and when you're hot, even the average ones taste great. But a few places are worth seeking out. On the East Side, the best is **Hawaiian Blizzard** (⊠ Kappaʻa Shopping Center, 4-1105 Kuhio Hwy.), a true shave ice stand that opens up midday in front of the Big-Save grocery store in Kappaʻa. In Līhuʻe, try **Halo Halo Shave Ice** (⊠ 2956 Kress St.). And on the hot, dry West Side, make a beeline for **Jo-Jo's Clubhouse** (⊠ Mile marker 23, Kaumualii, Hwy. 50), on the main drag in Waimea. All three places have benches where you can sit and slurp.

$$ ✕ **Sushi Blues.** If you've tried and liked Zelo's, you'll like this second-story restaurant and sushi bar, which is owned by the same folks. It has a nice ambience, with copper tabletops, lovely views of mountains streaked with waterfalls, and photos of international jazz greats lining the staircase. Regular entertainment, a full bar, and a sake menu add to its appeal. Choose from steaks, seafood dishes, and specialty sushi items such as the Las Vegas Roll, which is filled with tuna, yellowtail, and avocado and fried in a tempura batter. ⊠ *Ching Young Village, 5-5190 Kūhiō Hwy., Hanalei* ☎ *808/826-9701* ▭ *AE, D, DC, MC, V. $18–$25.*

$-$$ ✕ **Kīlauea Fish Market.** If you're not in a hurry, this tiny restaurant serves up fresh fish in quality preparations, including tucked into hearty wraps and salads, stir-fried and grilled with tasty sauces. The chicken plate lunch, with a choice of brown or white rice, is the best deal for the budget conscious. After placing your order inside, you can eat outside at covered tables, or take out. ⊠ *Kīlauea Lighthouse Rd., Kīlauea* ☎ *808/828–6244* ▭ *MC, V* ☉ *Closed Sun.*

THE EAST SIDE

Kapaʻa & Wailua

Since the East Side is the island's largest population center, it makes sense that it boasts the widest selection of restaurants. It's also a good place to get both cheaper meals, and the local-style cuisine that residents favor.

Most of the eateries are found along Kuhio Highway between Kapaʻa and Wailua; a few are tucked into shopping centers and resorts. In Lihuʻe, it's easier to find lunch than dinner because many restaurants cater to the business crowd.

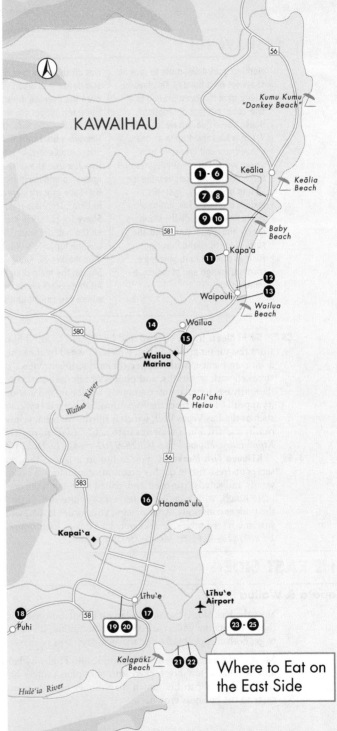

KAWAIHAU

Kumu Kumu
"Donkey Beach"

Keālia

Keālia
Beach

1-**6**

7 **8**

9 **10**

Baby
Beach

Kapa'a

11

12

13

Waipouli

Wailua
Beach

14

Wailua

15

Poli'ahu
Heiau

Wailua
Marina

Wailua River

16

Hanamā'ulu

Kapai'a

Līhu'e
Airport

23-**25**

Līhu'e

19 **20**

17

18

Puhi

21 **22**

Kalapākī
Beach

Hulē'ia River

Where to Eat on
the East Side

ROMANTIC DINING

Whether you're already feeling sparks, or trying to fan banked embers into flame, a romantic meal can help things along. Fortunately, Kaua'i has a number of restaurants that are conducive to love.

For divine sunsets, **The Beach House** (☎ 808/742-1424), in Kōloa, is tops, as it puts you right on the water. **La Cascata** (☎ 808/876-2761) and **Café Hanalei and Terrace** (☎ 808/826-2760), provide fabulous views and glamour, given their setting within the luxurious Princeville Hotel.

Café Portofino (☎ 808/245-2121), in Līhu'e, with its second-story view of Kalapaki Bay and harp music, practically caters to couples. Tops overall, though, is **Dondero's** (☎ 808/240-6456), in Kōloa, where the food, service and elegant setting come together to create a special evening. If it's a nice evening, by all means opt for the veranda.

Be sure to make reservations, and don't plan on pinching pennies. If you're on a budget, pick up some take-out food and spread a blanket on the beach for a sunset picnic and dessert beneath brilliant stars.

You'll find all the usual fast-food joints in both Kapa'a and Lihu'e, as well as virtually every ethnic cuisine available on Kaua'i. While fancy, gourmet restaurants are less abundant in this part of the island, there's plenty of good, solid food, and a few stellar attractions. But unless you're staying on the East Side, or passing through, it's probably not worth the long drive from the North Shore or Po'ipū resorts to eat here.

American–Casual

$–$$$ ✕ **Scotty's Beachside BBQ.** Ribs and other succulent smoked meats are the stars at this casual upstairs restaurant that has a large, often noisy dining room and lovely ocean view. While the BBQ is best here, the menu also has grilled steak, shrimp, chicken and burgers. You can choose your BBQ sauce and two side dishes; the coleslaw and baked beans are noteworthy. If you still have room for dessert, try the make your own s'mores or mango cheesecake. ⊠ *4-1546 Kūhiō Hwy., Kapa'a* ☎ *808/823–8480* ▤ *AE, D, MC, V* ☉ *Closed Sun.*

¢–$ ✕ **Eggbert's.** If you're big on breakfasts, try Eggbert's, which serves breakfast items until 3 PM daily. In the Coconut Marketplace, this family-friendly restaurant, with a sunny interior, lots of windows, and lānai seating, is a great spot for omelets, banana pancakes, and eggs Benedict in two sizes. Lunch selections include sandwiches, burgers, stir-fry, and fresh fish. Take-out orders are also available. ⊠ *Coconut Marketplace, 4-484 Kūhiō Hwy., Kapa'a* ☎ *808/822–3787* ▤ *MC, V* ☉ *No dinner. $6–$14.*

Contemporary

$$–$$$ ✕ **Hukilau Lana'i.** Relying heavily on super fresh island fish and locally
Fodor'sChoice grown vegetables, this restaurant offers quality food that is compe-
★ tently and creatively prepared. The fish—grilled, steamed or sautéed and served with succulent sauces—shines here. Other sound choices are the

savory meat loaf and prime rib. Chicken and a few pasta dishes round out the menu. The ahi nachos appetizer is not to be missed, nor is the warm chocolate dessert soufflé. The spacious dining room looks out to the ocean, and it's lovely to eat at the outdoor tables when the weather is nice. Overall, one of the best choices on the East Side. ⊠ *Kauai'i Coast Resort, Coconut Marketplace, Kūhiō Hwy., Kapa'a* ☎ *808/822–0600* ⊟ *AE, D, DC, MC, V* ☉ *No lunch. Closed Mon.*

$–$$ ✕ **Caffé Coco.** A restored plantation cottage set back off the highway and surrounded by tropical foliage is the setting for this island café. You'll know it by its bright lime-green storefront. An attached black-light art gallery and a vintage apparel shop called Bambulei make this a fun stop for any meal. Outdoor seating in the vine-covered garden is pleasant during nice weather, although on calm nights, it can get buggy. Acoustic music is offered regularly, attracting a laid-back local crowd. Pot stickers filled with tofu and chutney, 'ahi wraps, Greek and organic salads, fresh fish and soups, and a daily list of specials are complemented by a full espresso bar and wonderful desserts. Allow plenty of time, because the tiny kitchen can't turn out meals quickly. ⊠ *4-369 Kūhiō Hwy., Wailua* ☎ *808/822–7990* ⊟ *MC, V* ☉ *Closed Mon. $12–$20.*

Eclectic

¢–$ ✕ **Wailua Family Restaurant.** Catering to families, seniors, and folks on a budget, this restaurant offers basic fare in a basic setting. Hearty eaters will appreciate the self-serve, all-you-can-eat, hot-and-cold salad bar; tostada, taco, and pasta bar; and dessert bar. Steaks, chops, chicken, pasta, and seafood fill out the menu. Breakfast buffets on weekend mornings include eggs Benedict, a mahimahi-and-eggs combo, fresh tropical fruit, and corn-bread muffins. It gets crowded after church on Sunday mornings. This is a good way to sample some local foods. ⊠ *4-361 Kūhiō Hwy., Kapa'a* ☎ *808/822–3325* ⊟ *AE, D, MC, V. $5–$16.*

¢   ✕ **Ono Family Restaurant.** It's not always easy to grab a table at Ono, especially on weekend mornings. Dependable food and efficient service account for its popularity with locals and tourists alike. The decor is country diner, with wooden booths and tables, local antiques, and old-fashioned fixtures. The menu has a touch of Hawaiian style, including such local favorites as kimchi omelets, banana macadamia-nut pancakes, breakfast burritos, Portuguese sausage, and fried rice, offered alongside such all-American choices as eggs Canterbury (poached eggs, ham, turkey, jack cheese, tomato, hollandaise sauce, and mushrooms on an English muffin). Lunch is less interesting: the usual burgers, sandwiches, salads, and soups. You have a choice of indoor or sidewalk seating alongside busy Kuhio Highway in this downtown Kapa'a eatery. ⊠ *4-1292 Kūhiō Hwy., Kapa'a* ☎ *808/822–1710* ⊟ *AE, D, DC, MC, V* ☉ *No dinner. $5–$9.*

Italian

¢–$$ ✕ **Kaua'i Pasta.** If you don't mind a no-frills atmosphere for affordable five-star food, this is the place. The husband of the husband-and-wife team that run Kaua'i Pasta left his executive chef position at Roy's to open a catering business. He leased a kitchen that happened to have a small dining area, and rather than let it go to waste, they open for din-

AUTHENTIC TASTE OF HAWAI'I: LŪʻAU OR LAULAU?

The best place to sample Hawaiian food is at a backyard lūʻau. Aunts and uncles are cooking, the pig is from a cousin's farm, and the fish is from a brother's boat.

But even locals have to angle for invitations to those rare occasions. So your choice is most likely between a commercial lūʻau and a Hawaiian restaurant.

Most commercial lūʻau will offer you little of the authentic diet; they're more about umbrella drinks, laughs, spectacle, and fun. Expect to spend some time—most are far from Waikīkī—and no small amount of cash.

For greater authenticity, folksy experiences, and rock-bottom prices, visit a Hawaiian restaurant (most are in anonymous storefronts in residential neighborhoods). Expect rough edges and some effort negotiating the menu.

In either case, much of what is known today as Hawaiian food would be as foreign to a 16th-century Hawaiian as risotto or chow mien. The pre-contact diet was simple and healthy—mainly raw and steamed seafood and vegetables. Early Hawaiians used earth ovens and heated stones to cook seafood, taro, sweet potatoes, and breadfruit and seasoned their food with sea salt and ground kukui nuts. Seaweed, fern shoots, sweet potato vines, coconut, banana, sugarcane, and select greens and roots rounded out the diet.

Successive waves of immigrants added their favorites to the ti leaf-lined table. So it is that foods as disparate as salt salmon and chicken long rice are now Hawaiian—even though there is no salmon in Hawaiian waters and long rice (cellophane noodles) is Chinese.

AT THE LŪʻAU: KĀLUA PORK

The heart of any lūʻau is the *imu*, the earth oven in which a whole pig is roasted. The preparation of an imu is an arduous affair for most families, who tackle it only once a year or so, for a baby's first birthday or at Thanksgiving, when many Islanders prefer to imu their turkeys. Commercial lūʻau operations have it down to a science, however.

THE ART OF THE STONE

The key to a proper imu is the *pohaku*, the stones. Imu cook by means of long, slow, moist heat released by special stones that can withstand a hot fire without exploding. Many Hawaiian families treasure their imu stones, keeping them in a pile in the backyard and passing them on through generations.

PIT COOKING

The imu makers first dig a pit about the size of a refrigerator, then lay down *kiawe* (mesquite) wood and stones, and build a white-hot fire that is allowed to burn itself out. The ashes are raked away, and the hot stones covered with banana and ti leaves. Well-wrapped in ti or banana leaves and a net of chicken wire, the pig is lowered onto the leaf-covered stones. *Laulau* (leaf-wrapped bundles of meats, fish, and taro leaves) may also be placed inside. Leaves—ti, banana, even ginger—cover the pig followed by wet burlap sacks (to create steam). The whole is topped with a canvas tarp and left to steam for the better part of a day.

OPENING THE IMU

This is the moment everyone waits for: The imu is unwrapped like a giant present and the imu keepers gingerly wrestle out the steaming pig. When it's unwrapped, the meat falls moist and smoky-flavored from the bone, looking and tasting just like Southern-style pulled pork, but without the barbecue sauce.

WHICH LŪʻAU?

Germaine's Lūʻau. Widely regarded as most folksy and local.

Paradise Cove. Party-hearty atmosphere, kid-friendly.

Polynesian Cultural Center. The sharpest production values but no booze.

Royal Hawaiian Hotel. Gracious and relaxed, famous mai tais.

MEA 'AI 'ONO.
GOOD THINGS TO EAT.

LAULAU

Steamed meats, fish, and taro leaf in ti-leaf bundles: fork-tender, a medley of flavors; the taro resembles spinach.

Laulau

LOMI LOMI SALMON

Salt salmon in a piquant salad or relish with onions, tomatoes.

Lomi Lomi Salmon

POI (DON'T CALL IT LIBRARY PASTE.)

Islanders are beyond tired of jokes about poi, a paste made of pounded taro root.

Consider: The Hawaiian Adam is descended from *kalo* (taro). Young taro plants are called "keiki"–children. Poi is the first food after mother's milk for many Islanders. 'Ai, the word for food, is synonymous with poi in many contexts.

Not only that. We like it. "There is no meat that doesn't taste good with poi," the old Hawaiians said.

But you have to know how to eat it: with something rich or powerfully flavored. "It is salt that makes the poi go in," is another adage. When you're served poi, try it with a mouthful of smoky kālua pork or salty lomi lomi salmon. Its slightly sour blandness cleanses the palate. And if you don't like it, smile and say something polite. (And slide that bowl over to a local.)

Poi

E HELE MAI 'AI! COME AND EAT!

Hawaiian restaurants tend to be inconveniently located in well-worn storefronts with little or no parking, outfitted with battered tables and clattering Melmac dishes, open odd (and usually limited) hours and days, and often so crowded you have to wait. But they personify aloha, invariably run by local families who welcome tourists who take the trouble to find them.

Many are cash-only operations and combination plates are a standard feature: one or two entrées, a side such as chicken long rice, choice of poi or steamed rice and—if the place is really old-style—a tiny portion of coarse Hawaiian salt and some raw onions for relish.

Most serve some foods that aren't, strictly speaking, Hawaiian, but are beloved of

kama'āina, such as salt meat with watercress (preserved meat in a tasty broth), or *akubone* (skipjack tuna fried in a tangy vinegar sauce).

Our favorite: **Dani's Restaurant** (✉ 4201 Rice St., Līhu'e, ☎ 808/245-4991).

MENU GUIDE

Much of the Hawaiian language encountered during a stay in the Islands will appear on restaurant menus and lists of lū'au fare. Here's a quick primer.

'ahi: *yellowfin tuna.*

aku: *skipjack, bonito tuna.*

'ama'ama: *mullet; it's hard to get but tasty.*

bento: *a box lunch.*

chicken lū'au: *a stew made from chicken, taro leaves, and coconut milk.*

haupia: *a light, gelatinlike dessert made from coconut.*

imu: *the underground ovens in which pigs are roasted for lū'au.*

kālua: *to bake underground.*

kaukau: *food. The word comes from Chinese but is used in the Islands.*

kimchee: *Korean dish of pickled cabbage made with garlic and hot peppers.*

Kona coffee: *coffee grown in the Kona district of the Big Island.*

laulau: *literally, a bundle. Laulau are morsels of pork, chicken, butterfish, or other ingredients wrapped with young taro shoots in ti leaves for steaming.*

liliko'i: *passion fruit, a tart, seedy yellow fruit that makes delicious desserts and jellies.*

lomi lomi: *to rub or massage; also a massage. Lomi lomi salmon is fish that has been rubbed with onions and herbs, commonly served with minced onions and tomatoes.*

lū'au: *a Hawaiian feast, also the leaf of the taro plant used in preparing such a feast.*

lū'au leaves: *cooked taro tops with a taste similar to spinach.*

mahimahi: *mild-flavored dolphinfish, not the marine mammal.*

mai tai: *potent rum drink with orange and lime juice, from the Tahitian word for "good."*

malassada: *a Portuguese deep-fried doughnut without a hole, dipped in sugar.*

manapua: *dough wrapped around diced pork.*

manō: *shark.*

niu: *coconut.*

'ōkolehao: *a liqueur distilled from the ti root.*

onaga: *pink or red snapper.*

ono: *a long, slender mackerel-like fish; also called wahoo.*

'ono: *delicious; also hungry.*

'opihi: *a tiny shellfish, or mollusk, found on rocks; also called limpets.*

pāpio: *a young ulua or jack fish.*

pohā: *Cape gooseberry. Tasting a bit like honey, the pohā berry is often used in jams and desserts.*

poi: *a paste made from pounded taro root, a staple of the Hawaiian diet.*

poke: *chopped, pickled raw tuna, tossed with herbs and seasonings.*

pūpū: *Hawaiian hors d'oeuvre.*

saimin: *long thin noodles and vegetables in broth, often garnished with small pieces of fish cake, scrambled egg, luncheon meat, and green onion.*

sashimi: *raw fish thinly sliced and usually eaten with soy sauce.*

ti leaves: *a member of the agave family. The fragrant leaves are used to wrap food while cooking and removed before eating.*

uku: *deep-sea snapper.*

ulua: *a member of the jack family that also includes pompano and amberjack. Also called crevalle, jack fish, and jack crevalle.*

ner every evening except Monday. Specials, written on the whiteboard at the entrance, are always satisfying and delicious. The locals have this place figured out; they show up in droves. The food's fabulous, and the price is right. Bring your own bottle of wine; they will provide a corkscrew and wineglasses for a $5 corkage fee. ⊠ *4-939B Kūhiō Hwy., Kapa'a* ☎ *808/822–7447* ▭ *MC, V* ⌂ *BYOB* ☉ *Closed Mon. $8–$20.*

Japanese

$–$$$$ ✕ **Restaurant Kintaro.** If you want to eat someplace that's a favorite with locals, visit Kintaro's. But be prepared to wait, because the dining room and sushi bar are always busy. Try the Bali Hai, a roll of eel and smoked salmon, baked and topped with wasabi mayonnaise. For an "all-in-one-dish" meal, consider the *Nabemono,* a single pot filled with a healthful variety of seafood and vegetables. *Teppanyaki* dinners are meat, seafood, and vegetables flash-cooked on tabletop grills in an entertaining display. Tatami-mat seating is available behind shoji screens that provide privacy for groups. Like many longtime restaurants, it's an enduring favorite that doesn't always live up to expectations. ⊠ *4-370 Kūhiō Hwy., Wailua* ☎ *808/822–3341* ▭ *AE, D, DC, MC, V* ☉ *Closed Sun. No lunch. $14–$42.*

Steak & Seafood

$–$$$$ ✕ **Bull Shed.** The A-frame exterior of this popular restaurant imparts a distinctly rustic feel. Inside, light-color walls and a full wall of glass highlight an ocean view that is one of the best on Kaua'i. Come early for a window seat, where you can watch surf crashing on the rocks while you study the menu. The food is simple and basic—think white bread and iceberg lettuce—but they know how to do surf and turf. You can try both in one of several combo dinner platters or order fresh island fish and thick steaks individually. The restaurant is best known for its prime rib and Australian rack of lamb. Longtime visitors and locals love this place, which hasn't changed much in 20 years and coasts on the following it attained when the island had few restaurants. Arrive by 5:30 for early-bird specials. ⊠ *796 Kūhiō Hwy., Kapa'a* ☎ *808/822–3791 or 808/ 822–1655* ▭ *AE, D, DC, MC, V* ☉ *No lunch. $12–$38.*

$–$$$ ✕ **Wailua Marina Restaurant.** Offering the island's only river view, this marina restaurant—an island fixture for almost 40 years—is a good spot to stop for lunch after a boat ride up the Wailua River to the Fern Grotto and worth a visit on its own merit. With more than 40 selections, the menu is a mix of comfort food and more sophisticated dishes; portions are gigantic. The chef is fond of stuffing: you'll find stuffed baked pork chops, stuffed chicken baked in plum sauce, and 'ahi stuffed with crab. The steamed mullet is a classic island dish. ⊠ *Wailua River State Park, Wailua Rd., Wailua* ☎ *808/822–4311* ▭ *AE, D, DC, MC, V* ☉ *Closed Mon. $10–$28.*

Thai

¢–$$ ✕ **Mema Thai Chinese Cuisine.** Refined and intimate, Mema Thai serves its dishes on crisp white linens accented by tabletop orchid sprays. Menu items such as broccoli with oyster sauce and cashew chicken reveal Chinese origins, but the emphasis is on Thai dishes. A host of cur-

8

ries—red, green, yellow, and house—made with coconut milk and kaffir-lime leaves run from mild to mouth searing. The traditional green-papaya salad adds a cool touch for the palate. ⊠ *Wailua Shopping Plaza, 369 Kūhiō Hwy., Kapaʻa* ☎ *808/823–0899* ⊟ *AE, D, DC, MC, V* ⊗ *No lunch weekends. $7–$19.*

Vegetarian

¢–$$ ✕ **Blossoming Lotus.** There are other vegetarian restaurants on the island, but there are no other *vegan* restaurants. Blossoming Lotus has been known to convert die-hard meat lovers. The restaurant bills its fare as "vegan world fusion cuisine," and its menu lives up to the claim: curry, tacos, mung dal, baba ghanoush, and spring rolls—all made fresh, with loving attention. Try the enchilada casserole made from marinated and baked tempeh, beans, rice, chili sauce, and cashew cheese layered between sprouted-wheat tortillas and topped with carob mole, salsa, and nondairy sour cream. ⊠ *4504 Kukui St., Kapaʻa* ☎ *808/822–7678* ⊟ *AE, D, DC, MC, V. $9–$18.*

¢   ✕ **Papaya's.** Kauaʻi's largest natural foods market contains a buffet-style café whose good food and low prices make it popular. Food items change daily, but there's usually a breakfast burrito and oftentimes spinach lasagna, stuffed peppers, and fish tacos for lunch and dinner. The soup-and-salad bar, a daily fixture, has fresh, organic lettuce and vegetables, most grown nearby. You can order takeout, or eat at a covered table in the courtyard. ⊠ *Kauaʻi Village Shopping Center, 4-831 Kūhiō Hwy., Kapaʻa* ☎ *808/823–0190* ⊟ *AE, D, MC, V* ⊗ *Closed Sun. $6.50 per pound.*

THE EAST SIDE: LĪHUʻE

American–Casual

$–$$$ ✕ **Aroma's.** With its eclectic menu of Greek-Italian-Spanish and Pacific Rim–inspired fare, this upstairs restaurant near Nawiliwili Harbor has become one of the better places to eat in Līhuʻe. You can dine inside, or on a deck that faces a stream. Owner-chef Robert Moler competently prepares fresh fish specials, lamb with a tomato, apple and raisin chutney, filled crepes, honey-glazed grilled steak topped with sautéed onions and melted Gorgonzola cheese, among other creative entrées. Save room for the rich crème brûlée cheesecake. For breakfast, try the cherry and cream cheese crepes. ⊠ *3501 Rice St. Ste. 207, Līhuʻe* ☎ *808/245–9192* ⊟ *D, MC, V.*

$–$$$ ✕ **JJ's Broiler.** This spacious, low-key restaurant is almost like two eateries in one. Hearty American fare, including burgers and 2-pound buckets of steamer clams bathed in white wine, garlic, and herbs, is served in the bar and dining room downstairs. On sunny afternoons, ask for a table on the lānai overlooking Kalapakī Bay and try one of the generous salads. Upstairs you can feast on fancier Pacific Rim dishes, including sugarcane shrimp and Peking chicken tacos in a garlic oyster sauce. The house specialty is Slavonic steak, a broiled sliced tenderloin dipped in a buttery wine sauce. ■ TIP→ **Although the restaurant is open until 11 PM, making it one of the few places on Kauaʻi where you can eat late, it's better for lunch for two reasons: the view, and the fact that dinner options**

The Plate-Lunch Tradition

TO EXPERIENCE ISLAND HISTORY FIRSTHAND, take a seat at one of Hawaiʻi's ubiquitous "plate-lunch" eateries, and order a segmented Styrofoam plate piled with rice, macaroni salad, and maybe some fiery pickled vegetable condiment. On the sugar plantations, native Hawaiians and immigrant workers from many different countries came together in the fields, sharing food from their "kaukau kits," the utilitarian version of the Japanese *bento* lunchbox. From this "melting pot" came the vibrant language of pidgin and its equivalent in food: the plate lunch.

At beaches and events, you can probably see a few tiny kitchens-on-wheels, another excellent venue for sampling plate lunch. These portable restaurants are descendants of "lunch wagons" that began selling food to plantation workers in the 1930s. Try the deep-fried chicken *katsu* (rolled in Japanese panko flour and spices). The marinated beef teriyaki is another good choice, as is miso butterfish. The noodle soup, *saimin*, with its Japanese fish stock and Chinese red-tinted barbecue pork, is a distinctly local medley. Koreans have contributed spicy barbecue *kal-bi* ribs, often served with chili-laden *kimchi* (pickled cabbage). Portuguese bean soup and tangy Filipino *adobo* stew are also favorites. The most popular Hawaiian contribution to the plate lunch is the *laulau*, a mix of meat and fish and young taro leaves, wrapped in more taro leaves and steamed.

8

are hit and miss. ⊠ *Anchor Cove, 3146 Rice St., Nāwiliwili* ☎ *808/246–4422* ▭ *D, MC, V. $10–$30.*

$–$$ ✕ **Līhuʻe Barbecue Inn.** Few Kauaʻi restaurants are more beloved than this family-owned eatery, a mainstay of island dining since 1940. The menu runs from traditional American to Asian. Try the baby back ribs, macadamia-nut chicken, or Cajun seafood medley with king crab, or choose a full Japanese dinner from the other side of the menu. If you can't make up your mind, strike a compromise with the inn's tri-sampler. Opt for the fruit cup—fresh, not canned—instead of soup or salad, and save room for a hefty slice of homemade cream pie, available in all sorts of flavors. ⊠ *2982 Kress St., Līhuʻe* ☎ *808/245–2921* ▭ *MC, V. $10–$25.*

Eclectic

$$–$$$$ ✕ **Gaylord's.** Located in what was at one time Kauaʻi's most expensive plantation estate, Gaylord's pays tribute to the elegant dining rooms of 1930s high society. Tables with candlelight sit on a cobblestone patio surrounding a fountain and overlooking a wide lawn. The innovative menu features classic American cooking with an island twist. Try won-ton-wrapped prawns with a wasabi plum sauce, New Zealand venison, blackened prime rib, or fresh-fish specials. Lunches are a mix of salads, sandwiches, and pasta, enjoyed in a leisurely fashion. The lavish Sunday brunch may include such specialties as sweet-potato hash and Cajun 'ahi in addition to the standard omelets and pancakes. Before or after dining you can wander around the estate grounds or take a horse-drawn carriage ride. The unique setting makes up for the culinary gaps. ⊠ *Kilohana Plantation, 3-2087 Kaumuali'i Rd., Līhu'e* ☎ *808/245–9593* ▤ *AE, D, DC, MC, V. $24–$50.*

$–$$$ ✕ **Kukui's Restaurant and Bar.** The healthful choices and cross-cultural flavors on Kukui's menu are well matched with its casual, open-air setting. The meals are not very imaginative but have hints of Hawaiian, Asian, and contemporary American cuisines. Slow-roasted prime rib, fresh catch, *huli huli* chicken (a Hawaiian version of barbecued chicken), penne with sun-dried tomato and macadamia pesto, and a surf-and-turf option are representative of the well-rounded fare. A prime rib and king crab buffet ($38) is served on Friday and Saturday nights in addition to the regular menu. An extensive breakfast buffet ($20) is offered every morning, or choose from the à la carte menu. ⊠ *Kaua'i Marriott Resort & Beach Club, 3610 Rice St., Līhu'e* ☎ *808/245–5050* ▤ *AE, D, DC, MC, V. $16–$32.*

> **BUDGET-FRIENDLY EATS: EAST SIDE**
>
> At these small, local-style eateries, two people can generally eat dinner for less than $20.
>
> ■ **Garden Island BBQ and Chinese Restaurant.** ⊠ *4252-A Rice St., Līhu'e* ☎ *808/245–8868.*
>
> ■ **Hamura Saimin.** ⊠ *2956 Kress St., Līhu'e* ☎ *808/245-3271.*
>
> ■ **Korean BBQ.** ⊠ *4-356 Kūhiō Hwy., Wailua* ☎ *808/823–6744.*
>
> ■ **Papaya's.** ⊠ *4-831 Kūhiō Hwy., Kapa'a* ☎ *808/823-0190.*
>
> ■ **Waipouli Restaurant.** ⊠ *Waipouli Town Center, Kūhiō Hwy., Kapa'a* ☎ *808/822-9311.*

Hawaiian

¢ ✕ **Dani's Restaurant.** Kaua'i residents frequent this big, sparsely furnished eatery near the Līhu'e Fire Station for hearty, local-style food at breakfast and lunch. Dani's is a good place to try lū'au food without commercial lū'au prices. You can order Hawaiian-style *laulau* (pork and taro leaves wrapped in ti leaves and steamed) or kālua pig, slow roasted in an underground oven. Other island-style dishes include Japanese-prepared *tonkatsu* (pork cutlet) and teriyaki beef, and there's always the all-American New York steak. Omelets are whipped up with fish cake, kālua pig, or seafood; everything is served with rice. ⊠ *4201 Rice St., Līhu'e* ☎ *808/245–4991* ▤ *MC, V* ⊘ *Closed Sun. No dinner. $6–$9.*

¢ ✕ **Hamura Saimin.** Folks just love this funky old plantation-style diner. Locals and tourists stream in and out all day long, and neighbor islanders stop in on their way to the airport to pick up take-out orders for friends and family back home. *Saimen* is the big draw, and each day the Hiraoka family dishes up about 1,000 bowls of steaming broth and home-made noodles, topped with a variety of garnishes. The barbecued chicken and meat sticks adopt a smoky flavor during grilling. The landmark eatery is also famous for its *liliko'i* (passion fruit) chiffon pie. ■ TIP➔ **As one of the few island eateries open late, until 11 PM on weeknights and midnight**

on Friday and Saturday, it's favored by night owls. ⊠ *2956 Kress St., Līhu'e* ☎ *808/245-3271* 🖃 *No credit cards. $4–$7.*

Italian

★ **$–$$$** ✕ **Café Portofino.** The menu at this authentic northern Italian restaurant is as inspired as the views of Kalapakī Bay and the Hā'upu range. Owner Giuseppe Avocadi's flawless dishes have garnered a host of culinary awards and raves from dining critics. The fresh 'ahi carpaccio is a signature dish, and pasta, scampi, and veal are enhanced by sauces that soar like Avocadi's imagination. Linger over coffee and ice cream–filled profiteroles or traditional tiramisu while enjoying harp music. Excellent service and a soothing, dignified ambience complete the delightful dining experience, making this one of your best bets for a quality meal in Līhu'e. ⊠ *Kaua'i Marriott Resort & Beach Club, 3610 Rice St., Līhu'e* ☎ *808/245-2121* 🖃 *AE, D, DC, MC, V* ⊗ *No lunch. $17–$30.*

WORD OF MOUTH

"We went to Coconut Marketplace and finally tried Lappert's Ice Cream: Joe had mint-chip and I had turtle-cashew-cluster—both extremely yummy!" –CajunStorm

Japanese

¢–$ ✕ **Hanamā'ulu Restaurant, Tea House, Sushi Bar, and Robatayaki.** Business is brisk at this landmark Kaua'i eatery. The food is a mix of Japanese, Chinese, and local-style cooking, served up in hearty portions. The ginger chicken and fried shrimp are wildly popular, as are the fresh sashimi and sushi. Other choices include tempura, chicken *katsu* (Japanese-style fried chicken), beef broccoli, and *robatayaki* (grilled seafood and meat). The main dining room is rather unattractive, but the private rooms in back look out on the Japanese garden and fishponds and feature traditional seating on tatami mats at low tables. These tearooms can be reserved, and are favored for family events and celebrations. ⊠ *1-4291 Kūhiō Hwy., Rte. 56, Hanamā'ulu* ☎ *808/245-2511* 🖃 *MC, V* ⊗ *Closed Mon. $8–$16.*

Seafood

$–$$$$ ✕ **Duke's Canoe Club.** Surfing legend Duke Kahanamoku is immortalized at this casual bi-level restaurant set on Kalapakī Bay. Guests can admire surfboards, photos, and other memorabilia marking his long tenure as a waterman. It's an interesting collection, and an indoor garden and waterfall add to the pleasing ambience. Downstairs you can find simple fare ranging from fish tacos and stir-fried cashew chicken to hamburgers, served 11 AM to 11 PM. At dinner, upstairs, when prices increase, fresh fish prepared in a variety of styles is the best choice. Duke's claims to have the biggest salad bar on the island, though given the lack of competition that isn't saying much. A happy-hour drink and appetizer is a less expensive way to enjoy the moonrises and ocean views here— though it can get pretty crowded. The Barefoot Bar is a hot spot for after-dinner drinks, too. Still, the setting is more satisfying than the food at this popular eatery. ⊠ *Kaua'i Marriott Resort & Beach Club, 3610 Rice St., Līhu'e* ☎ *808/246-9599* 🖃 *AE, D, DC, MC, V. $13–$45.*

8

THE SOUTH SHORE & THE WEST SIDE

Although the South Shore and West Side are lumped together, they're two different worlds when it comes to dining. Most South Shore restaurants are expensive and located within the Po'ipū resorts, while West Side eateries tend to be more local-style and are generally found along Kaumuali'i Highway.

If you're looking for a gourmet meal in an upscale setting, this is where you'll find it. Po'ipū has a number of excellent restaurants in dreamy settings, and decidedly fewer family-style, lower-priced eateries.

Pickings start to get slimmer the farther west you travel, and dining choices often are dictated by what's open. Fortunately, West Side restaurants are generally worth patronizing, so you won't go too wrong if your hunger demands to be satisfied while you're out enjoying the sights.

American-Casual

¢–$$ ✕ **Camp House Grill.** A plantation-style camp house with squeaky wooden floors has become a simple, down-home restaurant with a funky atmosphere. The food is equally basic: hamburgers, chicken, pork ribs, and fresh fish aimed at families seeking familiar comfort food. Large breakfasts are available, and pies are baked fresh daily; you can eat a slice on the premises or take home an entire pie for a late-night craving. As you enter Kalāheo heading west toward Waimea Canyon, look for the blue building on the right. ⊠ *Kaumuali'i Hwy., Rte. 50, Kalāheo* ☎ *808/332–9755* ⊠ *Kaua'i Village, Kūhiō Hwy., Kapa'a* ☎ *808/822–2442* ▭ *AE, D, MC, V. $6–$19.*

Contemporary

$$–$$$
Fodor'sChoice
★

✕ **Beach House.** This restaurant partners a dreamy ocean view with impressive cuisine. Few Kaua'i experiences are more delightful than sitting at one of the outside tables and savoring a delectable meal while the sun sinks into the glassy blue Pacific. It's the epitome of tropical dining, and no other restaurant on Kaua'i can offer anything quite like it. Chef Todd Barrett's menu changes often, but the food

is consistently creative and delicious. A few trademark dishes appear regularly, such as Chinese-style roast duck, mint-coriander lamb rack, fire-roasted 'ahi, and lemongrass and kaffir-lime sea scallops. Seared macadamia-nut-crusted mahimahi, a dish ubiquitous on island menus, gets a refreshing new twist when served with a lilikoi-lemongrass beurre blanc. Save room for the signature molten chocolate desire, a decadent finale at this pleasing and deservedly popular restaurant. ⊠ *5022 Lāwa'i Rd., Kōloa* ☎ *808/742–1424* ⌂ *Reservations essential* ▭ *AE, DC, MC, V* ☉ *No lunch. $19–$32.*

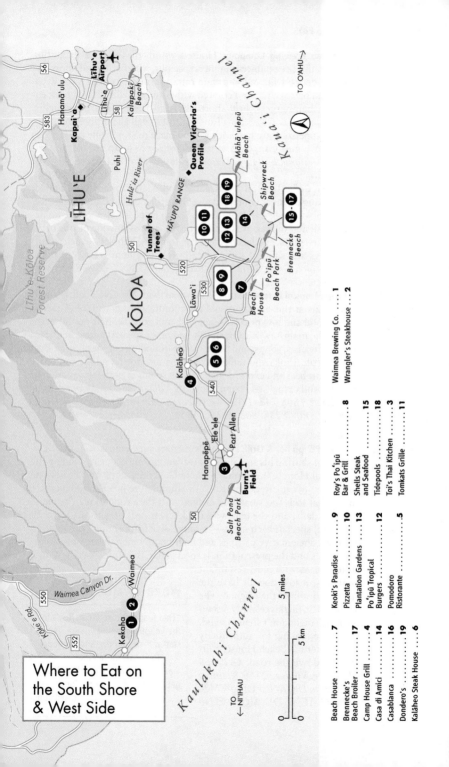

Where to Eat on the South Shore & West Side

Beach House **7**
Brennecke's
Beach Broiler **17**
Camp House Grill **4**
Casa di Amici **14**
Casablanca **16**
Dondero's **19**
Kalāheo Steak House **6**

Keoki's Paradise **9**
Pizzetta **10**
Plantation Gardens **13**
Po'ipū Tropical
Burgers **12**
Pomodoro
Ristorante **5**

Roy's Po'ipū
Bar & Grill **8**
Shells Steak
and Seafood **15**
Tidepools **18**
Toi's Thai Kitchen **3**
Tomkats Grille **11**

Waimea Brewing Co. **1**
Wrangler's Steakhouse ... **2**

¢–$$$ ✕ **Waimea Brewing Company.** Housed within the Waimea Plantation Cottages, this brewpub-restaurant is spacious, with hardwood floors and open-air decks. Dine indoors amid rattan furnishings or at a bar decorated with petroglyphs and colored with Kaua'i red dirt. Kālua pork enchiladas, hamburgers, beef short ribs, and fresh fish are highlights. Entrées come in two sizes (small and big!), although all portions are hearty and the appetizers are huge. It's a good place to stop while traveling to or from Waimea Canyon, and the microbrews on tap are worth a try. ✉ *9400 Kaumuali'i Hwy., Waimea* ☎ *808/338–9733* ▭ *AE, D, MC, V. $8–$30.*

¢–$$ ✕ **Tomkats Grille.** Tropical ponds, a waterfall, a large bar area, and a porch overlooking an inner courtyard give this grill a casual island ambience. Try the blackened "katch of the day" with tropical salsa, or the homemade chili and burger. Wash it down with a glass of wine or one of 35 ales, stouts, ports, and lagers. Plenty of Tomkats' Nibblers—such as buffalo wings and sautéed shrimp—enliven happy hour from 3 to 6 PM. ✉ *Old Kōloa Town, 5402 Kōloa Rd., Kōloa* ☎ *808/742–8887* ▭ *MC, V. $7–$26.*

$☺ ✕ **Po'ipū Tropical Burgers.** Families may find themselves returning for multiple meals at this all-day casual restaurant, with its children's menu, simple food and low prices. Veggie, fish and gourmet half-pound burgers are the mainstay, with fresh fish and other specials added at dinner and sandwiches, soups, and hearty salads rounding out the choices. Bottomless soft drinks and milk shakes are a nice touch; adults can order wine, draft beer and exotic drinks. Dining rooms at both locales are airy, cheerful and casual. ✉ *Po'ipū Shopping Village, 2360 Kiahuna Plantation Dr.* ☎ *808/742–1808.* ✉ *Coconut Marketplace, Kūhio Hwy., Kapa'a* ☎ *808/823–8808* ▭ *MC, V.*

Eclectic

$–$$$$ ✕ **Roy's Po'ipū Bar & Grill.** Hawai'i's culinary superstar, Roy Yamaguchi, is fond of sharing his signature Hawaiian fusion cuisine by cloning the successful Honolulu restaurant where he got his start. You'll find one of these copycat eateries on Kaua'i's South Shore in a shopping-center locale that feels too small and ordinary for the exotic food. The menu changes daily, and the hardworking kitchen staff dreams up 15 to 20 (or more) specials each night—an impressive feat. Though the food reflects the imaginative pairings and high-quality ingredients of the original Roy's and the presentation is spectacular, the atmosphere is a little different. As with most restaurant branches, it just doesn't have the heart and soul of the original. The visitors who fill this celebrity restaurant each night don't seem to mind, but those looking for authenticity may prefer the Beach House, a little way down the road. ✉ *Po'ipū Shopping Village, 2360 Kiahuna Plantation Dr., Kōloa* ☎ *808/742–5000* ▭ *AE, D, DC, MC, V* ☺ *No lunch. $15–$42.*

> **WORD OF MOUTH**
>
> "That first night we ate at Roy's in the Po'ipū Shopping Village. The staff was so friendly, and our food was great (we shared the macadamia-nut mahimahi). Must get the soufflé . . . to die for!"
>
> –travelisfun

Italian

$$–$$$$ ✕ **Dondero's.** The inlaid marble floors, ornate tile work, and Italianate
Fodor'sChoice murals that compose the elegant decor at this restaurant compete with
★ a stunning ocean view. And in addition to the beautiful setting, Don-
dero's offers outstanding food, a remarkable wine list, and impeccable
service, making this Kaua'i's best restaurant. Chef Vincent Pecoraro com-
bines old-world techniques with new energy to create menu selections
as enticing as the surroundings. Pistachio-crusted rack of lamb with a
root-vegetable fritter and pancetta mashed sweet potatoes, and lobster
piccata on a bed of fettuccine with sun-dried tomatoes and a truffle cream
sauce thrill the palate and delight the eye. Order a light, traditional tiramisu
or chocolate crème brûlée with fresh raspberries so you can linger over
coffee. The waitstaff deserves special praise for its thoughtful, discreet
service. ⊠ *Grand Hyatt Kaua'i Resort and Spa, 1571 Po'ipū Rd., Kōloa*
☎ *808/240–6456* ▭ *AE, D, DC, MC, V* ☉ *No lunch. $26–$42.*

$–$$$ ✕ **Casa di Amici.** Tucked away in a quiet neighborhood above Po'ipū
Beach, this "House of Friends" has live classical piano music on week-
ends and an outside deck open to sweeping ocean views. Entrées from
the internationally eclectic menu include a saffron-vanilla paella risotto
made with black tiger prawns, fresh fish, chicken breast, and homemade
Italian sausage. For dessert, take the plunge with a baked Hawai'i: a
chocolate-macadamia-nut brownie topped with coconut and passion-
fruit sorbet and flambéed Italian meringue. The food and setting are pleasant, but service can be maddeningly slow, especially when you're really
hungry. ⊠ *2301 Nalo Rd., Po'ipū* ☎ *808/742–1555* ▭ *AE, D, DC, MC,*
V ☉ *No lunch. $16–$27.*

★ **$$** ✕ **Plantation Gardens.** A historic plantation manager's home has been
converted to a restaurant that serves seafood and kiawe-grilled meats
with a Pacific Rim and Italian influence. You'll walk through a tropi-
cal setting of torchlighted orchid gardens and lotus-studded koi ponds
to a cozy, European-feeling dining room with cherrywood floors and
veranda dining. The menu is based on fresh, local foods: fish right off
the boat, herbs and produce picked from the plantation's gardens, fruit
delivered by neighborhood farmers. The result is Italian cuisine with an
island flair—seafood *laulau* (seafood wrapped in ti leaves and steamed)
served with mango chutney—served alongside traditional classics such
as rosemary-skewered pork tenderloin and pan-roasted scallops with
sticky-rice cakes. Definitely save room for dessert: the warm pineapple
upside-down cake is a dream. In short, the food is excellent and the set-
ting charming. ⊠ *Kiahuna Plantation, 2253 Po'ipū Rd., Kōloa* ☎ *808/*
742–2121 ▭ *AE, DC, MC, V* ☉ *No lunch. $19–$26.*

$–$$ ✕ **Pomodoro Ristorante Italiano.** Begin with prosciutto and melon, then
proceed directly to the multilayer meat lasagna, a favorite of the chefs—
two Italian-born brothers. Other highlights include eggplant or veal parmi-
giana, chicken saltimbocca, and scampi in a garlic, caper, and white wine
sauce. Two walls of windows brighten this intimate second-story restaurant in the heart of Kalāheo, where you'll find good food at reasonable
prices. ⊠ *Upstairs at Rainbow Plaza, Kaumuali'i Hwy., Rte. 50, Kalāheo*
☎ *808/332–5945* ▭ *MC, V* ☉ *Closed Sun. No lunch. $14–$24.*

8

$ ✕ **Pizzetta.** Solid food characterizes this family-style Italian restaurant, which serves up hearty portions of pasta, lasagna and eggplant Parmesan, along with calzones, pizza with numerous toppings and salads. The atmosphere is casual and lively and the food is good, especially for the price. The Kapaʻa location is a bit noisier than the Kōloa locale; both are busy. Neighborhood delivery. ✉ *5408 Kōloa Rd., Kōloa* ☎ *808/742—8881.* ✉ *4-1387 Kūhio Hwy., Kapaʻa* ☎ *808/823–8882* ▤ *MC, V.*

Mediterranean

$-$$$ ✕ **Casablanca at Kiahuna.** Outdoor dining in a pleasant garden setting and consistently good food make this restaurant at the Kiahuna Swim and Tennis Club worth a visit. The Moroccan lamb is noteworthy, or try the fresh mozzarella wrapped in prosciutto and served with poached figs in a distinctive pork-fig sauce. A tapas menu rounds out the offerings. ✉ *2290 Poʻipū Rd., Poʻipū* ☎ *808/742–2929* ▤ *AE, D, MC, V* ⊘ *No dinner Sun. or Mon.*

Thai

$-$$ ✕ **Toi's Thai Kitchen.** Country-style Thai cuisine, hearty portions, reasonable prices and a casual, clean simple dining room make this family-run eatery a solid choice on the restaurant-sparse West Side. Most dishes can be prepared vegetarian style, or with beef, pork, chicken or seafood. Try Toi's Temptation, a hearty mix of meats, pineapple, potatoes and lemon-grass in a sauce of red chili-heated coconut milk, or one of the excellent curries. Meals include a greeen papaya or lettuce salad and warm tapioca or black rice pudding. ✉ *Eleʻele Shopping Center, Kaumualii Hwy., Eleʻele* ☎ *808/335–3111.*

Steak & Seafood

★ $$$-$$$$ ✕ **Tidepools.** The Grand Hyatt Kauaʻi is notable for its excellent restaurants, which differ widely in their settings and cuisine. This one is definitely the most tropical and campy, sure to appeal to folks seeking a bit of island-style romance and adventure. Private grass-thatch huts seem to float on a koi-filled pond beneath starry skies while torches flicker in the lushly landscaped grounds nearby. The equally distinctive food has an island flavor that comes from the chef's advocacy of Hawaiʻi regional cuisine and extensive use of Kauaʻi-grown products. You won't go wrong ordering the fresh-fish specials or one of the signature dishes, such as wok-seared soy-, sake-, and ginger-marinated ʻahi; grilled mahimahi; or pan-seared beef tenderloin. Start with Tidepools' pūpū platter for two—with a lobster cake, peppered beef fillet, and ʻahi sashimi—to wake up your taste buds. If you're still hungry at the end of the meal, the ginger crème brûlée is sure to satisfy. ✉ *Grand Hyatt Kauaʻi Resort and Spa, 1571 Poʻipū Rd., Kōloa* ☎ *808/240–6456 Ext. 4260* ▤ *AE, D, DC, MC, V* ⊘ *No lunch. $29–$36.*

$$-$$$$ ✕ **Brennecke's Beach Broiler.** Brennecke's is decidedly casual and fun, with a busy bar, windows overlooking the beach, and a cheery blue-and-white interior. It specializes in big portions in a wide range of offerings, including New York steaks, lobster, crab legs, shrimp, and the fresh catch of the day. Can't decide? You can create your own combination meal. This place is especially good for happy hour (3 PM to 5 PM), as the drink and pūpū menus are tomes. There's a take-out deli downstairs. The stan-

dard surf and turf is not remarkable in any way, but the ocean view is nice. ⊠ *2100 Hoʻōne Rd., Poʻipū* ☎ *808/742–7588* ⊟ *AE, D, DC, MC, V. $20–$40.*

☺ $-$$$$ ✕ **Keoki's Paradise.** Built to resemble a dockside boathouse, this active, boisterous place fills up quickly on weekend nights thanks to the live music. Seafood appetizers span the tide from sashimi to Thai shrimp sticks, crab cakes, and scallops crusted in *panko* (Japanese-style bread crumbs). The day's fresh catch is available in half a dozen styles and sauces. And there's a sampling of beef, chicken, and pork-rib entrées for the committed carnivore. A lighter menu is available at the bar for lunch and dinner. ⊠ *Poʻipū Shopping Village, 2360 Kiahuna Plantation Dr., Kōloa* ☎ *808/742–7534* ⊟ *AE, D, DC, MC, V. $16–$30.*

$-$$$$ ✕ **Wrangler's Steakhouse.** Denim-cover seating, decorative saddles, and a stagecoach in a loft helped to transform the historic Ako General Store in Waimea into a West Side steak house. You can eat under the stars on the deck out back or inside the old-fashioned, wood-panel dining room. The 16-ounce New York steak comes sizzling, and the rib eye is served with capers. Those with smaller appetites might consider the vegetable tempura or the ʻahi served on penne pasta. Local folks love the special lunch: soup, rice, beef teriyaki, and shrimp tempura served in a three-tier *kaukau* tin, or lunch pail, just like the ones sugar-plantation workers once carried. A gift shop has local crafts (and sometimes a craftsperson doing demonstrations). ⊠ *9852 Kaumualiʻi Hwy., Waimea* ☎ *808/ 338–1218* ⊟ *AE, MC, V* ☉ *Closed Sun. $17–$38.*

$$-$$$ ✕ **Shells Steak and Seafood.** Chandeliers made from shells light the dining room and give this restaurant its name. The menu is upscale surf and turf, with prime cuts of steak and fresh fish enhanced by tropical spices and sauces. Shells is one of three signature restaurants in the Sheraton's Oceanfront Galleria. Each of these restaurants has been designed to embrace the view of the Pacific Ocean from sunrise to starlight. ⊠ *Sheraton Kauaʻi Resort, 2440 Hoʻonani Rd., Poʻipū Beach, Kōloa* ☎ *808/742–1661* ⊟ *AE, D, DC, MC, V* ☉ *No lunch. $20–$40.*

$-$$ ✕ **Kalāheo Steak House.** Prime rib, tender top sirloin, Cornish game hen in citrus marinade, Kalāheo shrimp, Alaskan king crab legs, and Portuguese bean soup are competently prepared and served up in hearty portions at this cozy, country-ranch-house-style restaurant. Weathered wood furnishings and artifacts pay tribute to Hawaiʻi's *paniolo* (cowboys), who can still be found in these parts. Fresh-baked rum cake comes with Lappert's ice cream (made at a factory up the road). Wines range from $8 to $25 a bottle. The food is good, but the prices are a bit high. ⊠ *4444 Pāpālina Rd., Kalāheo* ☎ *808/332–9780* ⊟ *AE, D, MC, V* ⊿ *Reservations not accepted* ☉ *No lunch. $20–$33.*

BUDGET-FRIENDLY EATS: SOUTH SHORE & WEST SIDE

- **Grind's Cafe and Espresso.** ⊠ *Rte. 50, ʻEleʻele* ☎ *808/335-6027.*

- **Taqueria Nortenos.** ⊠ *2827-A Poʻipū Rd., Kōloa* ☎ *808/742-7222.*

- **Wong's Chinese Restaurant.** ⊠ *Kaumualiʻi Hwy., Hanapēpē* ☎ *808/335-5066.*

8

Where to Stay

WORD OF MOUTH

"The North Shore is the most beautiful part of the island, and the South Shore has most of the resort choices. The East Side is where most of the residents live because it is so centrally located, so there are better prices for restaurants, gas, incidentals."

—Kellie

Updated
by Joan
Conrow

THE GARDEN ISLE HAS LODGINGS for every taste, from swanky resorts to rustic cabins, and from family-friendly condos to romantic bed-and-breakfasts. When choosing a place to stay, location is an important consideration—Kaua'i may look small, but it takes more time than you might think to get around. If at all possible, stay close to your desired activities. ■ TIP→ **Prices are highest near the ocean and in resort communities such as Princeville and Po'ipū.** Wherever you stay, the ubiquitous wild roosters crow a very early wake-up call and stray cats beg for handouts. Resist the urge to feed either.

As a rule, resorts offer a full roster of amenities and large, well-appointed rooms. They are all oceanfront properties that lean toward the luxurious. If you want to golf, play tennis, or hang at a spa, stay at a resort. You'll also be more likely to find activities for children at resorts, including camps that allow parents a little time off too. The island's hotels tend to be smaller and older, with fewer on-site amenities.

Individual condominium units are equipped with all the comforts of home, but each property offers different services, so inquire if you want tennis courts, golf, and on-site restaurants. They're ideal for families, couples traveling together, and longer stays.

Vacation rentals run the gamut from fabulous luxury estates to scruffy little dives. It's buyer-beware in this totally unregulated sector of the visitor industry, so choose carefully. Many lower-priced homes are in rural areas far from beaches, or in crowded neighborhoods that may be a bit too local-style for some tastes. ■ TIP→ **Condos and vacation rentals typically require a minimum stay of three nights to a week, along with a cleaning fee.**

The island's bed-and-breakfasts allow you to meet local residents and more directly experience the aloha spirit. They tend to be among the more expensive types of lodging, though, and don't assume you get a lavish breakfast unless it's a featured attraction. You'll usually get a very comfortable room in a private house along with a morning meal; some properties have stand-alone units on-site. ■ TIP→ **Even the best establishments may have the occasional gecko or cockroach; the alternative is heavy pesticide spraying, which is more common at resorts. Expect to see some kind of critter if you stay in a vacation rental.**

If you need help choosing a property, **Bed & Breakfast Kaua'i** (☎ 800/822–1176 🖷 808/826–9292 ⊕ www.bnbkauai.com) may prove helpful. Liz Hey, a longtime island resident, maintains a network of more than three dozen cottages, condos, and B&Bs that consider all lifestyles and budgets. Most large real estate companies also maintain a roster of vacation rentals.

WHAT IT COSTS				
$$$$	**$$$**	**$$**	**$**	**¢**
HOTELS	over $340	$261–$340	$181–$260	$100–$180	under $100

Hotel prices are for two people in a standard double room in high season. Condo price categories reflect studio and one-bedroom rates.

THE NORTH SHORE

The North Shore is mountainous and wet, which accounts for its rugged, lush landscape. Posh resorts and condominiums await you at Princeville, a community with dreamy views, excellent golf courses, and lovely sunsets. It maintains the lion's share of North Shore accommodations—primarily luxury hotel rooms and condos built on a plateau overlooking the sea. Hanalei, a bayside town in a broad valley, has a smattering of hotel rooms and numerous vacation rentals, many within walking distance of the beach. Prices tend to be high in this resort area. If you want to do extensive sightseeing of other parts of the island, be prepared for a long drive—one that's very dark at night.

> **WORD OF MOUTH**
>
> "For a breathtaking sunset, just sit back and watch from the Princeville grounds." -annahead

Hotels & Resorts

★ **$$$$** **Princeville Resort.** Built into the cliffs above Hanalei Bay, this sprawling resort offers expansive views of the sea and mountains, including Makana, the landmark peak immortalized as mysterious Bali Hai island in the film *South Pacific*. Spacious guest rooms are designed in bold colors to match those of Kaua'i's abundant yellow hibiscus, red 'ōhi'a flower, and dark green mokihana berry. Little details make a difference, such as lighted closets, dimmer switches on all lamps, original artwork, and door chimes. Bathrooms feature height-adjustable showerheads and a privacy window—flip a switch and it goes from clear to opaque so you can see the sights without becoming an attraction yourself. Two restaurants serve excellent food and excellent views, and the poolside lū'au is lavish. The Living Room, a swanky bar with nightly entertainment, has big windows that showcase gorgeous sunsets. There's shuttle service to the resort's two top-ranked golf courses, spa, and tennis center, none of which is on the hotel grounds. ✉ *5520 Ka Haku Rd., Princeville 96722* ☎ *808/826-9644 or 888/488-3535* 📠 *808/826-1166* 🌐 *www.starwood.com/hawaii* *201 rooms, 51 suites* *4 restaurants, room service, minibars, 2 18-hole golf courses, 8 tennis courts, pool, gym, health club, massage, spa, beach, 2 bars, children's programs (ages 5–12), dry cleaning, laundry service, business services, travel services* 💳 *AE, D, DC, MC, V. $500–$735.*

Condos & Vacation Rentals

$$–$$$$ **Hanalei Bay Resort.** This time-share condominium resort has a lovely location overlooking Hanalei Bay and Nā Pali Coast. Three-story buildings angle down the cliffs, making for some steep walking paths. Units are extremely spacious, with high, sloping ceilings and large private lānai. Rattan furniture and island art add a casual feeling to rooms. Studios have small kitchenettes not meant for serious cooking. The larger units have full kitchens. The resort's upper-level pool is one of the nicest on the island, with authentic lava-rock waterfalls, an open-air hot tub, and a kid-friendly sand "beach." The restaurant is expensive, but the food is reasonably good and the stunning views help justify the price. The friendly tropical bar offers live music. The tennis courts are on-site, and you have golf privileges at Princeville Resort. ⊠ *5380 Honoiki Rd., Princeville 96722* ☎ *808/826–6522 or 800/827–4427* 🖷 *808/826–6680* ⊕ *www.hanaleibayresort.com* ⇱ *134 units* ♨ *Restaurant, in-room safes, kitchenettes, refrigerators, cable TV, golf privileges, 8 tennis courts, 2 pools, hot tub, massage, beach, bar, shop, babysitting, children's programs (ages 5–12), laundry facilities* ▤ *AE, D, DC, MC, V. Studios $240, 1-bedroom $360–$400.*

$$$$ 🏠 **Kīlauea Lakeside Estate.** The world revolves around you at this pricey private-island retreat, where the amenities and activities are custom-designed to create your dream vacation. The proprietors can arrange for personal chefs, windsurfing lessons, lakeside spa treatments, and on-site weddings. A private 20-acre freshwater lake teeming with bass and catfish awaits your fishing pole. You can also have your own par-3 golf hole and putting green and 3 acres of botanical gardens to stroll through. The modern three-bedroom house includes a romantic master suite and bath. Expect to pay a cleaning fee of about $375. ⊠ *4613 Waiakalua Rd., Kīlauea 96754* ☎ *310/379–7842* 🖷 *310/379–0034* ⊕ *www.kauaihoneymoon.com* ⇱ *1 house* ♨ *BBQs, fans, kitchen, cable TV, in-room VCRs, beach, fishing, laundry facilities; no a/c* ▤ *AE, D, MC, V. $595–$850.*

$$–$$$ 🏠 **Hanalei Colony Resort.** This 5-acre property, the only true beachfront resort on Kaua'i's North Shore, is a laid-back, go-barefoot kind of place sandwiched between towering mountains and the sea. Its charm is in its simplicity. There are no phones, TVs, or stereos in the rooms, but you can get complimentary high-speed wireless Internet access in the resort's oceanfront common room. Each of the two-bedroom units can sleep a family of four, although this place is popular with the honeymoon crowd. The units are well maintained, with Hawaiian-style furnishings, full kitchens, and lānai. Amenities, such as cocktail receptions and cultural activities, vary from season to season. There's an art gallery with coffee bar on-site. ⊠ *5-7130 Kūhiō Hwy., Hā'ena 96714* ☎ *808/826–6235 or 800/ 628–3004* 🖷 *808/826–9893* ⊕ *www.hcr.com* ⇱ *48 units*

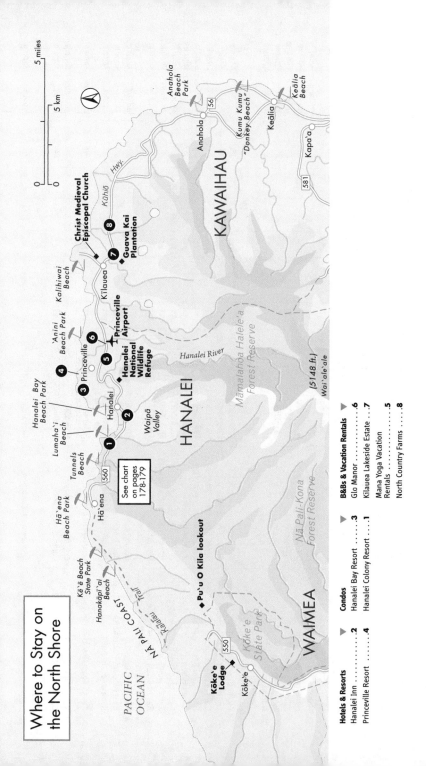

Where to Stay on the North Shore

PACIFIC OCEAN

NĀ PALI COAST

Kē'ē Beach State Park

Kē'ē Beach

Kalalau Trail

Hanakāpī'ai Beach

Hā'ena Beach Park

Hā'ena

Tunnels Beach

Lumaha'i Beach

Hanalei Bay Beach Park

'Anini Beach Park

Kalihiwai Beach

560

See chart on pages 178–179

Hanalei

Waipā Valley

Princeville

Hanalei Bay

Hanalei River

Princeville Airport

Kīlauea

Christ Medieval Episcopal Church

Guava Kai Plantation

Anahola Beach Park

Kūhiō Hwy.

Anahola

56

Kumu Kumu "Donkey Beach"

Kealia

Kealia Beach

Kapa'a

581

HANALEI

Mamalahoa Halele'a Forest Reserve

Nā Pali-Kona Forest Reserve

(5148 ft.) Wai'ale'ale

KAWAIHAU

WAIMEA

Kōke'e State Park

Kōke'e

550

◆ Pu'u O Kila lookout

Kōke'e Lodge

◆ Hanalei National Wildlife Refuge

N

0   5 miles

0   5 km

Hotels & Resorts ▶

Hanalei Inn **2**
Princeville Resort **4**

Condos ▶

Hanalei Bay Resort **3**
Hanalei Colony Resort **1**

B&Bs & Vacation Rentals ▶

Glo Manor **6**
Kilauea Lakeside Estate . . .**7**
Mana Yoga Vacation
Rentals **5**
North Country Farms **8**

WHERE TO STAY IN KAUA'I

HOTEL NAME	Worth Noting	Cost	Pools	Beach	Golf Course	Tennis Courts	Gym	Spa	Children's Programs	Rooms	Restaurants	Other	Location
The North Shore													
Hotels & Resorts													
★ Princeville Resort	Lavish poolside lū'au	$500–$735	1	yes	yes	8	yes	yes	5–12	252	4		Princeville
Condos & Vacation Rentals													
Glo Manor	Private	$65–$135								3		kitchens	Anini
Hanalei Bay Resort	Great views	Studios $240, 1-bedroom $360–$400	2	yes	yes	8		mass.	5–12	134	1	kitchens	Princeville
Hanalei Inn	Great location	$119								4		kitchens	Anini
Hanalei Colony Resort	Go-barefoot kind of place	$185–$300	1	yes						48		no A/C	Hā'ena
Kilauea Lakeside Estate	Private lake	$595–$850								1		no A/C	Kilauea
Mana Yoga	Views, yoga	$85–$150		yes						2		kitchens	Princeville
★ North Country Farms		$130								2		no A/C	Kilauea
The East Side													
Hotels & Resorts													
Aloha Beach Resort Kaua'i	Beach cottages available	$219–$359	2			1	yes			250	1		Kapa'a
Courtyard Kaua'i at Waipouli Beach	Popular nightly lū'au	$239–$409	1	yes		3				311	1		Kapa'a
Garden Island Inn	Beach across the street	$90–$135					yes			24		no A/C	Lihu'e
Hotel Coral Reef	Good location, low price	$99–$149		yes			yes			26		no A/C	Kapa'a
Kaua'i Hilton	Uncrowded beach	$219–$275	4	yes	yes	4	yes	yes		357	3		Lihu'e
Kaua'i Marriott Resort & Beach Club	26,000-sq-ft pool	$354–$469	1	yes	yes	7	yes	yes	5–12	599	2	shops	Lihu'e
Kaua'i Sands	Hawai'i-owned and operated	$125–$160	2	yes			yes			202		kitchens	Kapa'a
Resort Quest Islander on the Beach	Plantation-style design	$195–$295	1	yes						200			Kapa'a
Condos & Vacation Rentals													
★ Aloha Cottages	Oceanfront	$110–$300								2		no A/C	Kapa'a
Best Western Plantation Hale Suites	Beach across the street	1-bedroom $185–$205	3	yes						110		kitchens	Kapa'a
Kapa'a Sands	Hawai'i-owned and operated	Studios $110–$135, 2-bedroom $155–$175	1	yes						20		no A/C	Kapa'a
Kaua'i Coast Resort at the Beachboy	Uncrowded beach	1-bedroom $265–$305, 2-bedroom $340–$385	1	yes		1	yes	yes		108	1	kitchens	Kapa'a
Kaua'i Hostel	One block to the beach	$20–$50										kitchens	Kapa'a
Outrigger at Lae Nani	Cultural programs	1-bedroom $250–$310, 2-bedroom $270–$370	1	yes		1				84	3	no A/C	Kapa'a
B&Bs													
Rosewood Bed and Breakfast	Located on a plantation	$45–$135								7		no A/C	Kapa'a

The South Shore

Hotels & Resorts

Name	Comments	Price							Rooms			Location
★ Grand Hyatt Kaua'i Resort and Spa	5 acres of swimming lagoons	$485–$705	1	yes	4	yes	yes	5-12	602	6	shops	Kōloa
Sheraton Kaua'i Resort	Ocean wing right on water	$355–$655	2	yes	3	yes	mass.	5-12	413	4		Kōloa

Condos & Vacation Rentals

Name	Comments	Price							Rooms			Location
Garden Isle Cottages	Beautiful ocean view	$169–$190	1						4		no A/C	Kōloa
Hideaway Cove	Quiet	Studio $125–$140, 1-bedroom $160, 2-bedroom $220–$235, 3-bedroom $320							7		kitchens	Po'ipū
Kalaheo Inn	Close to town	$80–$120							14		kitchens	Kalaheo
Kaua'i Cove Cottages	Excellent snorkeling	$105–$145							3		no A/C	Po'ipū
Kōloa Landing Cottages	Walk to beach	$119							4		kitchens	Po'ipū
Makahuena at Po'ipū	Close to the center of Po'ipū	1-bedroom $260, 2-bedroom $265–$475, 3-bedroom $340–$410	1		1				78		no A/C	Po'ipū
Outrigger Kiahuna Plantation	Popular with families	1-bedroom $245–$479, 2-bedroom $385–$525	1	yes	6				333	1	no A/C	Kōloa
Po'ipū Crater	Close to beach	$115–$137	1	yes					30		kitchens	Po'ipū
Po'ipū Kapili	Deluxe PH suites available	1-bedroom $255–$285, 2-bedroom $335–$560	1		2				60		no A/C	Kōloa
Po'ipū Shores	Excellent whale-watching	1-bedroom $300, 2-bedroom $395, 3-bedroom $495	1						39		no A/C	Kōloa
Suite Paradise Po'ipū Kai	Short walk to beach	1-bedroom $133–$370, 2-bedroom $205–$416, 3-bedroom $275–$319, 4-bedroom $428	6		9				130		no A/C	Kōloa
Whalers Cove	Rocky beach	2-bedroom $355–$485	1	yes					30		no A/C	Kōloa

B&Bs

Name	Comments	Price							Rooms			Location
Gloria's Spouting Horn Bed & Breakfast	Romantic	$325	1	yes					3		no A/C	Po'ipū
Po'ipū Plantation Resort	Cottages available	$120–$190, 3-night minimum							12		kitchens	Po'ipū

The West Side

Hotels & Resorts

Name	Comments	Price							Rooms			Location
★ Waimea Plantation Cottages	Good for large groups	Studio $175, 1-bedroom $260–$350, 2-bedroom $330–$405, 3-bedroom $390–$455, 4-bedroom $505, 5-bedroom $775	1	yes			yes		48	1	no A/C	Waimea

Condos & Vacation Rentals

Name	Comments	Price							Rooms			Location
Kōke'e Lodge	Rustic wilderness cabins	$45							12	1	no A/C	Kekaha

⌂ *BBQs, fans, kitchens, pool, hot tub, beach, shop, laundry facilities; no a/c, no room phones, no room TVs* ⊟ *AE, MC, V. $210–$350.*

$ ✕ **Hanalei Inn.** If you're looking for low-price lodgings a block from gorgeous Hanalei Bay, look no further, as this is the only choice. While the accommodations are simple, they are clean, and the location is ideal. Each studio features a private bath and full kitchen, as well as a queen-size bed. Outside, share the picnic table, hammocks, soda machine, pay phone and lawn with other guests. ⊠ *5-5468 Kūhio Hwy., Hanalei 96714* ☎ *808/826–9333* ⊕ *www.hanaleiinn.com* ⇨ *4 studios* ⌂ *Cable TV, ceiling fan, full kitchen, hardwood floors.* ⊟ *AE, D, DC, MC, V. $119.*

★ $ ⊞ **North Country Farms.** These comfortable lodgings are tucked away on a tidy, 4-acre organic fruit, flower, and vegetable farm just east of Kīlauea. Although simple, they're clean and provide everything a couple or family might need, including kitchenettes. Owner Lee Roversi and her children are warm, friendly, and creative. You'll enjoy the thoughtful selection of videos, games, puzzles, and reading material. The setting is rural and quiet, with lush tropical landscaping around the two units. You are welcome to pick fresh produce. Several nice beaches are just a few minutes' drive away. ⊠ *Kahili Makai, Box 723, Kīlauea 96754* ☎ *808/828–1513* 🖷 *808/828–0899* ⊕ *www.northcountryfarms.com* ⇨ *2 cottages* ⌂ *Kitchenettes, cable TV, in-room VCRs; no a/c. $130.*

¢–$★ ✕ **Glo Manor.** Tucked into the lush vegetation at the end of beautiful Anini Beach, this delightful family-owned property is an 8,000-square-foot mansion converted into three separate units, each comfortably furnished with full bath, telephone, color TV and either a kitchenette or full kitchen, with laundry facilities. Choose from a studio, one-bedroom or two-bedroom unit (with a lānai overlooking a stream) at low rates not often found in these pricey parts. Very private and quiet. ⊠ *4453 Anini Beach Rd., Kilauea 96754* ☎ *808/828–6684* ⊕ *homepages.hawaiian.net/glomanor* ⇨ *3 units* ⊟ *MC, V. $65–$135.*

¢–$ ✕ **Mana Yoga Vacation Rentals.** If you enjoy yoga, or just a rural environment, these lodgings (a studio and 2-bedroom unit) offer peace and quiet, mountain views and all the amenities of home, as well as the services of yoga instructor and massage therapist Michaelle Edwards, who has a yoga studio on-site. Three-night minimum stay. ⊠ *3812 Ahonui Place, Princeville 96722* ☎ *808/826—9230* ⊕ *www.manayoga.com/ accomodations.htm* ⇨ *2 units* ⌂ *BBQ, wireless Internet, TV/VCR/ CD/DVD, laundry facilities, beach gear, mountain bikes, kayaks; no smoking.* ⊟ *MC, V. Studio $85–$95, 2-bedroom $130–$150.*

THE EAST SIDE

Kapa'a & Wailua

The East Side, or Coconut Coast, is a good centralized home base if you want to see and do it all. Since Kapa'a is the island's major population center, this area has a lived-in, real-world feel. It has a number of smaller, older properties that are modestly priced but still comfortable, as well as private vacation rentals in the hills behind the town that may be too rural and far from the beach for most visitors. This is also where you'll find some of the best deals on accommodations and a wider choice of inexpensive restaurants and shops than the resort areas. The beaches here are so-so for swimming but nice for sunbathing, walking, and watching the sun and moon rise.

Līhu'e is not the most desirable place to stay on Kaua'i, in terms of scenic beauty, although it does have it advantages, including easy access to the aiport. It's located smack dab in the middle of the island, too, giving you good access to sights and activities on all parts of the island. Restaurants and shops are also plentiful, and there's lovely Kalapakī Bay for beachgoers.

Hotels & Resorts

$$–$$$$ ▦ **Aloha Beach Resort Kaua'i.** Nestled between Wailua Bay and the Wailua River, this low-key, low-rise resort is an easy, convenient place to stay. Families will enjoy being within walking distance of Lydgate Beach Park. It's also close to shops and low-cost restaurants. Rooms are in two wings and have beach, mountain, or ocean views. The resort also offers one-bedroom beach cottages with kitchenettes. ✉ *3-5920 Kūhiō Hwy., Kapa'a 96746* ☎ *808/823–6000 or 888/823–5111* 🖷 *808/823–6666* ⊕ *www.abrkauai.com* ⇋ *216 rooms, 10 suites, 24 beach cottages* ⚐ *Restaurant, in-room data ports, in-room safes, tennis court, 2 pools, gym, hot tub, shuffleboard* ▭ *AE, D, DC, MC, V. $229–$359.*

$$–$$$$ ▦ **Courtyard Kaua'i at Waipouli Beach.** Formerly known as the Kaua'i Coconut Beach Resort, this popular oceanfront hotel was bought and refurbished by Courtyard by Marriott in 2005. The bright, spacious rooms face the ocean or pool and have been outfitted with modern amenities, including free wireless high-speed Internet access. Each oceanfront room has a large lānai. The 11-acre site has always been desirable, nestled as it is among ancient coconut groves and close to a coastal bike and walking path, shops, restaurants, the ocean, and the airport. The new owners wisely kept the best of the old resort, including its sunset torchlighting ceremony. ✉ *4-484 Kūhiō Hwy., Kapa'a 96746* ☎ *808/822–3455 or 800/760–8555* 🖷 *808/822–1830* ⊕ *www.marriott.com* ⇋ *311 rooms* ⚐ *Restaurant, in-room safes, Wi-Fi, 3 tennis courts, pool, hot tub, beach, shuffleboard, no-smoking rooms* ▭ *AE, D, DC, MC, V. $249–$420.*

$$–$$$$ ▦ **Resort Quest Islander on the Beach.** A Hawai'i-plantation-style design gives this 6-acre beachfront property a pleasant, low-key feeling. Rooms are spread over eight three-story buildings, with lānai that look out on lovely green lawns. Rooms have showers but not tubs. A free-form pool sits next to a golden-sand beach, and you can take the lounge chairs to the ocean's edge. ✉ *4-484 Kūhiō Hwy., Kapa'a 96746* ☎ *808/822–7417 or 877/977–6667* 🖷 *808/822–1947* ⇋ *198 rooms, 2 suites* ⚐ *In-room safes, cable TV, pool, hot tub, beach, bar, laundry facilities* ▭ *AE, D, DC, MC, V. $210–$325.*

> ### CONDO COMFORTS
>
> Foodland, in the Princeville Shopping Center, has the best selection of groceries, sundries, and other items needed to supply the kitchen. It's open daily from 7 AM to 11 PM. Be sure to ask for a discount card, as the prices may give you sticker shock.

9

$ ⚐ **Kaua'i Sands.** Hawaiian owned and operated, this oceanfront inn is an example of what island accommodations were like before the arrival of the megaresorts. This is basic, no-frills lodging. Furnishings are spare, simple, and clean. It's so retro it's unintentionally hip. A big grassy courtyard opens to the beach, and there's plenty of dining and shopping at the Coconut Marketplace. ✉ *420 Papaloa Rd., Kapa'a 96746* 📞 *808/822–4951 or 800/ 560–5553* 🖶 *808/822–0978* ⊕ *www.kauaisandshotel.com* ⬅ *200 rooms, 2 suites* ♿ *Some kitchenettes, cable TV, 2 pools, gym, beach, laundry facilities, no-smoking rooms* ▤ *AE, D, DC, MC, V.* *$145–$170.*

SAVING MONEY

If you're on a budget, take heart. Most of the lodgings on Kaua'i fall into the budget and standard range, which means less than $250 per night. Kapa'a and Wailua offer the greatest number of accommodations in the affordable category, while the North and South shores have the more luxury lodgings.

¢–$ ⚐ **Hotel Coral Reef.** Coral Reef has been in business since the 1960s and is something of a beachfront landmark. It went through a major renovation, and now the accommodations are on a par with the prime location. Besides remodeling the rooms, the owners added a large pool that looks onto the ocean. The two two-room units are good for families. ✉ *1516 Kūhiō Hwy., Kapa'a 96746* 📞 *808/822–4481 or 800/843– 4659* 🖶 *808/822–7705* ⊕ *www.hotelcoralreef.com* ⬅ *24 suites* ♿ *In-room safes, some refrigerators, cable TV, gym, sauna, beach, laundry facilities; no a/c, no room phones* ▤ *MC, V. $99–$149.*

Condos

Location, location, location. The Coconut Coast is one of the only resort areas on Kaua'i where you can actually walk to the beach, restaurants, and stores from your condo. It's not only convenient, but comparatively cheap. You pay less for lodging, meals, services, merchandise, and gas here—all because the reefy coastline isn't as ideal as the sandy-bottom bays that front the fancy resorts found elsewhere. We think the shoreline is just fine. There are pockets in the reef to swim in, and the coast is very scenic and uncrowded. It's a good choice for families because the prices are right and there's plenty to keep everyone happy and occupied.

$$$ ⚐ **Kaua'i Coast Resort at the Beachboy.** Fronting an uncrowded stretch of beach, this three-story primarily time-share resort is convenient and a bit more upscale than nearby properties. The fully furnished one- and two-bedroom condo units, each with a private lānai and well-equipped kitchen, are housed in three buildings. They are decorated in rich woods, tropical prints, and Hawaiian-quilt designs. The 8-acre property looks out on the ocean and offers a heated pool with waterscapes, a day spa, a children's pool, a good restaurant, and an oceanside hot tub. It's in the Coconut Marketplace, so it's within walking distance of shops, restaurants, and a movie theater. ✉ *520 Aleka Loop, Kapa'a 96746* 📞 *808/822–3441 or 877/977–4355* 🖶 *808/822–0843* ⊕ *www.*

shellhospitality.com ⟳ *108 units* ⚵ *Restaurant, in-room data ports, in-room safes, kitchens, microwaves, refrigerators, tennis court, pool, gym, hot tub, spa, beach* ☰ *AE, D, DC, MC, V. 1-bedroom $265–$305, 2-bedroom $340–$385.*

WHAT'S IN A NAME?

Name changes are extremely frequent among Island properties, especially condominiums, making it hard even for the Kaua'i Visitors Bureau to keep its lodging maps up to date. When making reservations, inquire if the property recently had a name change, and ask for directions that include landmarks, rather than street addresses, which are often difficult to find, anyway. That way, if you do get lost, you'll have a better chance of being properly guided by a resident who may not know the property's newest name, either.

$$–$$$ ▥ **Outrigger at Lae Nani.** Ruling Hawaiian chiefs once returned from ocean voyages to this spot, now host to condominiums comfortable enough for minor royalty. Hotel-sponsored Hawaiiana programs and a booklet for self-guided historical tours are nice extras. Units are all uniquely decorated, with bright, full kitchens and expansive lānai. Your view of landscaped grounds is interrupted only by a large pool before ending at a sandy, swimmable beach. You can find plenty of dining and shopping at the nearby Coconut Marketplace. ⊠ *410 Papaloa Rd., Kapa'a 96746* ☎ *808/822–4938 or 800/688–7444* 🖶 *808/822–1022* ⊕ *www.outriggerlaenani.com* ⟳ *84 units* ⚵ *BBQs, fans, in-room safes, kitchens, microwaves, cable TV, tennis court, pool, beach, laundry facilities; no a/c* ☰ *AE, D, DC, MC, V. 1-bedroom $215–$330, 2-bedroom $325–$390.*

$$ ▥ **Best Western Plantation Hale Suites.** These attractive plantation-style one-bedroom units have well-equipped kitchenettes and garden lānai. Rooms are clean and pretty, with white-rattan furnishings and pastel colors. You couldn't ask for a more convenient location for dining, shopping, and sightseeing: it's across from Waipouli Beach and near Coconut Marketplace. Request a unit away from noisy Kūhiō Highway. ⊠ *484 Kūhiō Hwy., Kapa'a 96746* ☎ *808/822–4941 or 800/775–4253* 🖶 *808/822–5599* ⊕ *www.plantation-hale.com* ⟳ *110 units* ⚵ *BBQs, in-room safes, kitchenettes, microwaves, cable TV with movies and video games, 3 pools, hot tub, shuffleboard, laundry facilities* ☰ *AE, D, DC, MC, V. 1-bedroom $195–$230.*

$ ▥ **Kapa'a Sands.** An old rock etched with *kanji*, Japanese characters, reminds you that the site of this condominium gem was formerly occupied by a Shinto temple. Two-bedroom rentals—equipped with full kitchens and private lānai—are a fair deal. Studios feature pull-down Murphy beds to create more daytime space. Ask for an oceanfront room to get the breeze. ⊠ *380 Papaloa Rd., Kapa'a 96746* ☎ *808/822–4901 or 800/222–4901* 🖶 *808/822–1556* ⊕ *www.kapaasands.com* ⟳ *20 units* ⚵ *Fans, kitchens, microwaves, cable TV, in-room VCRs, pool, beach; no a/c* ☰ *MC, V. Studios $120–$150, 2-bedroom $170–$185.*

B&Bs & Vacation Rentals

★ **$–$$$** ▥ **Aloha Cottages.** Owners Charlie and Susan Hoerner restored a three-bedroom plantation home on Kapa'a's Baby Beach to reflect the charm of yesteryear with the conveniences of today. Think plank flooring, gingerbread, and stained glass alongside a Wolf stove, Bosch dishwasher, and granite countertops. The orientation is due east; you won't have to leave your bed—or living room or lānai—to watch the sun rise, the whales breach, or the full moon rise. In addition to the main house, there's a cozy bungalow called Moonrise Cottage in back that's perfect for honeymooners. Rent both (weekly rentals only) to sleep a total of eight. Credit cards are accepted via PayPal only. ⊠ *1041 Moana Kai Rd., Kapa'a 96746* ☎ *808/823–0933 or 877/915–1015* ⊕ *www.alohacottages.com* ⤳ *2 cottages* ⟁ *BBQs, fans, kitchens, cable TV; no a/c* ▭ *MC, V. Sunrise Cottage $2,100/week with $250 cleaning fee; Moonrise Cottage $775/ week with $125 cleaning fee.*

★ ¢–$ 🏠 **Rosewood Bed and Breakfast.** This charming B&B on a macadamia-nut plantation estate offers four separate styles of accommodations, including a two-bedroom Victorian cottage, a little one-bedroom grass-thatch cottage, a bunkhouse with three rooms and a shared bath, and the traditional main plantation home with two rooms, each with private bath. The bunkhouse and thatched cottage feature outside hot-cold private shower areas hidden from view by a riot of tropically scented foliage. ⊠ *872 Kamalu Rd., Kapa'a 96746* ☎ *808/822–5216* 🖶 *808/822–5478* ⊕ *www.rosewoodkauai.com* ⤳ *2 cottages, 3 rooms in bunkhouse, 2 rooms in main house* ⟁ *Kitchens, some cable TV; no a/c, no room phones, no smoking* ▭ *No credit cards. $45–$145.*

¢ ✕ **Kaua'i International Hostel.** If price is your only concern, the hostel is the place. Yes, it's funky and worn, but it's close to the beach, shops and the bus route, and conveniently located on the north end of Kapa'a town. You can bunk in the dormitory or splurge on the private room with double bed. In either case, you'll share the bathroom, as well as the amenities in the common room. ⊠ *4532 Lehua St., Kapa'a 96746* ☎ *808/ 823–6142* ⊕ *www.hostels.com/kauaihostel* ⟁ *Cable TV, pool table, laundry facilities* ▭ *No credit cards. $20–$50.*

Līhu'e

Hotels & Resorts

☾ $$$$ 🏠 **Kaua'i Marriott Resort & Beach Club.** An elaborate tropical garden, waterfalls right off the lobby, Greek statues and columns, and an enormous 26,000-square-foot swimming pool characterize the grand—and grandiose—scale of this resort on Kalapakī Bay, which looks out at the dramatic Hā'upu mountains. This resort has it all—fine dining, shopping, a spa, golf, tennis, and water activities of all kinds. Rooms have tropical decor, and most have expansive ocean views. It's comfortable and convenient, though the airport noise can be a turnoff. Many of the rooms have been converted to time shares, too. ⊠ *3610 Rice St., Kalapakī Beach, Līhu'e 96766* ☎ *808/245–5050 or 800/220–2925* 🖶 *808/ 245–5148* ⊕ *www.marriotthotels.com* ⤳ *356 rooms, 11 suites, 232 time-share units* ⟁ *2 restaurants, room service, minibars, 2 18-hole golf courses, 7 tennis courts, pool, health club, outdoor hot tub, spa, beach, boating, shops, children's programs (ages 5–12), airport shuttle* ▭ *AE, D, DC, MC, V. $372–$490.*

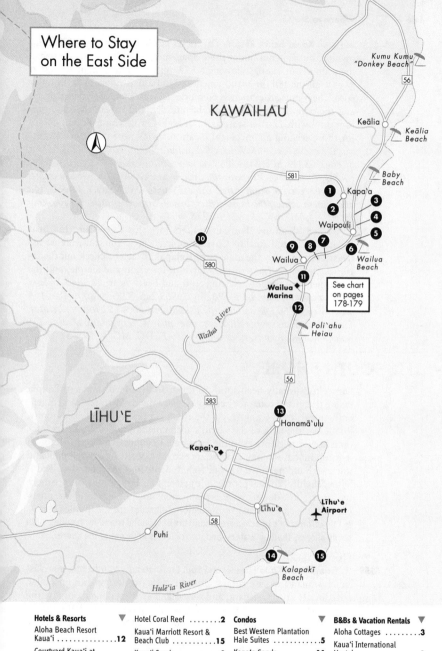

Where to Stay on the East Side

KAWAIHAU

Kumu Kumu
"Donkey Beach"

56

Keālia

Keālia
Beach

581

① Kapaʻa

② ③

Waipouli
④

⑩

⑨ ⑧ ⑦ ⑤

Wailua ⑥ Wailua
Beach

580

⑪

Wailua
Marina

See chart
on pages
178-179

⑫

Poliʻahu
Heiau

56

583

⑬

Hanamāʻulu

LĪHUʻE

Kapaiʻa

Līhuʻe
Airport

Līhuʻe

58

Puhi

⑭ ⑮

Kalapakī
Beach

Huleʻia River

$$-$$$ ✕ **Hilton Kauai Beach Resort.** This hotel has had a number of different owners, but is again under the management of Hilton, which opened the property in 1986, following a $14 million renovation in 2006 that gave it all the Hilton brand amenities and a luxurious, upscale ambience. The rooms are extremely comfortable, with a relaxed tropical decor, and the oceanfront grounds are beautifully landscaped; the sand-bottom pool with 12-foot waterfall is a highlight. It's an excellent choice for those seeking a convenient location, as it's near the airport, without the noise. ⊠ *3445 Wilcox Rd., Līhu'e 96766* ☎ *808/245–1955 or 888/805–3843 808/246–9085* ⊕ *www.hiltonkauairesort.com* ⬦ *350 rooms, 7 suites* ⟋ *3 restaurants, room service, A/C, in-room wireless Internet access, in-room safes, cable TV with DVD player, 4 pools, spa and fitness center, business center, beach, airport shuttle, no smoking* ▭ *AE, D, DC, MC, V. $219–$275.*

¢-$ 🏨 **Garden Island Inn.** Bargain hunters love this three-story inn near Kalapakī Bay and Anchor Cove shopping center. You can walk across the street and enjoy the majesty of Kalapakī Beach or check out the facilities and restaurants of the Marriott. It's clean and simple, and the innkeepers are friendly, sharing fruit and beach gear. ⊠ *3445 Wilcox Rd., Kalapakī Beach, Līhu'e 96766* ☎ *808/245–7227 or 800/648–0154* 🖷 *808/245–7603* ⊕ *www.gardenislandinn.com* ⬦ *21 rooms, 2 suites, 1 condo* ⟋ *Fans, some kitchens, microwaves, refrigerators, cable TV; no a/c in some rooms, no smoking* ▭ *AE, DC, MC, V. $95–$150.*

THE SOUTH SHORE

Sunseekers usually head south to the condo-studded shores of Po'ipū, where three- and four-story complexes line the coast and the surf is generally ideal for swimming. As the island's primary resort community, Po'ipū has the bulk of the island's accommodations, and more condos than hotels, with prices in the moderate to expensive range. Although it accommodates many visitors, its extensive, colorful landscaping and low-rise buildings save it from feeling dense and overcrowded, and it has a delightful coastal promenade perfect for sunset strolls. Surprisingly, the South Shore doesn't have as many shops and restaurants as one might expect for such a popular resort region, but there are still ample choices. ■ TIP➔ **The area's beaches are among the best on the island for families, with sandy shores, shallow waters, and grassy lawns adjacent to the shore.**

Hotels & Resorts

☾ **$$$$**   🏨 **Grand Hyatt Kaua'i Resort and Spa.** Dramatically handsome, this clas-
Fodor'sChoice   sic Hawaiian low-rise is built into the cliffs overlooking an unspoiled
★   coastline. It's open, elegant, and very island-style, making it our favorite of the megaresorts. It has four very good restaurants, including Dondero's, the best on Kaua'i. Spacious rooms, two-thirds with ocean views, have a plantation theme with bamboo and wicker furnishings and island art. Five acres of meandering fresh- and saltwater-swimming lagoons—a big hit with kids—are beautifully set amid landscaped grounds. While adults enjoy treatments at the first-rate ANARA Spa, kids can check out Camp Hyatt. ⊠ *1571 Po'ipū Rd., Kōloa 96756* ☎ *808/742–1234 or 800/633–7313* 🖷 *808/742–1557* ⊕ *www.kauai.hyatt.com*

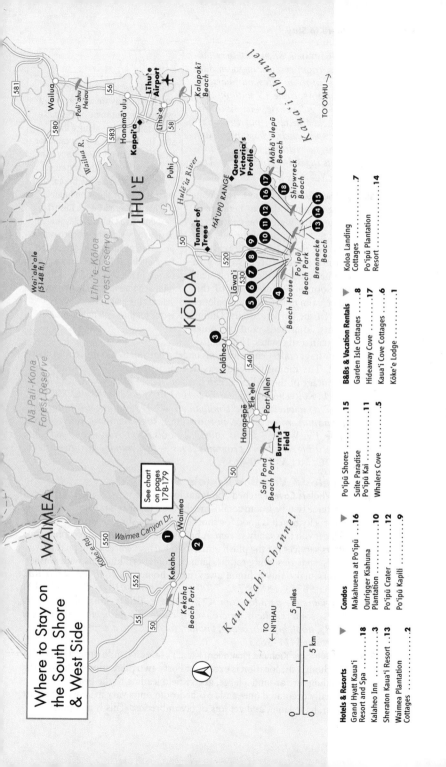

Where to Stay on
the South Shore
& West Side

Hotels & Resorts ▶

Grand Hyatt Kaua'i
Resort and Spa **18**
Kalaheo Inn **3**
Sheraton Kaua'i Resort ...**13**
Waimea Plantation
Cottages **2**

Condos ▶

Makahuena at Po'ipū **16**
Outrigger Kiahuna
Plantation **10**
Po'ipū Crater **12**
Po'ipū Kapili **9**

Po'ipū Shores **15**
Suite Paradise
Po'ipū Kai **11**
Whalers Cove **5**

B&Bs & Vacation Rentals ▶

Garden Isle Cottages **8**
Hideaway Cove **17**
Kaua'i Cove Cottages ...**6**
Kōke'e Lodge **1**

Koloa Landing
Cottages **7**
Po'ipū Plantation
Resort **14**

565 rooms, 37 suites *6 restaurants, room service, in-room data ports, in-room safes, minibars, refrigerators, cable TV with movies, 18-hole golf course, 4 tennis courts, pool, health club, hot tub, massage, spa, beach, 4 bars, nightclub, shops, babysitting, children's programs (ages 5–12)* ☐ *AE, D, DC, MC, V. $505–$705.*

$$$$ 🏨 **Sheraton Kaua'i Resort.** The ocean wing accommodations here are so close to the water you can practically feel the spray of the surf as it hits the rocks below. Beachfront rooms have muted sand and eggshell colors, which complement the soothing atmosphere of this quiet, calm resort. Brighter palettes enliven the garden rooms. Dining rooms, king beds, and balconies differentiate the suites. Hawaiian artisans stage crafts demonstrations under a banyan tree in the central courtyard. The dining Galleria was designed so that all restaurants take advantage of the endless ocean horizon. ☒ *2440 Ho'onani Rd., Po'ipū Beach, Kōloa 96756* ☎ *808/742–1661 or 888/488–3535* 🖷 *808/742–9777* ⊕ *www.starwood.com/hawaii* *399 rooms, 14 suites* *7 restaurants, room service, in-room safes, some minibars, refrigerators, cable TV, Wi-Fi, 3 tennis courts, 2 pools, gym, massage, beach, bar, babysitting, children's programs (ages 5–12), laundry facilities* ☐ *AE, D, DC, MC, V. $390–$655.*

Condos & Vacation Rentals

$$$$ 🏨 **Whalers Cove.** Perched about as close to the water's edge as they can get, these two-bedroom condos are the most luxurious on the South Shore. The rocky beach is good for snorkeling, and a short drive or brisk walk will get you to a sandy stretch. A handsome koa-bedecked reception area offers services for the plush units. Two barbecue areas, big picture windows, spacious living rooms, lānai, and modern kitchens with washer-dryers make this a home away from home. ☒ *2640 Pu'uholo Rd., Kōloa 96756* ☎ *808/742–7400 or 800/367–8020* 🖷 *808/742–9121* ⊕ *www.suite-paradise.com* *30 units* *BBQs, fans, in-room data ports, some kitchens, microwaves, cable TV with movies, in-room VCRs, pool, hot tub, beach, laundry facilities; no a/c* ☐ *AE, MC, V. 2-bedroom $411–$655.*

$$–$$$$ 🏨 **Outrigger Kiahuna Plantation.** Kaua'i's largest condo project is lackluster, though the location is excellent. Forty-two plantation-style, low-rise buildings arc around a large, grassy field leading to the beach. The individually decorated one- and two-bedroom units vary in style, but all are clean, have lānai, and get lots of ocean breezes. This is a popular destination for families who take advantage of the swimmable beach and lawn for picnics and games. Great sunset and ocean views are bonuses in some units. ⊠ *2253 Poʻipū Rd., Kōloa 96756* ☎ *808/742–6411 or 800/688–7444* 🖷 *808/742–1698* 🌐 *www.outrigger.com* ↘ *333 units* ☖ *Restaurant, fans, kitchens, cable TV, in-room VCRs, in-room broadband, 18-hole golf course, 6 tennis courts, pool, beach; no a/c* ☰ *AE, DC, MC, V. 1-bedroom $265–$385, 2-bedroom $339–$405.*

\$–\$\$\$\$ 🏨 **Suite Paradise Poʻipū Kaī.** Condominiums, many with cathedral ceilings and all with big windows overlooking the lawns, give this property the feeling of a spacious, quiet retreat inside and out. Large furnished lānai have views to the ocean and across the 110-acre grounds. All the condos are furnished with modern kitchens. Some units are two-level; some have sleeping lofts. One-to four-bedroom units are also available. A two-night minimum stay is required. Walking paths connect to both Brennecke and Shipwreck beaches. ⊠ *1941 Poʻipū Rd., Kōloa 96756* ☎ *808/742–6464 or 800/ 367–8020* 🖷 *808/742–9121* 🌐 *www.suite-paradise.com* ↘ *130 units* ☖ *Restaurant, fans, in-room data ports, in-room safes, kitchens, cable TV, in-room VCRs, 9 tennis courts, 6 pools, hot tub; no a/c in some rooms* ☰ *AE, D, DC, MC, V. 1-bedroom $133–$370, 2-bedroom $205–$416, 3-bedroom $275–$319, 4-bedroom $145–$385.*

\$\$\$ 🏨 **Poʻipū Shores.** Sitting on a rocky point above pounding surf, this is a perfect spot for whale- or turtle-watching. Weddings are staged on a little lawn beside the ocean, and a sandy swimming beach is a 10-minute walk away. There are three low-rise buildings, with a pool in front of the middle one. Condo units are individually owned and decorated. All have large windows, and many of them have bedrooms on the ocean side; each unit either shares a sundeck or has a lānai. ⊠ *1775 Peʻe Rd., Kōloa 96756* ☎ *808/742–7700 or 800/367–5004* 🖷 *808/742–9720* 🌐 *www. castleresorts.com* ↘ *39 units* ☖ *Fans, kitchens, microwaves, cable TV, pool, laundry facilities; no a/c* ☰ *AE, MC, V. 1-bedroom $303, 2-bedroom $400, 3-bedroom $505.*

★ \$\$–\$\$\$ 🏨 **Poʻipū Kapili.** Spacious one- and two-bedroom condo units are minutes from Poʻipū's restaurants and beaches. White-frame exteriors and double-pitched roofs complement the tropical landscaping. Interiors include full kitchens and entertainment centers. There are garden and across-the-street ocean views to choose from. Three deluxe 2,600-square-foot penthouse suites have enormous lānai, private elevators, and cathedral ceilings. You can mingle at a weekly coffee hour held beside the ocean-view pool or grab a good read from the resort library. Fresh seasonings are ready to be picked from the herb garden, and there's a bar-

TIME-SHARE HEAVEN

For reasons no one can quite explain, Kauaʻi has more time-share units than any other island. You can expect to be enticed into attending a vacation ownership seminar with promises of free gifts, discount rates on activities and other perks. If you have an extra couple of hours to burn, and can extricate yourself from high-pressure sales tactics, it may be worth attending. Otherwise, you might find those freebies aren't such a bargain, after all.

9

becue poolside. In winter you can whale-watch as you cook. ✉ *2221 Kapili Rd., Kōloa 96756* ☎ *808/742–6449 or 800/443–7714* 🖷 *808/742–9162* ⊕ *www.poipukapili.com* 🖙 *60 units* ♿ *BBQ, fans, kitchens, microwaves, cable TV, in-room VCRs, in-room broadband, 2 tennis courts, pool, library; no a/c* ▭ *MC, V. 1-bedroom $230–$295, 2-bedroom $350–$550.*

WORD OF MOUTH

"Po'ipū—this is my personal favorite. You have easy access to outstanding (though sometimes crowded) beaches, top-notch condos and hotels, restaurants, and a resort feel."   –alanwar

$$ 🖻 **Makahuena at Po'ipū.** Situated close to the center of Po'ipū, on a rocky point over the ocean, the Makahuena is near Shipwreck and Po'ipū beaches. It's a better deal for the price than some of the nearby properties. Large, tastefully decorated one-, two-, and three-bedroom suites with white-tile and sand-color carpets are housed in white-wood buildings on well-kept lawns. Each unit has a kitchen and washer and dryer; there's also a small pool and shared barbecue area on the property. ✉ *1661 Pe'e Rd., Po'ipū 96756* ☎ *808/742–2482 or 800/367–5004* 🖷 *808/742–2379* ⊕ *www.castleresorts.com* 🖙 *78 units* ♿ *BBQs, fans, kitchens, in-room VCRs, tennis court, pool, hot tub, laundry facilities; no a/c* ▭ *AE, MC, V. 1-bedroom $260, 2-bedroom $305–$345, 3-bedroom $400.*

$ ✕ **Pōipu Crater Resort.** These two-bedroom condominium units are fairly spacious, and the large windows and high ceilings add to the sense of space and light. They're also well-furnished, with full kitchens and all the comforts of home. The condos are set within a nicely landscaped resort built on an extinct volcanic crater known as Piha Keakua, or place of the gods. It's one of the best-priced properties with ocean proximity, located just 700 yards from Keoniloa Bay (Shipwrecks), which is a famous bodysurfing spot with a snapping shore break. ✉ *2330 Hoohu Rd., Po'ipū 96756* ☎ *808/742–7260* ⊕ *www.suite-paradise.com* 🖙 *30 units* ♿ *Pool, lighted tennis courts, cable TV, full kitchen* ▭ *AE, DC, MC, V. $115–$137.*

B&Bs & Vacation Rentals

$–$$ 🖻 **Garden Isle Cottages.** Tropical fruit trees and flower gardens surround these spacious oceanside cottages. Contemporary Hawaiian furnishings include some rattan; amenities include kitchens with microwaves, ceiling fans, and washers and dryers. The restaurants of nearby Po'ipū are a five-minute walk away. The best part of staying here is the ocean view. A $50 cleaning fee is charged. ✉ *2660 Pu'uholo Rd., Kōloa 96756* ☎ *808/742–6717 or 800/742–6711* ⊕ *www.oceancottages.com* 🖙 *4 cottages* ♿ *Fans, kitchens, microwaves, laundry facilities, color TV with DVD, gas barbecue, phones in room; no a/c* ▭ *No credit cards. $189–$220.*

$–$$ 🖻 **Po'ipū Plantation Resort.** Plumeria, ti, and other tropical foliage create a lush landscape for this resort, which has one B&B-style plantation home and nine one- and two-bedroom cottage apartments. All cottage units have wood floors and full kitchens and are decorated in light, airy shades. The 1930s plantation home has two rooms with private baths and two suites. A full complimentary breakfast is served daily for those staying in the main house. A minimum three-night stay is required, but rates decrease with the length of stay. ✉ *1792 Pe'e Rd., Po'ipū 96756* ☎ *808/742–6757 or 800/634–0263* 🖷 *808/742–8681* ⊕ *www. poipubeach.com* ᗰ *3 rooms, 9 cottages* ♨ *BBQs, fans, kitchens, in-room VCRs, hair salon, hot tub, laundry facilities* ▤ *D, MC, V. $135–$210, 3-night minimum.*

$–$$ ✕ **Koloa Landing Cottages.** These four studio units, tucked into lush vegetation to provide privacy, are good choices for South Shore vacationers on a budget. While they aren't deluxe, the prices aren't, either, and you're within walking distance of the great beaches that make this area a prime destination. Two of the units have two bedrooms (one with twin beds) and two baths, and can comfortably accommodate four persons, while the others are a studio and one-bedroom unit designed for couples or solo travelers. ✉ *2704 Hoonani Rd., Po'ipū 96756* ☎ *808/742–1470 or 800/779–8773* ⊕ *www.www.koloa-landing.com* ᗰ *4 studios* ♨ *Cable TV, ceiling fan, full kitchen, gas BBQ.* ▤ *AE, D, DC, MC, V. $119.*

$ ⊞ **Hideaway Cove.** On a residential street ending in a cul-de-sac, Hideaway Cove is very quiet, even though it's one block from the ocean's edge in the heart of Po'ipū. What was once two homes has been converted to seven complete vacation homes. Owner Herb Lee appointed each with resort-quality furniture and furnishings—even original artwork. The two-bedroom Seabreeze villa comes with a hot tub on the lānai. The three-bedroom Oceanview villa connects via an internal staircase with the two-bedroom Aloha villa to provide a large five-bedroom home with two complete living areas—perfect for two families traveling together. Rates drop with a seven-night stay, effectively making the seventh night free. ✉ *2307 Nalo Rd., Po'ipū 96756* ☎ *808/635–8785 or 866/849–2426* ⊕ *www.hideawaycove.com* ᗰ *7 units* ♨ *BBQs, fans, kitchens, cable TV, in-room DVD/VCR, laundry facilities* ▤ *AE, D, MC, V. Studio $160–$185, 1-bedroom $200, 2-bedroom $280–$290, 3-bedroom $395–$475.*

$ ⊞ **Kaua'i Cove Cottages.** Three modern studio cottages sit side by side at the mouth of Waikomo Stream, beside an ocean cove that offers super snorkeling. The studios have airy tropical decor under cathedral ceilings; each has a complete kitchen. Private patios on the ocean side have gas barbecue grills. There's a $25 cleaning fee for stays of fewer than three nights. VCRs are available on request. ✉ *2672 Pu'uholo Rd., Po'ipū 96756* ☎ *808/651–0279 or 800/624–9945* ⊕ *www.kauaicove.com* ᗰ *3 cottages* ♨ *BBQs, fans, kitchens, cable TV, snorkeling; no a/c* ▤ *D, MC, V. $105–$145.*

THE WEST SIDE

If you want to do a lot of hiking or immerse yourself in the island's history, find a room in Waimea, although the pickings are slim, because this is not a resort area. There's one resort that's unlike any other resort in the Islands, and a few very spartan cabins are rented in nearby Kōke'e State Park. As a result, you won't find a lot of restaurants and shops, but you will encounter dark skies, quiet days, miles of largely deserted beach, and a rural ambience that speaks to the area's deep roots in cattle ranching and sugar.

Hotels & Resorts

$–$$$$
Fodor'sChoice
★

🏨 **Waimea Plantation Cottages.** History buffs will adore these reconstructed sugar-plantation cottages, which offer a vacation experience unique in all Hawai'i. The one- to five-bedroom cottages are tucked among coconut trees along a lovely stretch of coastline on the sunny West Side. (Note that swimming waters here are sometimes murky, depending on weather conditions.) ■ TIP→ **It's a great property for family reunions or other large gatherings.** These cozy little homes, replete with porches, feature plantation-era furnishings, modern kitchens, and cable TV. Barbecues, hammocks, porch swings, a gift shop, a spa, and a museum are on the property. Complimentary wireless Internet access is available in the main building; in-room data ports are available if requested in advance. ⊠ *9400 Kaumuali'i Hwy., Box 367, Waimea 96796* ☎ *808/338–1625 or 800/992–4632* 🖷 *808/338–2338* ⊕ *www.waimea-plantation.com* 🛏 *48 cottages* ⚐ *Restaurant, fans, some kitchens, cable TV, pool, spa, beach, horseshoes, bar, shop, Internet room; no a/c* 🖃 *AE, D, DC, MC, V. Studio $175, 1-bedroom $260–$350, 2-bedroom $330–$405, 3-bedroom $390–$455, 4-bedroom $505, 5-bedroom $775.*

$
✕ **Kalaheo Inn.** It isn't easy to find lodgings on the West Side, but this old-fashioned inn does the job in Kahaheo town, where accommodations are otherwise unavailable. You can choose from studios, or one-, two-, and three-bedroom suites. The suites also have a fridge and microwave, and a few have gas stoves if you want to eat at home. The rooms are very basic, but clean, with pillow-top beds for extra comfort. This property is a ways from the beach, but there's a great little hilltop 9-hole golf course just up the road, and it's an easy drive to Koke'e State Park. One nice touch is the tropical fruit picked on-site and offered free to guests, local style. ⊠ *4444 Papalina Rd., Kalaheo 96741* ☎ *808/332–6032 or 888/332–6023* ⊕ *www.kalaheoinn.com* 🛏 *14 units* ⚐ *BBQ grills, beach towels, mats, chairs, snorkel gear, coolers, golf clubs, games and books* 🖃 *MC, V. $80–$120.*

Vacation Rentals

¢
🏨 **Kōke'e Lodge.** If you're an outdoor enthusiast, you can appreciate Kaua'i's mountain wilderness from the 12 rustic cabins that make up this lodge. They are austere, to say the least, but more comfortable than a tent, and the mountain setting is grand. Wood-burning stoves ward off the chill and dampness (wood is a few dollars extra). If you aren't partial to dormitory-style sleeping, request the cabins with two bedrooms; both styles sleep six and have kitchenettes. The lodge restaurant serves a light breakfast and lunch between 9 and 3:30 daily. ⊠ *3600 Kōke'e Rd., at mile marker 15, Kekaha* ⊙ *Box 819, Waimea 96796* ☎ *808/ 335–6061* 🛏 *12 cabins* ⚐ *Restaurant, some kitchenettes, hiking, shops; no a/c, no room phones, no room TVs* 🖃 *D, DC, MC, V. $55.*

UNDERSTANDING KAUA'I

HAWAI'I AT A GLANCE

THE ALOHA SHIRT: A
COLORFUL SWATCH OF
ISLAND HISTORY

THESE VOLCANIC ISLES

HAWAIIAN
VOCABULARY

HAWAI'I AT A GLANCE

Fast Facts

Nickname: Aloha State
Capital: Honolulu
State song: "Hawai'i Pono'i"
State bird: The nēnē, an endangered land bird and variety of goose
State flower: Yellow Hibiscus Brackenridgii
State tree: Kukui (or candlenut), a Polynesian-introduced tree
Administrative divisions: There are four counties with mayors and councils: City and County of Honolulu (island of O'ahu), Hawai'i County (Hawai'i Island), Maui County (islands of Maui, Moloka'i, Lāna'i and Kahoolawe), and Kaua'i County (islands of Kaua'i and Ni'ihau)
Entered the Union: August 21, 1959, as the 50th state
Population: 1,334,023
Life expectancy: Female 82, male 76

Literacy: 81%
Ethnic groups: Hawaiian/part Hawaiian 22.1%; Caucasian 20.5%; Japanese 18.3%; Filipino 12.3%; Chinese 4.1%
Religion: Roman Catholic 22%; Buddhist, Shinto and other East Asian religions 15%; Mormon 10%; Church of Christ 8%; Assembly of God and Baptist 6% each; Episcopal, Jehovah's Witness and Methodist 5% each
Language: English is the first language of the majority of residents; Hawaiian is the native language of the indigenous Hawaiian people and an official language of the state; other languages spoken include Samoan, Chinese, Japanese, Korean, Spanish, Portuguese, Filipino, and Vietnamese

The loveliest fleet of islands that lies anchored in any ocean.
Mark Twain

Geography & Environment

Land area: An archipelago of 137 islands encompassing a land area of 6,422.6 square mi in the north-central Pacific Ocean (about 2,400 mi from the West Coast of the continental U.S.).
Coastline: 750 mi
Terrain: Volcanic mountains, tropical rain forests, verdant valleys, sea cliffs, canyons, deserts, coral reefs, sand dunes, sandy beaches
Natural resources: Dimension limestone, crushed stone, sand and gravel, gemstones
Natural hazards: Hurricanes, earthquakes, tsunamis
Flora: More than 2,500 species of native and introduced plants throughout the islands.
Fauna: Native mammals include the hoary bat, Hawaiian monk seal, and

Polynesian rat. The humpback whale migrates to Hawaiian waters every winter to mate and calve. More than 650 fish and 40 different species of shark live in Hawaiian waters. Freshwater streams are home to hundreds of native and alien species. The humuhumunukunukuāpua'a (Hawaiian triggerfish) is the unofficial state fish.
Environmental issues: Plant and animal species threatened and endangered due to hunting, overfishing, overgrazing by wild and introduced animals, and invasive alien plants.

Hawai'i is not a state of mind, but a state of grace.
Paul Theroux

Economy

Tourism and federal defense spending continue to drive the state's economy. Efforts to diversify in the areas of science and technology, film and television production, sports, ocean research and development, health and education, tourism, agriculture, and floral and specialty food products are ongoing.

GSP: $40.1 billion
Per capita income: $30,000
Inflation: 1%
Unemployment: 4.3%
Work force: 595,450
Debt: $7.3 billion
Major industries: Tourism, federal government (defense and other agencies)
Agricultural products: Sugar, pineapple, papayas, guavas, flower and nursery products, asparagus, alfalfa hay, macadamia nuts, coffee, milk, cattle, eggs, shellfish, algae
Exports: $616 million
Major export products: Aircraft and parts, naphthas, medical equipment and supplies, fruit, steel scrap, electronic components, unleaded gasoline, artwork, cocoa, coffee, flowers, macadamia nuts
Imports: $2.6 billion
Major import products: Crude oil, electronic and digital equipment, coal, passenger motor vehicles

In what other land save this one is the commonest form of greeting not "Good day," or How d'ye do," but "Love?" That greeting is "Aloha"—love, I love, my love to you . . .It is a positive affirmation of the warmth of one's own heart, giving.

Jack London

Debate has waxed and waned for more than a century over how and when to return to native Hawaiians more than 1 million acres of land and other assets seized when American business interests overthrew the island monarchy in 1893. Certain native factions still advocate a return to independent nationhood. Sovereignty gained new momentum in the 1990s with the passage of a federal law formally apologizing for the overthrow and urging reconciliation. Momentum has since fizzled. Hawai'i's current governor has renewed efforts to have Congress recognize Hawaiians as an indigenous people, much like Native Americans and Alaskans. The governor also has pledged to support continued funding of health care, language, and other cultural programs, and to achieve state and federal obligations to distribute homestead lands to qualified Hawaiians.

Did You Know?

- Hawai'i is home to the world's most active volcano: Kīlauea, on the Big Island.

- 'Iolani Palace had electricity and telephones installed several years before the White House, and is the only palace on U.S. soil.

- Hawai'i has about 12% of all endangered plants and animals in the United States; 75% of the country's extinct plants and birds were Hawaiian.

- The Royal Hawaiian Band is the only intact organization from the time of Hawaiian monarchy that is fully functional and still preserves Hawai'i's musical history.

THE ALOHA SHIRT: A COLORFUL SWATCH OF ISLAND HISTORY

ELVIS PRESLEY had an entire wardrobe of them in the '60s films *Blue Hawaii* and *Paradise, Hawaiian Style*. During the '50s, entertainer Arthur Godfrey and bandleader Harry Owens often sported them on television shows. John Wayne loved to lounge around in them. Mick Jagger felt compelled to buy one on a visit to Hawai'i in the 1970s. Dustin Hoffman, Steven Spielberg, and Bill Cosby avidly collect them.

The roots of the aloha shirt go back to the early 1930s, when Hawai'i's garment industry was just beginning to develop its own unique style. Although locally made clothes did exist, they were almost exclusively for plantation workers and were constructed of durable palaka or plain cotton material.

Out of this came the first stirrings of fashion: Beachboys and schoolchildren started having sport shirts made from colorful Japanese kimono fabric. The favored type of cloth was the kind used for children's kimonos—bright pink and orange floral prints for girls; masculine motifs in browns and blues for boys. In Japan, such flamboyant patterns were considered unsuitable for adult clothing, but in the Islands such rules didn't apply, and it seemed the flashier the shirt, the better—for either sex. Thus, the aloha shirt was born.

It was easy and inexpensive in those days to have garments tailored to order; the next step was moving to mass production and marketing. In June 1935 Honolulu's best-known tailoring establishment, Musa-Shiya, advertised the availability of "Aloha shirts—well tailored, beautiful designs and radiant colors. Ready-made or made to order . . . 95¢ and up." This is the first known printed use of the term that would soon refer to an entire industry. By the following year, several local manufacturers had begun full-scale production of "aloha wear." One of them, Ellery Chun of King-Smith, registered as local trademarks the terms "Aloha Sportswear" and "Aloha Shirt" in 1936 and 1937, respectively.

These early entrepreneurs were the first to create uniquely Hawaiian designs for fabric as well—splashy patterns that would forever symbolize the Islands. A 1939 *Honolulu Advertiser* story described them as a "delightful confusion [of] tropical fish and palm trees, Diamond Head and the Aloha Tower, surfboards and leis, 'ukuleles and Waikīkī beach scenes."

The aloha wear of the late 1930s was intended for—and mostly worn by—tourists, and interestingly, a great deal of it was exported to the mainland and even Europe and Australia. By the end of the decade, for example, only 5% of the output of one local firm, the Kamehameha Garment Company, was sold in Hawai'i.

World War II brought this trend to a halt, and during the postwar period aloha wear really came into its own in Hawai'i itself. A strong push to support local industry gradually nudged island garb into the workplace, and kama'āina began to wear the clothing that previously had been seen as attire for visitors.

In 1947, for example, male employees of the City and County of Honolulu were first allowed to wear aloha shirts "in plain shades" during the summer months. Later that year, the first observance of Aloha Week started the tradition of "bankers and bellhops . . . mix[ing] colorfully in multihued and tapa-designed Aloha shirts every day," as a local newspaper's Sunday magazine supplement noted in 1948. By the 1960s, "Aloha Friday," set aside specifically for the wearing of aloha attire, had become a tradition. In the following decade the suit and tie practically disappeared as work attire in Hawai'i, even for executives.

Most of the Hawaiian-theme fabric used in manufacturing aloha wear was designed in the Islands, then printed on the mainland or in Japan. The glowingly vibrant rayons of the late '40s and early '50s (a period now seen as aloha wear's heyday) were at first printed on the East Coast, but manufacturers there usually required such large orders that local firms eventually found it impossible to continue using them. By 1964, 90% of Hawaiian fabric was being manufactured in Japan—a situation that still exists today.

Fashion trends usually move in cycles, and aloha wear is no exception. By the 1960s the "chop suey print" with its "tired clichés of Diamond Head, Aloha Tower, outrigger canoes [and] stereotyped leis" was seen as corny and garish, according to an article published in the *Honolulu Star-Bulletin*. But it was just that outdated aspect that began to appeal to the younger crowd, who began searching out old-fashioned aloha shirts at the Salvation Army and Goodwill thrift stores. These shirts were dubbed "silkies," a name by which they're still known, even though most of them were actually made of rayon.

Before long, what had been 50¢ shirts began escalating in price, and a customer who had balked at paying $5 for a shirt that someone had already worn soon found the same item selling for $10—and more. By the late 1970s, aloha-wear designers were copying the prints of yesteryear for their new creations.

The days of bargain silkies are now gone. The few choice aloha shirts from decades past that still remain are offered today by specialized dealers for hundreds of dollars apiece, causing many to look back to the time when such treasures were foolishly worn to the beach until they fell apart. The best examples of vintage aloha shirts are now rightly seen as art objects, worthy of preservation for the lovely depictions they offer of Hawai'i's colorful and unique scene.

— DeSoto Brown

THESE VOLCANIC ISLES

DAWN AT THE CRATER ON HORSEBACK. It's cold at 10,023 feet above the warm Pacific—maybe 45°F. The horses' breath condenses into smoky clouds, and the riders cling to their saddles. It's eerily quiet except for the creak of straining leather and the crunch of volcanic cinders underfoot, sounds that are absurdly magnified in the vast empty space that yawns below.

This is Haleakalā, the "house of the sun." It's the crown of East Maui and the largest dormant volcanic depression in the world. The park encompasses 28,665 acres, and the valley itself is 21 mi in circumference and 19 square mi in area. At its deepest, it measures 3,000 feet from the summit, and could accommodate all of Manhattan. What you see here isn't actually a crater at all but something called a caldera, formed by the collapsing of the main cone, the result of eons of wind and rain wearing down what was once a small dip at the original summit peak. The small hills within the valley are volcanic cinder cones, each the site of an eruption.

Every year thousands of visitors drive the world's steepest auto route to the summit of Haleakalā National Park. Sunrise is extraordinary here. Mark Twain called it "the sublimest spectacle" he had ever witnessed.

But sunrise is only the beginning.

Hiking Haleakalā is like walking on the moon, with 32 mi of trails weaving around volcanic rubble, crater cones, frozen lava flows, vents, and tubes. The colors are muted yet dramatic—black, yellow, russet, orange, lavender, brown, even a pinkish blue—and change throughout the day.

This ecosystem sustains the surefooted mountain goat; the rare *nēnē* goose (no webbing between its toes, the better to negotiate this rugged terrain); and the strange, delicate silversword. A spiny, metallic-leaf plant, the silversword once grew abundantly on Haleakalā's slopes. Today it survives in small numbers at Haleakalā and at high elevations on the Big Island of Hawaiʻi. The plants live up to 40 years, bloom only once, scatter their seeds, and die.

It's not difficult to see this place as a bubbling, sulfurous cauldron, a direct connection to the core of the earth. Haleakalā's last—and probably final—eruption occurred in 1790, a few years after a Frenchman named Jean-François de Galaup, Comte de La Pérouse, became the first European to set foot on Maui. The rocky area on the southwest side of East Maui known as La Pérouse Bay is the result of that flow.

Large and small, awake or sleeping, volcanoes are Hawaiʻi's history and heritage. Behind their beauty is the story of the flames that created this ethereal island chain. The islands in the Hawaiian archipelago are actually the upper bodies of immense mountains rising from the bottom of the sea. Formed by molten rock known as magma, the islands have slowly grown from the earth's volatile mantle, lava forced through a "hot spot" in the thin crust of the ocean floor. The first ancient eruptions cooled and formed pools on the Pacific bottom. Then as magma spilled from the vents over millions of years, the pools became ridges and grew into crests. The latter built upon themselves over the eons, until finally they towered above the surface of the sea. This type of volcano, with its slowly formed, gently sloping sides, is known as a shield volcano. All of the Hawaiian Islands were created this way.

As the Islands cooled in the Pacific waters, the lava slopes slowly bloomed, over centuries, with colorful flora. About once every 35,000 years a seed, spore, bird, or insect arrived here on the winds or waves. They found a fertile, sun-and-rain–drenched home, free of predators. Over time, these migrants developed into highly specialized organisms. A land with no predatory species breeds a population of plants and animals devoid of biological protections, making them especially fragile and vulnerable to foreign species and human development. Today Hawai'i suffers from one of the world's highest species extinction rates; eighty percent of native Hawaiian birds are now gone.

But for all the talk of geology, Hawaiian myth casts a different history of the islands. Pele, the beautiful and tempestuous daughter of Haumea, the Earth Mother, and Wakea, the Sky Father, is the Hawaiian goddess of fire, the maker of mountains, melter of rock, eater of forests—a creator and a destroyer. Legend has it that Pele came to the Islands long ago to flee from her cruel older sister, Na Maka o Kahai, goddess of the sea. Pele ran first to the small island of Ni'ihau, making a crater home there with her digging stick. But Na Maka found her and destroyed her hideaway, so Pele again had to flee. On Kaua'i she delved deeper, but Na Maka chased her from that home as well. Pele ran on—from O'ahu to Moloka'i, Lāna'i to Kaho'olawe, Molokini to Maui—but always Na Maka pursued her.

Pele came at last to *Halema'uma'u,* the vast fire-pit crater of Kīlauea, and there, on the Big Island, she dug deepest of all. There she is said to remain, all-powerful, quick to rage, and often unpredictable; the mountain is her impenetrable fortress and domain—a safe refuge, at least for a time, from Na Maka o Kahai.

The chronology of the old tales of Pele's flight from isle to isle closely matches the reckonings of modern volcanologists regarding the ages of the various craters. Today, the Big Island's Kīlauea and Mauna Loa retain the closest links with the earth's superheated core and are active and volatile. The other volcanoes have been

carried beyond their magma supply by the movement of the Pacific Plate. Those on Kaua'i, O'ahu, and Moloka'i are completely extinct. Those at the southeasterly end of the island chain—Haleakalā, Mauna Ke'a, and Hualālai—are dormant and slipping away, so that the implacable process of volcanic death has begun. As erosion continues, the islands will someday melt back into the sea.

The largest island of the archipelago, the Big Island of Hawai'i rises some 13,796 feet above sea level at the summit of Mauna Ke'a. Mauna Loa is nearly as high at 13,667 feet. Geologists believe it required more than 3 million years of steady volcanic activity to raise these peaks up above the waters of the Pacific. From their bases on the ocean floor, these shield volcanoes are the largest mountain masses on the planet.

Mauna Loa's little sister, Kīlauea, at about 4,077 feet, is the most active volcano in the world. Between the two volcanoes, they have covered nearly 200,000 acres of land with their red-hot lava flows over the past 200 years. In the process, they have ravished trees, fields, meadows, villages, and more than a few unlucky humans. For generations, Kīlauea, in a continually eruptive state, has pushed molten lava up from the earth's magma at 1,800°F and more. But as active as she and Mauna Loa are, their eruptions are comparatively safe and gentle, producing continuous small flows rather than large bursts of fire and ash. The exceptions were two explosive displays during recorded history— one in 1790, the other in 1924. During these eruptions, Pele came close to destroying the Big Island's largest city, Hilo.

It is around these major volcanoes that the island's Hawai'i Volcanoes National Park was created. A sprawling natural preserve, the park attracts visitors from around the world for the unparalleled opportunity to view lava up-close and personal. Geology experts and volcanologists have been coming for a century or more to study and to improve methods for predicting the times and sites of eruptions.

Thomas Augustus Jaggar, preeminent volcanologist and student of Kīlauea, built his home on stilts wedged into cracks in the volcanic rock of the crater rim. Harvard-trained and universally respected, he was the driving force behind the establishment of the Hawaiian Volcano Observatory at Kīlauea in 1912. When he couldn't raise research funds from donations, public and private, he raised pigs to keep the scientific work going. After Jaggar's death, his wife scattered his ashes over the great fiery abyss.

The park is on the Big Island's southeastern flank, about 30 minutes out of Hilo on the aptly named Volcano Highway. Wear sturdy walking shoes and carry a warm sweater. It can be a long hike across the lava flats to see Pele in action, and at 4,000 feet above sea level temperatures can be brisk, however hot the volcanic activity. So much can be seen at close range along the road circling the crater that Kīlauea has been dubbed the "drive-in volcano."

At the park's visitor center sits a large display case. It contains dozens of lava-rock "souvenirs"—removed from Pele's grasp and then returned, accompanied by letters of apology. They are sent back by visitors who say they regret having broken the *kapu* (taboo) against removing even the smallest grain of native volcanic rock from Hawai'i. A typical letter might say: "I never thought Pele would miss just one little rock, but she did, and now I've wrecked two cars . . . I lost my job, my health is poor, and I know it's because I took this stone." The letters can be humorous, or poignant and remorseful, requesting Pele's forgiveness.

It is surprisingly safe at the crater's lip. Unlike Japan's Mount Fuji or Washington State's Mount St. Helens, Hawai'i's shield volcanoes spew their lava downhill, along the sides of the mountain. Still, the clouds of sulfur gas and fumes produced during volcanic eruptions are noxious and heady and can make breathing unpleasant, if not difficult. It has been pointed out that the chemistry of volcanoes—sulfur, hydrogen, oxygen, carbon dioxide—closely resembles the chemistry of the egg.

It's an 11-mi drive around the Kīlauea crater via the Crater Rim Road, and the trip takes about an hour. But it's better to walk a bit. There are at least eight major trails in the park, ranging from short 15-minute strolls to the three-day, 18-mi (one way) Mauna Loa Trail. An easy, comfortable walk is Sulfur Banks, with its many steaming vents creating halos of clouds around the rim of Kīlauea. The route passes through a forest of sandalwood, flowers, and ferns.

Just ahead is the main attraction: the center of Pele's power, Halema'uma'u. This yawning pit of flame and burning rock measures some 3,000 feet wide and is a breathtaking sight. When Pele is in full fury, visitors come in droves, on foot and by helicopter, to see her crimson expulsions coloring the dark earth and smoky sky. Kīlauea's most recent violent activity has occurred at mountainside vents instead of at the summit crater. Known as rift zones, they are lateral conduits that often open in shield volcanoes.

Kīlauea has two rift zones, one extending from the summit crater toward the southwest, through Kau, the other to the east-northeast through Puna, past Cape Kumakahi, into the sea. In the last two decades, repeated eruptions in the east rift zone have blocked off 12 mi of coastal road—some under more than 300 feet of rock—and have covered a total of 10,000 acres with lava. Where the flows entered the ocean, roughly 200 acres have been added to the Big Island.

Farther along the Crater Rim Road is the Thurston Lava Tube, an example of a strangely beautiful volcanic phenomenon common on the Islands. Lava tubes form when lava flows rapidly downhill. The sides and top of this river of molten rock cool, while the fluid center flows on. Most formations are short and shallow, but some measure 30 to 50 feet high and hundreds of yards long. Lava tubes were often used to store remains of the ancient Hawaiian royalty—the *ali'i*. The Thurston Lava Tube sits in a beautiful prehistoric fern forest.

Throughout the park, new lava formations are continually being created. These volcanic deposits exhibit the different types of lava produced by Hawai'i's volcanoes: *'a'ā,* the dark, rough lava that solidifies as cinders of rock; and the more common *pāhoehoe,* the smooth, satiny lava that forms the vast plains of black rock in ropy swirls known as lava flats, which in some areas go on for miles. Other terms that help identify what may be seen in the park include *caldera,* which are the open, bowl-like lips of a volcano summit; *ejecta,* the cinders and ash that float through the air around an eruption; and *olivine,* the semiprecious chrysolite (greenish in color) found in volcanic ash.

But this volcanic landscape isn't all fire and flash, cinders, and devastation. Hawai'i Volcanoes National Park is also the home of some of the most beautiful of the state's black-sand beaches; forest glens full of lacy butterflies and colorful birds such as the dainty flycatcher, called the *'elepaio*; and exquisite grottoes sparked with bright wild orchid sprays and crashing waterfalls. Even as the lava cools, still bearing a golden, glassy skin, lush, green native ferns—*ama'uma'u, kupukupu,* and *'ōkupukupu*—spring up in the midst of Pele's fallout, as if defying her destructiveness or simply confirming the fact that after fire she brings life.

Some 12 centuries ago, in fact, Pele brought humans to her verdant islands: the fiery explosions that lit Kīlauea and Mauna Loa probably guided the first explorers to Pele's side from the Marquesas Islands, some 2,400 mi away across the ocean.

Once settled, they worshiped her from a distance. Great numbers of religious *heiau* (outdoor stone platforms) dot the landscapes near the many older and extinct craters scattered throughout Hawai'i, demonstrating the reverence the native islanders have always held for Pele and her creations. But the ruins of only two *heiau* are to be found near the very active crater at Halema'uma'u. There, at the center of the capricious Pele's power, native Hawaiians caution one even today to "step lightly, for you are on holy ground."

In future ages, when mighty Kīlauea is no more, this area will still be a volcanic isle. Beneath the blue Pacific waters, fiery magma flows and new mountains form and grow. Off the south coast of the Big Island, a new island is forming. Still ½ mi below the water's surface, it won't be making an appearance any time soon, but already has a name: Lōihi.

— Gary Diedrichs

HAWAIIAN VOCABULARY

Although an understanding of Hawaiian is by no means required on a trip to the Aloha State, a *malihini*, or newcomer, will find plenty of opportunities to pick up a few of the local words and phrases. Traditional names and expressions are widely used in the Islands, thanks in part to legislation enacted in the early '90s to encourage the use of the Hawaiian language. You're likely to read or hear at least a few words each day of your stay. Such exposure enriches a trip to Hawai'i.

With a basic understanding and some uninhibited practice, anyone can have enough command of the local tongue to ask for directions and to order from a restaurant menu. One visitor announced she would not leave until she could pronounce the name of the state fish, the *humuhumunukunukuāpua'a*. Luckily, she had scheduled a nine-day stay.

Simplifying the learning process is the fact that Hawaiian contains only eight consonants—*H, K, L, M, N, P, W*, and the silent *'okina*, or glottal stop, written '—plus one or more of the five vowels. All syllables end in a vowel. Each vowel, except a few diphthongized double vowels such as *au* (pronounced "ow") or *ai* (pronounced "eye"), is pronounced separately. Thus *'Iolani* is four syllables (ee-oh-la-nee), not three (yo-la-nee). Although some Hawaiian words have only vowels, most also contain some consonants, which are never doubled.

Pronunciation is simple. Pronounce *A* "ah" as father; *E* "ay" as in weigh; *I* "ee" as in marine; *O* "oh" as in no; *U* "oo" as in true.

Consonants mirror their English equivalents, with the exception of *W*. When the letter begins any syllable other than the first one in a word, it is usually pronounced as a *V*. *'Awa*, the Polynesian drink, is pronounced "ava," *'ewa* is pronounced "eva."

Nearly all long Hawaiian words are combinations of shorter words; they are not difficult to pronounce if you segment them into shorter words. *Kalaniana'ole*, the highway running east from Honolulu, is easily understood as *Kalani ana 'ole*. Apply the standard pronunciation rules—the stress falls on the next-to-last syllable of most two- or three-syllable Hawaiian words—and Kalaniana'ole Highway is as easy to say as Main Street.

Now about that fish. Try *humu-humu nuku-nuku āpu a'a*.

The other unusual element in Hawaiian language is the *kahakō*, or macron, written as a short line ‾ placed over a vowel. Like the accent ´ in Spanish, the kahakō puts emphasis on a syllable that would normally not be stressed. The most familiar example is probably *Waikīkī*. With no macrons, the stress would fall on the middle syllable; with only one macron, on the last syllable, the stress would fall on the first and last syllables. Some words become plural with the addition of a macron, often on a syllable that would have been stressed anyway. No Hawaiian word becomes plural with the addition of an *S*, since that letter does not exist in the *'ōlelo Hawai'i* (which is Hawaiian for "Hawaiian language").

What follows is a glossary of some of the most commonly used Hawaiian words. Don't be afraid to give them a try. Hawaiian residents appreciate visitors who at least try to pick up the local language.

'a'ā: rough, crumbling lava, contrasting with *pāhoehoe*, which is smooth.

'ae: yes.

aikane: friend.

āina: land.

akamai: smart, clever, possessing savoir faire.

akua: god.

ala: a road, path, or trail.

ali'i: a Hawaiian chief, a member of the chiefly class.

aloha: love, kindness; also a salutation meaning greetings and farewell.

'**ānuenue:** rainbow.

'**a'ole:** no.

'**apōpō:** tomorrow.

'**auwai:** a ditch.

auwē: alas, woe is me!

'**ehu:** a red-haired Hawaiian.

'**ewa:** in the direction of 'Ewa plantation, west of Honolulu.

hala: the pandanus tree, whose leaves (*lau hala*) are used to make baskets and mats.

hālau: school.

hale: a house.

hale pule: church, house of worship.

ha mea iki or **ha mea 'ole:** you're welcome.

hana: to work.

haole: ghost. Since the first foreigners were Caucasian, *haole* now means a Caucasian person.

hapa: a part, sometimes a half; often used as a short form of *hapa haole,* to mean a person who is part-Caucasian; thus, the name of a popular local band, whose members represent a variety of ethnicities.

hau'oli: to rejoice. *Hau'oli Makahiki Hou* means Happy New Year. *Hau'oli lā hānau* means Happy Birthday.

heiau: an outdoor stone platform; an ancient Hawaiian place of worship.

holo: to run.

holoholo: to go for a walk, ride, or sail.

holokū: a long Hawaiian dress, somewhat fitted, with a yoke and a train. Influenced by European fashion, it was worn at court, and at least one local translates the word as "expensive mu'umu'u."

holomū: a post–World War II cross between a *holokū* and a mu'umu'u, less fitted than the former but less voluminous than the latter, and having no train.

honi: to kiss; a kiss. A phrase that some tourists may find useful, quoted from a popular hula, is *Honi Ka'ua Wikiwiki:* Kiss me quick!

honu: turtle.

ho'omalimali: flattery, a deceptive "line," bunk, baloney, hooey.

huhū: angry.

hui: a group, club, or assembly. A church may refer to its congregation as a *hui* and a social club may be called a *hui.*

hukilau: a seine; a communal fishing party in which everyone helps to drive the fish into a huge net, pull it in, and divide the catch.

hula: the dance of Hawai'i.

iki: little.

ipo: sweetheart.

ka: the. This is the definite article for most singular words; for plural nouns, the definite article is usually *nā.* Since there is no S in Hawaiian, the article may be your only clue that a noun is plural.

kahuna: a priest, doctor, or other trained person of old Hawai'i, endowed with special skills that often included the gift of prophecy or other supernatural powers; the plural is *kāhuna.*

kai: the sea, saltwater.

kalo: the taro plant from whose root poi is made.

kama'āina: literally, a child of the soil; it refers to people who were born in the Islands or have lived there for a long time.

kanaka: originally a man or humanity in general, it's now used to denote a male Hawaiian or part-Hawaiian, but is occasionally taken as a slur when used by non-Hawaiians. *Kanaka maoli,* originally a full-blooded Hawaiian person, is used by some native Hawaiian rights activists to embrace part-Hawaiians.

kāne: a man, a husband. If you see this word on a door, it's the men's room. If you see *kane* on a door, it's probably a misspelling; that is the Hawaiian name for the skin fungus tinea.

kapa: also called by its Tahitian name, *tapa,* a cloth made of beaten bark, usually dyed and stamped with a repeat design.

kapakahi: crooked, cockeyed, uneven. You've got your hat on *kapakahi.*

kapu: keep out, prohibited. This is the Hawaiian version of the more widely known Tongan word *tabu* (taboo).

kapuna: grandparent; elder.

kēia lā: today.

keiki: a child; *keikikāne* is a boy, *keikiwahine* a girl.

kona: the leeward side of the Islands, the direction (south) from which the *kona* wind and *kona* rain come.

kula: upland.

kuleana: a homestead or small plot of ground on which a family has been installed for some generations without necessarily owning it. By extension, *kuleana* is used to denote any area or department in which one has a special interest or prerogative. You'll hear it used this way: If you want to hire a surfboard, see Moki; that's his *kuleana.* And conversely: I can't help you with that; that's not my *kuleana.*

lā: sun.

lamalama: to fish with a torch.

lānai: a porch, a balcony, an outdoor living room. Almost every house in Hawai'i has one. Don't confuse this two-syllable word with the three-syllable name of the island, Lāna'i.

lani: heaven, the sky.

lau hala: the leaf of the *hala,* or pandanus tree, widely used in Hawaiian handicrafts.

lei: a garland of flowers.

limu: sun.

lolo: stupid.

luna: a plantation overseer or foreman.

mahalo: thank you.

makai: toward the ocean.

malihini: a newcomer to the Islands.

mana: the spiritual power that Hawaiians believe inhabits all things and creatures.

manō: shark.

manuwahi: free, gratis.

mauka: toward the mountains.

mauna: mountain.

mele: a Hawaiian song or chant, often of epic proportions.

Mele Kalikimaka: Merry Christmas (a transliteration from the English phrase).

Menehune: a Hawaiian pixie. The *Menehune* were a legendary race of little people who accomplished prodigious work, such as building fishponds and temples in the course of a single night.

moana: the ocean.

mu'umu'u: the voluminous dress in which missionaries enveloped Hawaiian women. Now made in bright printed cottons and silks, it is an indispensable garment in a Hawaiian woman's wardrobe. Culturally sensitive locals have embraced the Hawaiian spelling but often shorten the spoken word to "mu'u." Most English dictionaries include the spelling "muumuu."

nani: beautiful.

nui: big.

ohana: family.

'ono: delicious.

pāhoehoe: smooth, unbroken, satiny lava.

Pākē: Chinese. This *Pākē* carver makes beautiful things.

palapala: document, printed matter.

pali: a cliff, precipice.

pānini: prickly pear cactus.

paniolo: a Hawaiian cowboy, a rough transliteration of *español,* the language of the Islands' earliest cowboys.

pau: finished, done.

pilikia: trouble. The Hawaiian word is much more widely used here than its English equivalent.

puka: a hole.

pupule: crazy, like the celebrated Princess Pupule. This word has replaced its English equivalent in local usage.

pu'u: volcanic cinder cone.

waha: mouth.

wahine: a female, a woman, a wife, and a sign on the ladies' room door; the plural form is *wāhine.*

wai: freshwater, as opposed to saltwater, which is *kai.*

wailele: waterfall.

wikiwiki: to hurry, hurry up (since this is a reduplication of *wiki,* quick, neither W is pronounced as a V).

Note: Pidgin is the unofficial language of Hawai'i. It is a Creole language, with its own grammar, evolved from English, Hawaiian, Japanese, Portuguese, and other languages spoken in 19th-century Hawai'i. You'll hear it everywhere: on ranches, in warehouses, on beaches, and in the hallowed halls of the University of Hawai'i.

Kaua'i Essentials

PLANNING TOOLS, EXPERT INSIGHT,
GREAT CONTACTS

There are planners, and there are those who fly by the seat of their pants. We happily place ourselves among the planners. Our writers and editors try to anticipate all the issues you may face before and during any journey, and then they do their research. This section is the product of their efforts. Use it to get excited about your trip to Hawai'i, to inform your travel planning, or to guide you on the road should the seat of your pants start to feel threadbare.

GETTING STARTED

We're really proud of our Web site: Fodors. com is a great place to begin any journey. Scan Travel Wire for suggested itineraries, travel deals, restaurant and hotel openings, and other up-to-the-minute info. Check out Booking to research prices and book plane tickets, hotel rooms, rental cars, and vacation packages. Head to Talk for on-the-ground pointers from travelers who frequent our message boards. You can also link to loads of other travel-related resources.

▌ RESOURCES

ONLINE TRAVEL TOOLS

For more information on Kaua'i, visit ⊕ www.kauaidiscovery.com (Kaua'i Visitors Bureau). Other sites to check out for more general Hawai'i information include ⊕ www.gohawaii.com, the official Web site of the Hawai'i Visitors & Convention Bureau; ⊕ www.bestplaceshawaii.com for the Hawai'i State Vacation Planner; and ⊕ www.hawaii.gov, the state's official Web site. For information on other islands visit ⊕ www.bigisland.org (Big Island Visitors Bureau); ⊕ www.visitmaui. com (Maui County Visitors Bureau); ⊕ www.visit-oahu.com (O'ahu Visitors Bureau); and ⊕ www.molokai-hawaii. com (Moloka'i Visitors Association). **Safety Transportation Security Administration** (TSA) ⊕ www.tsa.gov. **Time Zones Timeanddate.com** ⊕ www. timeanddate.com/worldclock can help you figure out the correct time anywhere in the world.

Weather Accuweather.com ⊕ www. accuweather.com is an independent weather-forecasting service with especially good coverage of hurricanes. **Weather.com** ⊕ www. weather.com is the Web site for the Weather Channel.
Other Resources CIA World Factbook ⊕ www.odci.gov/cia/publications/factbook/ index.html has profiles of every country in the world. It's a good source if you need some quick facts and figures.

VISITOR INFORMATION

Before you go, contact the Kaua'i Visitors Bureau for a free travel planner that has information on accommodations, transportation, sports and activities, dining, arts and entertainment, and culture. You can also take a virtual tour of the island that includes great photos and helpful planning information.
Kaua'i Visitors Bureau ☎ 800/262-1400 ⊕ www.kauaidiscovery.com.

▌ THINGS TO CONSIDER

GOVERNMENT ADVISORIES

If you travel frequently, look into the TSA's Registered Traveler program. The program, which is still being tested in several U.S. airports, is designed to cut down on gridlock at security checkpoints by allowing prescreened travelers to pass quickly through kiosks that scan an iris and/or a fingerprint. How sci-fi is that?

GEAR

Hawai'i is casual: sandals, bathing suits, and comfortable, informal clothing are the norm. In summer synthetic slacks and shirts, although easy to care for, can be uncomfortably warm.

Probably the most important thing to tuck into your suitcase is sunscreen. This is the tropics, and the ultraviolet rays are powerful, even on overcast days. Doctors advise putting on sunscreen when you get up

---

WORD OF MOUTH

After your trip, be sure to rate the places you visited and share your experiences and travel tips with us and other Fodorites in Travel Ratings and Talk on www.fodors.com.

PACKING 101

Why do some people travel with a convoy of huge suitcases yet never have a thing to wear? How do others pack a duffel bag with a week's worth of outfits *and* supplies for every contingency? We realize that packing is a matter of style, but there's a lot to be said for traveling light. These tips help fight the battle of the bulging bag.

MAKE A LIST. In a recent Fodor's survey, 29% of respondents said they make lists (and often pack) a week before a trip. You can use your list to pack and to repack at the end of your trip. It can also serve as a record of the contents of your suitcase—in case it disappears in transit.

THINK IT THROUGH. What's the weather like? Is this a business trip? A cruise? Going abroad? In some places dress may be more or less conservative than you're used to. As you create your itinerary, note outfits next to each activity (don't forget accessories).

EDIT YOUR WARDROBE. Plan to wear everything twice (better yet, thrice) and to do laundry along the way. Stick to one basic look—urban chic, sporty casual, etc. Build around one or two neutrals and an accent (e.g., black, white, and olive green). Women can freshen looks by changing scarves or jewelry. For a week's trip, you can look smashing with three bottoms, four or five tops, a sweater, and a jacket.

BE PRACTICAL. Put comfortable shoes atop your list. (Did we need to say this?) Pack lightweight, wrinkle-resistant, compact, washable items. (Or this?) Stack and roll clothes, so they'll wrinkle less. Unless you're on a guided tour or a cruise, select luggage you can readily carry. Porters, like good butlers, are hard to find these days.

CHECK WEIGHT AND SIZE LIMITATIONS. In the United States you may be charged extra for checked bags weighing more than 50 pounds. Abroad some airlines don't allow you to check bags over 60 to 70 pounds, or they charge outrageous fees for every excess pound—or bag. Carry-on size limitations can be stringent, too.

CHECK CARRY-ON RESTRICTIONS. Research restrictions with the TSA. Rules vary abroad, so check them with your airline if you're traveling overseas on a foreign carrier. Consider packing all but essentials (travel documents, prescription meds, wallet) in checked luggage. This leads to a "pack only what you can afford to lose" approach that might help you streamline.

RETHINK VALUABLES. On U.S. flights, airlines are liable for only about $2,800 per person for bags. On international flights, the liability limit is around $635 per bag. But items such as computers, cameras, and jewelry aren't covered, and because gadgetry can go on and off the list of carry-on no-no's, you can't count on keeping things safe by keeping them close. Although comprehensive travel policies may cover luggage, the liability limit is often a pittance. Your home-owner's policy may cover you sufficiently when you travel—or not.

LOCK IT UP. If you must pack valuables, use TSA-approved locks (about $10) that can be unlocked by all U.S. security personnel.

TAG IT. Always tag your luggage; use your business address if you don't want people to know your home address. Put the same information (and a copy of your itinerary) inside your luggage, too.

REPORT PROBLEMS IMMEDIATELY. If your bags—or things inside them—are damaged or go astray, file a written claim with your airline *before leaving the airport*. If the airline is at fault, it may give you money for essentials until your luggage arrives. Most lost bags are found within 48 hours, so alert the airline to your whereabouts for two or three days. If your bag was opened for security reasons in the United States and something is missing, file a claim with the TSA.

Trip Insurance Resources

INSURANCE COMPARISON SITES		
Insure My Trip.com		www.insuremytrip.com.
Square Mouth.com		www.quotetravelinsurance.com.
COMPREHENSIVE TRAVEL INSURERS		
Access America	866/807-3982	www.accessamerica.com.
CSA Travel Protection	800/873-9855	www.csatravelprotection.com.
HTH Worldwide	610/254-8700 or 888/243-2358	www.hthworldwide.com.
Travelex Insurance	888/457-4602	www.travelex-insurance.com.
Travel Guard International	715/345-0505 or 800/826-4919	www.travelguard.com.
Travel Insured International	800/243-3174	www.travelinsured.com.
MEDICAL-ONLY INSURERS		
International Medical Group	800/628-4664	www.imgglobal.com.
International SOS	215/942-8000 or 713/521-7611	www.internationalsos.com.
Wallach & Company	800/237-6615 or 504/687-3166	www.wallach.com.

in the morning, whether it's cloudy or sunny. Don't forget to reapply sunscreen periodically during the day, since perspiration can wash it away. Consider using sunscreens with a sun protection factor (SPF) of 15 or higher. There are many tanning oils on the market in Hawai'i, including coconut and *kukui* (the nut from a local tree) oils, but they can cause severe burns. Too many Hawaiian vacations have been spoiled by sunburn and even sun poisoning. Hats and sunglasses offer important sun protection, too. Both are easy to find in island shops, but if you already have a favorite packable hat or sun visor, bring it with you, and don't forget to wear it. All major hotels provide beach towels.

As for clothing in the Hawaiian Islands, there's a saying that when a man wears a suit during the day, he's either going for a loan or he's a lawyer trying a case. Only a few upscale restaurants require a jacket for dinner. The aloha shirt is accepted dress in Hawai'i for business and most social occasions. Shorts are acceptable daytime attire, along with a T-shirt or polo shirt. There's no need to buy expensive sandals on the mainland—here you can get flip-flops for a couple of dollars and off-brand sandals for $20. Golfers should remember that many courses have dress codes requiring a collared shirt; call courses you're interested in for details. If you're not prepared, you can pick up appropriate clothing at resort pro shops. If you're visiting in winter, bring a sweater or light-to medium-weight jacket. A polar fleece pullover is ideal, and makes a great impromptu pillow.

TRIP INSURANCE

What kind of coverage do you honestly need? Do you even need trip insurance at all? Take a deep breath and read on.

We believe that comprehensive trip insurance is especially valuable if you're booking a very expensive or complicated trip (particularly to an isolated region) or if you're booking far in advance. Who knows what could happen six months down the road? But whether or not you get insurance has more to do with how comfortable you are assuming all that risk yourself.

Comprehensive travel policies typically cover trip cancellation and interruption, letting you cancel or cut your trip short because of a personal emergency, illness, or, in some cases, acts of terrorism in your destination. Such policies also cover evacuation and medical care. Some also cover you for trip delays because of bad weather or mechanical problems as well as for lost or delayed baggage. Another type of coverage to look for is financial default—that is, when your trip is disrupted because a tour operator, airline, or cruise line goes out of business. Generally you must buy this when you book your trip or shortly thereafter, and it's available to you only if your operator isn't on a list of excluded companies.

If you're going abroad, consider buying medical-only coverage at the very least. Neither Medicare nor some private insurers cover medical expenses anywhere outside the United States besides Mexico and Canada (including time aboard a cruise ship, even if it leaves from a U.S. port). Medical-only policies typically reimburse you for medical care (excluding that related to preexisting conditions) and hospitalization abroad, and provide for evacuation. You still have to pay the bills and await reimbursement from the insurer, though.

Expect comprehensive travel insurance policies to cost about 4% to 7% of the total price of your trip (it's more like 12% if you're over age 70). A medical-only policy may or may not be cheaper than a comprehensive policy. Always read the fine print of your policy to make sure that you are covered for the risks that are of most concern to you. Compare several policies to make sure you're getting the best price and range of coverage available.

■ TIP→ OK. You know you can save a bundle on trips to warm-weather destinations by traveling in rainy season. But there's also a chance that a severe storm will disrupt your plans. The solution? Look for hotels and resorts that offer storm/hurricane guarantees. Although they rarely allow refunds, most guarantees do let you rebook later if a storm strikes.

BOOKING YOUR TRIP

Unless your cousin is a travel agent, you're probably among the millions of people who make most of their travel arrangements online. But have you ever wondered just what the differences are between an online travel agent (a Web site through which you make reservations instead of going directly to the airline, hotel, or car-rental company), a discounter (a firm that does a high volume of business with a hotel chain or airline and accordingly gets good prices), a wholesaler (one that makes cheap reservations in bulk and then resells them to people like you), and an aggregator (one that compares all the offerings so you don't have to)? Is it truly better to book directly on an airline or hotel Web site? And when does a real live travel agent come in handy?

ONLINE

You really have to shop around. A travel wholesaler such as Hotels.com or Hotel-Club.net can be a source of good rates, as can discounters such as Hotwire or Priceline, particularly if you can bid for your hotel room or airfare. Indeed, such sites sometimes have deals that are unavailable elsewhere. They do, however, tend to work only with hotel chains (which makes them just plain useless for getting hotel reservations outside major cities) or big airlines (so that often leaves out upstarts such as jetBlue and some foreign carriers such as Air India). Also, with discounters and wholesalers you must generally prepay, and everything is nonrefundable. And before you fork over the dough, be sure to check the terms and conditions, so you know what a given company will do for you if there's a problem and what you'll have to deal with on your own.

■ TIP→ To be absolutely sure everything was processed correctly, confirm reservations made through online travel agents, discounters, and wholesalers directly with your hotel before leaving home.

Booking engines such as Expedia, Travelocity, and Orbitz are actually travel agents, albeit high-volume, online ones. And airline travel packagers such as American Airlines Vacations and Virgin Vacations—well, they're travel agents, too. But they may still not work with all the world's hotels.

An aggregator site will search many sites and pull the best prices for airfares, hotels, and rental cars from them. Most aggregators compare the major travel-booking sites such as Expedia, Travelocity, and Orbitz; some also look at airline Web sites, though rarely the sites of smaller budget airlines. Some aggregators also compare other travel products, including complex packages—a good thing, as you can sometimes get the best overall deal by booking an air-and-hotel package.

WITH A TRAVEL AGENT

If you use an agent—brick-and-mortar or virtual—you'll pay a fee for the service. And know that the service you get from some online agents isn't comprehensive. For example Expedia and Travelocity don't search for prices on budget airlines such as jetBlue, Southwest, or small foreign carriers. That said, some agents (online or not) *do* have access to fares that are difficult to find otherwise, and the savings can more than make up for any surcharge.

A knowledgeable brick-and-mortar travel agent can be a godsend if you're booking a cruise, a package trip that's not available to you directly, an air pass, or a complicated itinerary including several overseas flights. What's more, travel agents who specialize in a destination may have exclusive access to certain deals and insider information on things such as charter flights. Agents who specialize in types of travelers (senior citizens, gays and lesbians, naturists) or types of trips (cruises, luxury travel, safaris) can also be invaluable.

Online Booking Resources

AGGREGATORS

Kayak	www.kayak.com	looks at cruises and vacation packages
Mobissimo	www.mobissimo.com	
Qixo	www.qixo.com	compares cruises, vacation packages, travel insurance
Sidestep	www.sidestep.com	compares vacation packages and lists travel deals
Travelgrove	www.travelgrove.com	compares cruises and vacation packages

BOOKING ENGINES

Cheap Tickets	www.cheaptickets.com	discounter
Expedia	www.expedia.com	large online agency charges booking fee for airline tickets
Hotwire	www.hotwire.com	discounter
lastminute.com	www.lastminute.com	specializes in last-minute travel; link to U.S. site
Luxury Link	www.luxurylink.com	auctions and offers on high-end side
Onetravel.com	www.onetravel.com	discounter for hotels, car rentals, airfares, packages
Orbitz	www.orbitz.com	booking fee for airline tickets; clear breakdown of fees and taxes
Priceline.com	www.priceline.com	discounter that also allows bidding
Travel.com	www.travel.com	allows you to compare its rates with other booking engines
Travelocity	www.travelocity.com	booking fee for airline tickets

ONLINE ACCOMMODATIONS

Hotelbook.com	www.hotelbook.com	focuses on independent hotels worldwide
Hotel Club	www.hotelclub.net	good for major cities worldwide
Hotels.com	www.hotels.com	Expedia-owned wholesaler
Quikbook	www.quikbook.com	"pay when you stay" reservations that allow you to settle your bill when you check out, not when you book

OTHER RESOURCES

Bidding For Travel	www.biddingfortravel.com

A top-notch agent planning your trip may get you a room upgrade or a resort food and beverage credit; the one booking your cruise may arrange to have a bottle of champagne chilling in your cabin when you embark. And complain about the surcharges all you like, but when things don't work out the way you'd hoped, it's nice to have an agent to put things right.

■ TIP➔ Remember that Expedia, Travelocity, and Orbitz are travel agents, not just booking engines. To resolve any problems with a reservation made through these companies, contact them first.

If this is your first visit to Kaua'i, a travel agent or vacation packager specializing in Hawai'i can be extremely helpful in planning a memorable vacation. Not only do they have knowledge of the destination, but they can save you money by packaging the costs of airfare, hotel, activities, and car rental. In addition, many of the Hawai'i travel agents may offer added values or special deals (i.e., resort food and beverage credit, a free night's stay, etc.) when you book a package with them. The Hawai'i Visitors & Convention Bureau provides a list of member travel agencies and tour operators.

Agent Resources **American Society of Travel Agents** ☎ 703/739-2782 ⊕ www.travelsense. org.

Hawai'i Travel Agents **AA Vacations** ☎ 800/ 321-2121 ⊕ www.aavacations.com. **AAA Travel** ☎ 800/436-4222 ⊕ www.aaa.com. **All About Hawaii** ☎ 800/274-8687 ⊕ www. allabouthawaii.com. **Delta Vacations** ☎ 800/ 654-6559 ⊕ www.deltavacations.com. **Flying Dutchmen Travel** ☎ 800/514-5194 ⊕ www. flyingdutchmentravel.com. **Funjet Vacations** ☎ 888/558-6654 ⊕ www.funjet.com. **United Vacations** ☎ 800/699-6122 ⊕ www. unitedvacations.com.

■ ACCOMMODATIONS

Before booking accommodations, think hard about what kind of experience you want to have for your island vacation. There are several top-notch resorts on Kaua'i, including the Princeville Resort on the North Shore, where rooms can run more than $700 per night, and the Hyatt Regency Kaua'i on the South Shore for about the same, but Kaua'i also has a wide variety of condos, vacation rentals, and bed-and-breakfasts to choose from. The Kaua'i Visitors Bureau provides a comprehensive listing of accommodation choices to help you decide.

Most hotels and other lodgings require you to give your credit-card details before they will confirm your reservation. If you don't feel comfortable e-mailing this information, ask if you can fax it (some places even prefer faxes). However you book, get confirmation in writing and have a copy of it handy when you check in.

Be sure you understand the hotel's cancellation policy. Some places allow you to cancel without any kind of penalty—even if you prepaid to secure a discounted rate—if you cancel at least 24 hours in advance. Others require you to cancel a week in advance or penalize you the cost of one night. Small inns and B&Bs are most likely to require you to cancel far in advance. Most hotels allow children under a certain age to stay in their parents' room at no extra charge, but others charge for them as extra adults; find out the cutoff age for discounts.

■ TIP➔ Assume that hotels operate on the European Plan (EP, no meals) unless we specify that they use the Breakfast Plan (BP, with full breakfast), Continental Plan (CP, Continental breakfast), Full American Plan (FAP, all meals), Modified American Plan (MAP, breakfast and dinner), or are all-inclusive (AI, all meals and most activities).

BED & BREAKFASTS

For many travelers, nothing compares to the personal service and guest interaction offered at bed-and-breakfasts. A handful of B&Bs throughout Kaua'i offer charming accommodations in country and oceanfront settings and breakfasts with everything from tropical fruits and juices, Kaua'i coffee, and macadamia waffles to breads made with local bananas and mangoes. Some have pools, hot tubs, services such as *lomilomi* massage, and breakfasts delivered to your lānai.

Reservation Services **Bed & Breakfast.com** ☎ 512/322-2710 or 800/462-2632 ⊕ www. bedandbreakfast.com also sends out an on-line newsletter. **Bed &Breakfast Honolulu (Statewide)** ☎ 808/595-7533 or 800/288-4666 ⊕ www.hawaiibnb.com. **Bed & Break-fast Inns Online** ☎ 615/868-1946 or 800/215-7365 ⊕ www.bbonline.com. **BnB Finder. com** ☎ 212/432-7693 or 888/547-8226 ⊕ www.bnbfinder.com. **Better Bed and Breakfasts** ⊕ www.betterbedandbreakfasts. com. **Hawaii's Best Bed & Breakfasts** ☎ 808/263-3100 or 800/262-9912 ⊕ www. bestbnb.com.

CONDOMINIUM & HOUSE RENTALS

Vacation rentals are perfect for couples, families, and friends traveling together who like the convenience of staying at a home away from home. Whether you are seeking a condominium for a week or a large house for a month, you should be able to find the perfect getaway on Kaua'i. Properties managed by individual owners can be found on online vacation rental listing directories such as CyberRentals and Vacation Rentals By Owner, as well as on the Kaua'i Visitors Bureau's Web site. There are also several Kaua'i-based management companies with vacation rentals.

Inventories are greatest along the north and south shores, but there are some properties on the east and west shores as well. Compare companies, as some offer Internet specials and free night stays when booking. Policies vary, but most require a minimum stay, usually greater during peak travel seasons.

Island contacts **Aloha Rental Management** ☎ 808/826-7288 or 800/487-9833 ⊕ www. hanalei-vacations.com. **Blue Sky Kauai Vaca-tion Rentals** ☎ 888/894-1486 ⊕ www. blueskykauai.com. **CyberRentals Vacation Properties** ☎ 512/684-1098 ⊕ www. cyberrentals.com. **Grantham Resorts-Hawaii** ☎ 800/325-5701 ⊕ www.grantham-resorts.

10 WAYS TO SAVE

1. Join "frequent guest" programs. You may get preferential treatment in room choice and/or upgrades in your favorite chains.

2. Call direct. You can sometimes get a better price if you call a hotel's local toll-free number (if available) rather than a central reservations number. And don't be afraid to ask to speak to a manager to inquire about getting a better rate.

3. Check online. Check hotel Web sites, as not all chains are represented on all travel sites.

4. Look for specials. Always inquire about packages and corporate rates.

5. Be flexible. Although one hotel in your desired resort area might be booked, check others nearby.

6. Think about your room view. Ocean-view rooms tend to be much more expensive than garden-view rooms. If the hotel isn't fully booked when you arrive, sometimes you can get an upgrade just by asking, even though you booked a lower category.

7. Ask about taxes. Verify whether local hotel taxes are included in quoted rates. Currently, the hotel tax in Hawai'i is 11.42%, and that's usually added to the bill.

8. Read the fine print. Watch for add-ons, including resort fees, energy surcharges, and "convenience" fees for such things as unlimited local phone service you won't use, valet parking, or newspaper delivery.

9. Know when to go. In Hawai'i, rates at major hotels and resorts, as well as at vacation rentals, can be higher during holidays and from December through April. If you're trying to book, say, in late April, you might save money by changing your dates by a week or two. Ask when rates go down, though: if your dates straddle peak and off-peak seasons, a property may still charge peak-season rates for the entire stay.

10. Weigh your options (we can't say this enough). Weigh transportation times and costs against the savings of staying in a hotel that's cheaper because it's out of the way.

com. **Garden Island Properties** ☎ 808/822–4871 or 800/801–0378 ⊕ www.kauaiproperties.com. **Garden Island Rentals** ☎ 808/742–9537 or 800/247–5599 ⊕ www.kauairentals.com. **Kauai Vacation Rentals** ⊕ www.kauaivacationresorts.com. **Hanalei North Shore Properties** ☎ 800/488–3336 ⊕ www.hanaleinorthshoreproperties.com. **Kauai Vacation Rentals & Real Estate Inc.** ☎ 808/245–8841 or 800/367–5025 ⊕ www.kauaivacationrentals.com. **Vacation Rentals By Owner** ⊕ www.vrbo.com.

HOME EXCHANGES

With a direct home exchange you stay in someone else's home while they stay in yours. Some outfits also deal with vacation homes, so you're not actually staying in someone's full-time residence, just their vacant weekend place.

Exchange Clubs Home Exchange.com ☎ 800/877–8723 ⊕ www.homeexchange.com; $59.95 for a 1-year online listing. **HomeLink International** ☎ 800/638–3841 ⊕ www.homelink.org; $80 yearly for Web-only membership; $125 includes Web access and two catalogs. **Intervac U.S.** ☎ 800/756–4663 ⊕ www.intervacus.com; $78.88 for Web-only membership; $126 includes Web access and a catalog.

HOSTELS

Hostels offer bare-bones lodging at low, low prices—often in shared dorm rooms with shared baths—to people of all ages, though the primary market is young travelers, especially students. Some hostels

> **WORD OF MOUTH**
>
> Did the resort look as good in real life as it did in the photos? Did you sleep like a baby, or were the walls paper thin? Did you get your money's worth? Rate hotels and write your own reviews in Travel Ratings or start a discussion about your favorite places in Travel Talk on www.fodors.com. Your comments might even appear in our books. Yes, you, too, can be a correspondent!

serve breakfast; dinner and/or shared cooking facilities may also be available. In some hostels you aren't allowed to be in your room during the day, and there may be a curfew at night. Nevertheless, hostels provide a sense of community, with public rooms where travelers often gather to share stories. Those seeking intimacy or privacy should seek out a B&B.

Spread out over 2 acres in Kōkeʻe State Park, Camp Sloggett is a lodge, cottage, campground, and hostel owned by the YWCA of Kauaʻi. If you've got a group of 25 or more, you can rent the entire property, including the Sloggett Lodge, which is on the National Historic Register and has a commercial kitchen and dining/table settings for 48 people.

Hostels.com has an online listing of other hostels on the island that cater to a lively international crowd of backpackers, hikers, surfers, and windsurfers.

Hostels.com ⊕ www.hostels.com. **YWCA of Kauaʻi** ☎ 808/245–5959 ⊕ www.campingkauai.com.

▮ AIRLINE TICKETS

Most domestic airline tickets are electronic; international tickets may be either electronic or paper. With an e-ticket the only thing you receive is an e-mailed receipt citing your itinerary and reservation and ticket numbers. The greatest advantage of an e-ticket is that if you lose your receipt, you can simply print out another copy or ask the airline to do it for you at check-in. You usually pay a surcharge (up to $50) to get a paper ticket, if you can get one at all. The sole advantage of a paper ticket is that it may be easier to endorse over to another airline if your flight is canceled and the airline with which you booked can't accommodate you on another flight.

■ TIP→ Discount air passes that let you travel economically in a country or region must often be purchased before you leave home. In some cases you can get them only through a travel agent.

Check local and community newspapers when you're on Kaua'i for deals and coupons on interisland flights, should you wish to visit neighboring islands. Aloha Airlines, go! Airlines, Hawaiian Airlines, and IslandAir offer regular service between the islands. In addition to offering very competitive rates and online specials, all have free frequent-flier programs that will entitle you to rewards and upgrades the more you fly. Be sure to compare prices offered by all of the interisland carriers. If you are somewhat flexible with your days and times for island-hopping, you should have no problem getting a very affordable round-trip ticket.

Interisland Carriers Aloha Airlines ☎ 800/367-5250 ⊕ www.alohaairlines.com. **go! Airlines** ☎ 888/435-9462 ⊕ www.iflygo.com. **Hawaiian Airlines** ☎ 800/367-5320 ⊕ www.hawaiianair.com. **IslandAir** ☎ 800/323-3345 ⊕ www.islandair.com.

CHARTER FLIGHTS

Paragon Air offers 24-hour private charter service to and from the Līhu'e airport. In business since 1981, the company prides itself on its perfect safety record and has served a number of celebrities, including Bill Gates, Michael Douglas, and Kevin Costner, among others. You can arrange a customized tour of Kaua'i or neighboring islands, as well as air service from any airport in Hawai'i. Charter prices start at $475.

Paragon Air ☎ 800/428-1231 ⊕ www.paragon-air.com.

▌RENTAL CARS

Should you plan to do any sightseeing on Kaua'i, it is best to rent a car. Even if all you want to do is relax at your resort, you may want to hop in the car to check out one of the island's popular restaurants.

While on Kaua'i, you can rent anything from an econobox to a Ferrari. Rates are usually better if you reserve through a rental agency's Web site. It's wise to make reservations far in advance and make sure

11 WAYS TO SAVE

1. Nonrefundable is best. If saving money is more important than flexibility, then nonrefundable tickets work. Just remember that you'll pay dearly (as much as $100) if you change your plans.

2. Comparison shop. Web sites and travel agents can have different arrangements with the airlines and offer different prices for exactly the same flights.

3. Beware those prices. Many airline Web sites—and most ads—show prices *without* taxes and surcharges. Don't buy until you know the full price.

4. Stay loyal. Stick with one or two frequent-flier programs. You'll rack up free trips faster and you'll accumulate more quickly the perks that make trips easier.

5. Watch those ticketing fees. Surcharges are usually added when you buy your ticket anywhere but on an airline Web site. (That includes by phone—even if you call the airline directly—and paper tickets regardless of how you book.)

6. Check early and often. Start looking for cheap fares up to a year in advance, and keep looking until you see something you can live with.

7. Don't work alone. Some Web sites have tracking features that will e-mail you immediately when good deals are posted.

8. Jump on the good deals. Waiting even a few minutes might mean paying more.

9. Fly midweek. Look for departures on Tuesday, Wednesday, and Thursday, typically the cheapest days to travel.

10. Be flexible. Check on prices for departures at different times and to and from alternative airports.

11. Weigh your options. What you get can be as important as what you save. A cheaper flight might have a long layover rather than being nonstop, or it might land at a secondary airport, where your ground transportation costs might be higher.

Car Rental Resources

AUTOMOBILE ASSOCIATIONS		
American Automobile Association	315/797-5000	www.aaa.com
National Automobile Club	650/294-7000	www.thenac.com; CA residents only
MAJOR AGENCIES		
Alamo	800/462-5266	www.alamo.com
Avis	800/230-4898	www.avis.com
Budget	800/527-0700	www.budget.com
Hertz	800/654-3131	www.hertz.co
National Car Rental	800/227-7368	www.nationalcar.com

that a confirmed reservation guarantees you a car, especially if you're visiting during peak seasons or for major conventions or sporting events. Rates begin at about $25 to $35 a day for an economy car with air-conditioning, automatic transmission, and unlimited mileage, depending on your pickup location. This does not include the airport concession fee, general excise tax, rental vehicle surcharge, or vehicle license fee. When you reserve a car, ask about cancellation penalties and drop-off charges should you plan to pick up the car in one location and return it to another. Many rental companies in Hawai'i offer coupons for discounts at various attractions that could save you money later on in your trip.

In Hawai'i you must be 21 years of age to rent a car and you must have a valid driver's license and a major credit card. Those under 25 will pay a daily surcharge of $15–$25. Request car seats and extras such as GPS when you book. Hawai'i's Child Restraint Law requires that all children three years and younger be in an approved child safety seat in the backseat of a vehicle. Children ages 4–7 must be seated in a rear booster seat or child restraint such as a lap and shoulder belt. Car seats and boosters range from $5 to $8 per day.

In Hawai'i, your unexpired mainland driver's license is valid for rental for up to 90 days.

Since the road circling the island is mostly two lanes, be sure to allow plenty of time to return your vehicle so that you can make your flight. Traffic can be bad during morning and afternoon rush hour. Give yourself about 3½ hours before departure time to return your vehicle.

CAR-RENTAL INSURANCE

Everyone who rents a car wonders whether the insurance that the rental companies offer is worth the expense. No one—including us—has a simple answer. It all depends on how much regular insurance you have, how comfortable you are with risk, and whether or not money is an issue.

If you own a car and carry comprehensive car insurance for both collision and liability, your personal auto insurance will probably cover a rental, but read your policy's fine print to be sure. If you don't have auto insurance, then you should probably buy the collision- or loss-damage waiver (CDW or LDW) from the rental company. This eliminates your liability for damage to the car. Some credit cards offer CDW coverage, but it's usually supplemental to your own insurance and rarely covers SUVs, minivans, luxury models, and the like. If your coverage is secondary, you may still be liable for loss-of-use costs from the car-rental company (again, read the fine print). But no credit-card insurance is valid unless you use that card for *all* transactions, from reserving to paying the final bill.

■ TIP➔ Diners Club offers primary CDW coverage on all rentals reserved and paid for with the card. This means that Diners Club's company—not your own car insurance—pays in case of an accident. It *doesn't* mean that your car-insurance company won't raise your rates once it discovers you had an accident.

You may also be offered supplemental liability coverage; the car-rental company is required to carry a minimal level of liability coverage insuring all renters, but it's rarely enough to cover claims in a really serious accident if you're at fault. Your own auto-insurance policy will protect you if you own a car; if you don't, you have to decide whether you are willing to take the risk.

U.S. rental companies sell CDWs and LDWs for about $15 to $25 a day; supplemental liability is usually more than $10 a day. The car-rental company may offer you all sorts of other policies, but they're rarely worth the cost. Personal accident insurance, which is basic hospitalization coverage, is an especially egregious rip-off if you already have health insurance.

■ TIP➔ You can decline the insurance from the rental company and purchase it through a third-party provider such as Travel Guard (www.travelguard.com)—$9 per day for $35,000 of coverage. That's sometimes just under half the price of the CDW offered by some car-rental companies.

■ VACATION PACKAGES

Packages *are not* guided excursions. Packages combine airfare, accommodations, and perhaps a rental car or other extras (theater tickets, guided excursions, boat trips, reserved entry to popular museums, transit passes), but they let you do your own thing. During busy periods packages may be your only option, as flights and rooms may be sold out otherwise. Packages will definitely save you time. They can also save you money, particularly in peak seasons, but—and this is a really big

10 WAYS TO SAVE

1. Beware of cheap rates. Those great rates aren't so great when you add in taxes, surcharges, and insurance. Such extras can double or triple the initial quote.

2. Rent weekly. Weekly rates are usually better than daily ones. Even if you want to rent for only five or six days, ask for the weekly rate; it may very well be cheaper than the daily rate for that period of time.

3. Don't forget the locals. Price local companies as well as the majors.

4. Airport rentals can cost more. Airports often add surcharges, which you can sometimes avoid by renting from an agency whose office is just off airport property.

5. Wholesalers can help. Investigate wholesalers, which don't own fleets but rent in bulk from firms that do, and which frequently offer better rates (note that you must usually pay for such rentals before leaving home).

6. Look for rate guarantees. With your rate locked in, you won't pay more, even if the price goes up in the local currency.

7. Fill up farther away. Avoid hefty refueling fees by filling the tank at a station well away from where you plan to turn in the car.

8. Pump it yourself. Don't buy the tank of gas that's in the car when you rent it unless you plan to do a lot of driving.

9. Get all your discounts. Find out whether a credit card you carry or organization or frequent-renter program to which you belong has a discount program. And confirm that such discounts really are a deal. You can often do better with special weekend or weekly rates offered by a rental agency.

10. Check out package rates. Adding a car rental onto your air/hotel vacation package may be cheaper than renting a car separately on your own.

"but"—you should price each part of the package separately to be sure. And be aware that prices advertised on Web sites and in newspapers rarely include service charges or taxes, which can up your costs by hundreds of dollars.

■ TIP→ Some packages and cruises are sold only through travel agents. Don't always assume that you can get the best deal by booking everything yourself.

Each year consumers are stranded or lose their money when packagers—even large ones with excellent reputations—go out of business. How can you protect yourself? First, always pay with a credit card; if you have a problem, your credit-card company may help you resolve it. Second, buy trip insurance that covers default. Third, choose a company that belongs to the United States Tour Operators Association, whose members must set aside funds to cover defaults. Finally, choose a company that also participates in the Tour Operator Program of the American Society of Travel Agents (ASTA), which will act as mediator in any disputes. You can also check on the tour operator's reputation among travelers by posting an inquiry on one of the Fodors.com forums.

About half the visitors to the island of Kaua'i travel on package tours. All of the wholesalers specializing in Hawai'i offer a range of packages from the low to the high end. Because of the volume of business they do, wholesalers typically have great deals. Combine that with their knowledge of the destination and wholesale packages to Kaua'i make a lot of sense. However, shop around and compare before you book to make sure you are getting a good deal.

Organizations American Society of Travel Agents (ASTA) ☎ 703/739–2782 or 800/965–2782 ⊕ www.astanet.com. **United States Tour Operators Association** (USTOA) ☎ 212/599-6599 ⊕ www.ustoa.com.

Hawai'i Tour Operators American Express Vacations ☎ 800/528–4800 www.american expressvacations.com. **Apple Vacations**

⊕ www.applevacations.com. **Classic Vacations** ☎ 866/230–2540 ⊕ www. classicvacations.com. **Creative Leisure** ☎ 800/413–1000 ⊕ www.creativeleisure. com. **Pleasant Holidays** ☎ 800/742–9244 ⊕ www.pleasantholidays.com.

■ TIP→ Local tourism boards can provide information about lesser-known and small-niche operators that sell packages to only a few destinations.

▌ GUIDED TOURS

Guided tours are a good option when you don't want to do it all yourself. You travel along with a group (sometimes large, sometimes small), stay in prebooked hotels, eat with your fellow travelers (the cost of meals is sometimes included in the price of your tour, sometimes not), and follow a schedule. But not all guided tours are an if-it's-Tuesday-this-must-be-Belgium experience. A knowledgeable guide can take you places that you might never discover on your own, and you may be pushed to see more than you would have otherwise. Tours aren't for everyone, but they can be just the thing for first-time travelers to Kaua'i or those who enjoy the group traveling experience. Whenever you book a guided tour, find out what's included and what isn't. A "land-only" tour includes all your travel (by bus, in most cases) in the destination, but not necessarily your flights to and from or even within it. Also, in most cases prices in tour brochures don't include fees and taxes. And remember that you'll be expected to tip your guide (in cash) at the end of the tour.

Globus has four Hawai'i itineraries that include Kaua'i, one of which is an escorted cruise on Norwegian Cruise Lines' *Pride of Aloha* that includes two days on the garden island. Tauck Travel offers an 11-night "Best of Hawai'i" tour that includes two nights on Kaua'i with leisure time for either relaxation or exploration.

EscortedHawaiiTours.com, owned and operated by Atlas Cruises & Tours, sells more than a dozen Hawai'i trips ranging from 7 to 12 nights operated by various guided tour companies including Globus, Tauck, and Trafalgar. Several of these trips include two to three nights on Kaua'i.

Recommended Companies Atlas Cruises & Tours ☎ 800/942-3301 ⊕ www.Escorted HawaiiTours.com. **Globus** ☎ 866/755-8581 ⊕ www.globusjourneys.com. **Tauck Travel** ☎ 800/788-7885 ⊕ www.tauck.com.

SPECIAL-INTEREST TOURS

ART

"Painting in Paradise" is a seven-night, land-only tour offered by go On Tour, a company owned by Davisville Travel (a division of Carlisle Travel Management) that creates educational and cultural trips for small groups. Included are workshops with watercolor artists Sandy Delehanty and Kathy Young-Ross, shared accommodations at Waimea Plantation Cottages, shared car, meals, and free time for exploration. Prices start at about $1,500/person, based on 16 participants. This price does not include round-trip airfare between Kaua'i and your gateway city.

go On Tour ☎ 800/255-4567 ⊕ www.goontour.com.

BIRD-WATCHING

Hawai'i boasts more than 150 species of birds that live in the Hawaiian Islands. Offered in association with the University of Hawai'i at Hilo, "A Birder's Paradise: Kauai and Hawaii" is a seven-night land-only Elderhostel tour with three of those nights spent in Līhu'e. There are daily field lectures to bird-watching sites, including Waimea Canyon, Koke'e State Park, Kilauea Point, and Hakalau Forest National Wildlife Preserve; discussions of Hawai'i's plant and animal species and geologic wonders; and a presentation by a world-renowned birder and photographer. Included in the tour are accommodations, meals, ground transportation, and interisland airfare between Kaua'i and the Big Island. Travelers must purchase their own round-trip ticket from their gateway city. Prices start at around $1,740 per person.

Elderhostel, a nonprofit educational travel organization, has been leading all-inclusive learning adventures around the world for more than 20 years.

Field Guides has a three-island (O'ahu, Kaua'i, and the Big Island), 11-day guided bird-watching trip for 14 birding enthusiasts that focuses on endemic landbirds and specialty seabirds. While on Kaua'i, birders will visit Kōke'e State Park, Alaka'i Wilderness Preserve, and Kīlauea Point. The trip costs about $4,000 per person and includes accommodations, meals, ground transportation, interisland air, an eight-hour pelagic boat trip, and guided bird-watching excursions. Travelers must purchase their own airfare from/to their gateway city. Field Guides has been offering worldwide birding tours since 1984.

Fall Hawaii is a nine-day birding trip to O'ahu, Kaua'i, and the Big Island offered by Victor Emanuel Nature Tours, the largest company in the world specializing in birding tours. The guide for this tour is Bob Sundstrom, a skilled birder with a special interest in birdsong who has been leading birding tours in Hawai'i and other destinations since 1989. Birders will see Kaua'i honeycreepers and Hawaiian short-eared owls at Koke'e State Park and Alaka'i Swamp and seabirds at the National Wildlife Refuges at Kīlauea and Hanalei. Priced at about $4,000/person, the trip includes accommodations, meals, interisland air, ground transportation, and guided excursions. Travelers must purchase their own airline ticket from/to their gateway city.

Elderhostel ☎ 800/454-5768 ⊕ www.elderhostel.org. **Field Guides** ☎ 800/728-4953 ⊕ www.fieldguides.com. **Victor Emanuel Nature Tours** ☎ 800/328-8368 ⊕ www.ventbird.com.

CULTURE

Elderhostel also offers several land-only cultural and educational tours. "Best of Kaua'i's Natural and Cultural Wonders" is a six-night tour presented in association with the Kaua'i Historical Consortium.

You'll visit Hanalei, Kīlauea Point National Wildlife Refuge, Grove Farm Homestead Museum, Kaua'i Museum, and Koke'e Natural History Museum. You'll learn *lauhala* weaving and other traditional arts and crafts and discover why the island truly is like no other. The cost of this tour starts at $1,002 per person and includes accommodations, meals, ground transportation, and admission fees.

"Nature, History and Culture on Kaua'i and Hawai'i" is a 10-night trip that includes 5 nights on each island. Presented in association with the Kaua'i Historical Consortium and University of Hawai'i, Hilo, highlights of the tour include field trips to Kīlauea Point National Wildlife Refuge, Waimea Canyon, and the National Tropical Botanical Garden. Field interpreters from the Kaua'i Museum, Kaua'i Historical Society, and Grove Farm Homestead Museum will share the island's history and cultural traditions with travelers. Prices start at $1,946/person and include accommodations, meals, ground transportation, admission fees, and interisland air between Kaua'i and the Big Island.

Kaua'i also is included in several multi-island tours: a five-island, 15-night "Islands of Life in the Pacific" (2 nights at Kapa'a with visits to Waimea Canyon and Kīlauea Point National Wildlife Refuge); "Tropical Splendor," a four-island, 10-night adventure-afloat study cruise on board Norwegian Cruise Lines' *Pride of Aloha* with a port of call in Nawiliwili; the 21-night, four-island "Hawai'i: Spectacular Beauty & Vibrant History" (3 nights in Waipouli Beach with a visit to Waimea Canyon); the three-island, 11-night "Par-adise Adventure from Mountains to Sea," (3 nights in Kapa'a), where you'll hike, kayak, snorkel, and surf; and "Submarines, Volcanoes and Tropical Forests: Intergenerational Hawaii," a multi-island cruise tour designed for grandparents and their grandchildren. Check out the Elderhostel Web site for price information on these tours.

With all of these tours, travelers must purchase their own airline tickets between their gateway cities and the island where the tour starts.

Elderhostel ☎ 800/454-5768 ⊕ www.elderhostel.org.

ECO TOURS

Want to spend a week in Kaua'i hiking, snorkeling, surfing, and paddling? Kayak Kaua'i has a seven-day "Discovery Tour" where you will explore Kaua'i's peaks and canyons, rivers and coastlines, and discover lagoons with crystal-clear water and breathtaking waterfalls, sacred trails, and miles of ivory-white sand beaches. Tours are offered every month and include accommodations, airport shuttles, van support during the week, communal gear, linens, all meals, guides, day tours, and activities. "Discovery Tour" is rated moderate, but can be challenging at times, and participants should be in good physical condition. For two people, the cost is $2,500 per person; with a group of four or more, it is priced at $1,750 per person. Travelers must purchase their own airline tickets between their gateway cities and Kaua'i.

Kayak Kaua'i ☎ 800/437-3507 ⊕ www.kayakkauai.com.

TRANSPORTATION

▌ BY AIR

Flying time is about 10 hours from New York, 8 hours from Chicago, and 5 hours from Los Angeles.

Hawai'i is a major destination link for flights traveling to and from the U.S. mainland, Asia, Australia, New Zealand, and the South Pacific. Some of the major airline carriers serving Hawai'i fly direct to Kaua'i, allowing you to bypass connecting flights out of Honolulu. For the more spontaneous traveler, island-hopping is easy, with flights departing every 20 to 30 minutes daily until mid-evening. International travelers also have options: O'ahu and the Big Island are gateways to the United States.

Although Līhu'e Airport is smaller and more casual than Honolulu International, it can also be quite busy during peak times. Allot extra travel time during morning and afternoon rush-hour traffic periods.

Plan to arrive at the airport 60 to 90 minutes before departure for interisland flights.

Plants and plant products are subject to regulation by the Department of Agriculture, both on entering and leaving Hawai'i. Upon leaving the islands, you'll have to have your bags X-rayed and tagged at one of the airport's agricultural inspection stations before you proceed to check-in. Pineapples and coconuts with the packer's agricultural inspection stamp pass freely; papayas must be treated, inspected, and stamped. All other fruits are banned for export to the U.S. mainland. Flowers pass except for gardenias, rose leaves, jade vine, and mauna loa. Also banned are insects, snails, soil, cotton, cacti, sugarcane, and all berry plants.

You'll have to leave dogs and other pets at home. A 120-day quarantine is imposed to keep out rabies, which is nonexistent in Hawai'i. If specific pre- and post-arrival requirements are met, animals may qualify for a 30-day or 5-day-or-less quarantine.

Airlines & Airports **Airline and Airport Links.com** ⊕ www.airlineandairportlinks.com has links to many of the world's airlines and airports.

Airline Security Issues **Transportation Security Administration** ⊕ www.tsa.gov has answers for almost every question that might come up.

Air Travel Resources in Hawai'i **State of Hawaii Airports Division Offices** ☎ 808/836-6417 ⊕ www.hawaii.gov/dot/airports.

AIRPORTS

Honolulu International Airport (HNL) is the main stopover for most domestic and international flights. From Honolulu, there are interisland flights to Kaua'i departing regularly from early morning until evening. In addition, some carriers now offer non-stop service directly from the mainland to Līhu'e Airport (LIH) on a limited basis.

> ■ TIP→ **Long layovers don't have to be only about sitting around or shopping. These days they can be about burning off vacation calories. Check out www.airportgyms.com for lists of health clubs that are in or near many U.S. and Canadian airports.**

HONOLULU/O'AHU AIRPORT

Hawai'i's major airport is Honolulu International, on O'ahu, 20 minutes (9 mi) west of Waikīkī. To travel interisland from Honolulu, you can depart from either the interisland terminal or the commuter-airline terminal, located in two separate structures adjacent to the main overseas terminal building. A free bus service, the Wiki Wiki Shuttle, operates between terminals.

Honolulu International Airport (HNL) ☎ 808/836-6413 ⊕ www.hawaii.gov/dot/airports.

KAUA'I

On Kaua'i, visitors fly into Līhu'e Airport, on the East Side of the island. Visitor Information Booths are outside each baggage claim area. Visitors will also find

FLYING 101

Flying may not be as carefree as it once was, but there are some things you can do to make your trip smoother.

MINIMIZE THE TIME SPENT STANDING IN LINE. Buy an e-ticket, check in at an electronic kiosk, or check in on your airline's Web site before leaving home. Pack light and limit carry-on items to essentials.

ARRIVE WHEN YOU NEED TO. Research your airline's policy. It's usually at least an hour before domestic flights and two to three hours before international flights. But airlines at some busy airports have more stringent requirements. Check the TSA Web site for estimated security waiting times at major airports.

GET TO THE GATE. If you aren't at the gate at least 10 minutes before your flight is scheduled to take off (sometimes earlier), you won't be allowed to board.

DOUBLE-CHECK YOUR FLIGHT TIMES. Do this especially if you reserved far in advance. Schedules change, and alerts may not reach you.

DON'T GO HUNGRY. Ask whether your airline offers anything to eat; even when it does, be prepared to pay.

GET THE SEAT YOU WANT. Often, you can pick a seat when you buy your ticket on an airline Web site. But it's not guaranteed; the airline could change the plane after you book, so double-check. You can also select a seat if you check in electronically. Avoid seats on the aisle directly across from the lavatories. Frequent fliers say those are even worse than back-row seats that don't recline.

GOT KIDS? GET INFO. Ask the airline about its children's menus, activities, and fares. Sometimes infants and toddlers fly free if they sit on a parent's lap, and older children fly for half price in their own seats. Also inquire about policies involving car seats; having one may limit seating options. Also ask about seat-belt extenders for car

seats. And note that you can't count on a flight attendant to produce an extender; you may have to ask for one when you board.

CHECK YOUR SCHEDULING. Don't buy a ticket if there's less than an hour between connecting flights. Schedules are padded, but if anything goes wrong, you might miss your connection. If you're traveling to an important function, consider departing a day early.

BRING PAPER. Even when using an e-ticket, always carry a hard copy of your receipt; you may need it to get your boarding pass, which most airports require to get past security.

COMPLAIN AT THE AIRPORT. If your baggage goes astray or your flight goes awry, complain before leaving the airport. Most carriers require that you file a claim immediately.

BEWARE OF OVERBOOKED FLIGHTS. If a flight is oversold, the gate agent will usually ask for volunteers and offer some sort of compensation for taking a different flight. If you're bumped from a flight *involuntarily,* the airline must give you some kind of compensation if an alternate flight can't be found within one hour.

KNOW YOUR RIGHTS. If your flight is delayed because of something within the airline's control (bad weather doesn't count), the airline must get you to your destination on the same day, even if they have to book you on another airline and in an upgraded class. Read the Contract of Carriage, which is usually buried on the airline's Web site.

BE PREPARED. The Boy Scout motto is especially important if you're traveling during a stormy season. To quickly adjust your plans, program a few numbers into your cell: your airline, an airport hotel or two, your destination hotel, your car service, and/or your travel agent.

news and lei stands, an HMS Host restaurant, and a Travel Traders gift shop at the airport.

Kaua'i: Līhu'e Airport (LIH) ☎ 808/246-1448 ⊕ www.hawaii.gov/dot/airports.

GROUND TRANSPORTATION

Marriott Kaua'i and Radisson Kaua'i Beach Resort provide airport shuttles to and from the Līhu'e Airport. In addition, travelers who've booked a tour with Kaua'i Island Tours, Roberts Hawai'i, or Polynesian Adventure Tours will be picked up at the airport.

If you're not renting a car, you'll need to take a taxi or limousine. Cabs are available curbside at baggage claim. Cab fares to locations around the island are estimated as follows: Poipu $35–$41, Wailua-Waipouli $17–$20, Līhu'e–Kukui Grove $10, Princeville-Haena $72–$95. There are three limousine companies that service Līhu'e Airport: Any Time Shuttle, Custom Limousine, and Kaua'i Limousine. **Any Time Shuttle** ☎ 808/927-1120. **Custom Limousine** ☎ 808/246-6318. **Kaua'i Limousine** ☎ 808/245-4855.

FLIGHTS

ATA, Continental, and Northwest fly into O'ahu (Honolulu). American Airlines offers a daily, nonstop Los Angeles–Kaua'i flight, in addition to its service into Honolulu, Maui, and the Big Island. United Airlines provides direct service to Līhu'e Airport from Los Angeles and San Francisco. The carrier also flies into Honolulu, Maui, and the Big Island. From the U.S. mainland, Delta serves O'ahu (Honolulu) and Maui.

Aloha Airlines offers direct flights from Oakland and Orange County to Kona and connecting service from Las Vegas, Reno, Sacramento, and San Diego. Hawaiian Airlines flies from Arizona (Phoenix), California (Los Angeles, Sacramento, San Diego, San Francisco, San Jose), Nevada (Las Vegas), Oregon (Portland), and Washington (Seattle). All of these flights stop in either Honolulu or Maui and require a

change of planes for flights to Līhu'e. Hawaiian also services Australia, American Samoa, and Tahiti.

Aloha, go! Airlines, and Hawaiian offer regular service between the islands. Paragon Airlines offers private charter service to all the islands.

Airline Contacts Aloha Airlines ☎ 800/367-5250 ⊕ www.alohaairlines.com. **American Airlines** ☎ 800/433-7300 ⊕ www.aa.com. **America West** ☎ 800/327-7810 ⊕ www.americawest.com. **ATA** ☎ 800/435-9282 or 317/282-8308 ⊕ www.ata.com. **Continental Airlines** ☎ 800/523-3273 ⊕ www.continental.com. **Delta Airlines** ☎ 800/221-1212 ⊕ www.delta.com. **Hawaiian Airlines** ☎ 800/367-5320 ⊕ www.hawaiianair.com. **Northwest Airlines** ☎ 800/225-2525 ⊕ www.nwa.com. **Southwest Airlines** ☎ 800/435-9792 ⊕ www.southwest.com. **United Airlines** ☎ 800/864-8331 ⊕ www.united.com.

Interisland Flights Aloha Airlines ☎ 800/367-5250 ⊕ www.alohaairlines.com. **go! Airlines** ☎ 888/434-5946 ⊕ www.iflygo.com. **Hawaiian Airlines** ☎ 800/367-5320 ⊕ www.hawaiianair.com. **Island Air** ☎ 800/323-3345 ⊕ www.islandair.com. **Paragon Airlines** ☎ 800/428-1231 ⊕ www.paragon-air.com.

❚ BY BOAT

At this writing, a high-speed ferry service that will run between O'ahu (Honolulu), Kaua'i, and Maui is scheduled to begin in July 2007.

❚ BY BUS

BUS TRAVEL ON KAUA'I

On Kaua'i, the County Transportation Agency operates the Kaua'i Bus, which provides service between Hanalei and Kekaha. It also provides service to the airport and limited service to Kōloa and Po'ipū. The fare is $1.50 for adults, and frequent-rider passes are available. **Kaua'i Bus** ☎ 808/241-6410 ⊕ www.kauai.gov/OCA/Transportation.

❚ BY CAR

The best way to experience all of Kaua'i's stunning beauty is to get in a car and explore. The 15-mi stretch of Nā Pali Coast, with its breathtaking, verdant green sheer cliffs, is the only part of the island that's not accessible by car. Otherwise, one main road can get you from Barking Sands Beach on the west coast to Haena on the north coast.

Asking for directions will almost always produce a helpful explanation from the locals, but you should be prepared for an island term or two. Instead of using compass directions, remember that Hawai'i residents refer to places as being either *mauka* (toward the mountains) or *makai* (toward the ocean) from one another. Hawai'i has a strict seat belt law. Those riding in the front seat must wear a seat belt, and children under the age of 17 in the backseats must be belted. The fine for not wearing a seat belt is $92. Jaywalking is also very common in the islands, so please pay careful attention to the roads. It also is considered rude to honk your horn, so be patient if someone is turning or proceeding through an intersection. While driving on Kaua'i, you will come across several one-lane bridges. If you are the first to approach a bridge, the car on the other side will wait while you cross. If a car on the other side is closer to the bridge, then you should wait while the driver crosses. If you're enjoying the island's dramatic views, pull over to the shoulder so you don't block traffic.

GASOLINE

You can count on having to pay more at the pump for gasoline on Kaua'i than on the U.S. mainland.

ROAD CONDITIONS

Kaua'i has a well-maintained highway running south from Līhu'e to Barking Sands Beach; a spur at Waimea takes you along Waimea Canyon to Kōke'e State Park. A northern route also winds its way from Līhu'e to end at Hā'ena, the beginning of the rugged and roadless Nā Pali Coast. Opt for a four-wheel-drive vehicle if dirt-road exploration holds any appeal.

ROADSIDE EMERGENCIES

If you find yourself in an emergency or accident while driving on Kaua'i, pull over if you can. If you have a cell phone with you, call the roadside assistance number on your rental-car contract or AAA Help. If you find that your car has been broken into or stolen, report it immediately to your rental-car company and they can assist you. If it's an emergency and someone is hurt, call 911 immediately and stay there until medical personnel arrive.

Emergency Services AAA Help ☎ 800/222-4357.

ON THE GROUND

▮ COMMUNICATIONS

INTERNET

If you've brought your laptop with you to Kaua'i, you should have no problem checking e-mail or connecting to the Internet. Most of the major hotels and resorts offer high-speed access in rooms and/or lobbies. You should check with your hotel in advance to confirm that access is wireless; if not, ask whether in-room cables are provided. In some cases an hourly charge will be posted to your room that averages about $15 per hour. If you're staying at a small inn or B&B without Internet access, ask the proprietor for the nearest café or coffee shop with wireless access. **Cybercafes** ⊕ www.cybercafes.com lists more than 4,000 Internet cafés worldwide.

▮ EATING OUT

Whether it's a romantic candlelit dinner for two or a hole-in-the-wall with the island's best *saimin* (noodle soup), Kaua'i has something for every taste bud and every budget. With chefs using abundant locally grown fruits and vegetables, vegetarians often have many exciting choices for their meals. And because Kaua'i is popular among families, restaurants almost always have a kids' menu. When you're booking your accommodations or making a reservation at a hotel dining establishment, ask if they have free or reduced meals for children with paying adults.

MEALS & MEALTIMES

Food in Hawai'i is a reflection of the state's diverse cultural makeup and tropical location. Fresh seafood, organic fruits and vegetables, free-range poultry and meat, and locally grown products such as cocoa and macadamia nuts are the hallmarks of Hawai'i regional cuisine. Its preparations are drawn from across the Pacific Rim, including Japan, the Philippines,

Korea, and Thailand—and now, Hawaiian food is a cuisine in its own right.

Whether you're eating at a freestanding or hotel restaurant, breakfast is usually served from 6 or 7 AM to 9:30 or 10 AM and will often feature à la carte and/or buffet options. Enjoy tropical fresh fruit and juices; banana, mango, or coconut breads; Kona coffee; and specialties such as island-style French toast made with Portuguese sweet bread or *mochi* waffles made with sweet rice flour.

Of the thousands of McDonald's restaurants across the country, only in Hawai'i will you find menu items created for the local community. If you happen to visit a McDonald's for breakfast while you are on Kaua'i, you may want to try the egg, rice, and Portuguese sausage breakfast meal or the *saimin* bowl with its hot broth, noodles, Spam, and fish cake.

Lunch typically runs from 11:30 AM to around 1:30 or 2 PM, and will include salads, sandwiches, and lighter fare. The "plate lunch" is a favorite of many local residents, and usually consists of grilled teriyaki chicken, beef, or fish, served with two scoops of white rice and two side salads, with a big ladle of gravy over the meat and rice. The phrase "broke da mouth" is often used to describe these plates and refers not only to their size, but also to their tastiness.

Dinner typically is served from 5 to 9 PM and, depending on the restaurant, can be a simple or lavish affair. Stick to the chef specials if you can, because they usually represent the best of the season. *Poke* (marinated raw tuna) is a local hallmark and can often be found on *pūpū* (appetizer) menus.

Unless otherwise noted, the restaurants listed in this guide are open daily for lunch and dinner.

LOCAL DO'S & TABOOS

GREETINGS

Hawai'i is a very friendly place, and this is reflected in the day-to-day encounters with friends, family, and even business associates. Women often hug and kiss one another on the cheek, and men shake hands and sometimes combine that with a friendly hug. When a man and a woman are greeting each other and are good friends, it is not unusual for them to hug and kiss on the cheek. Children are taught to call any elders "auntie" or "uncle," even if they aren't related. It's a way to show respect and can result in a local Hawaiian child having dozens of aunties or uncles. It's also reflective of the strong sense of family that exists in the islands.

When you walk off a long flight, perhaps a bit groggy and stiff, nothing quite compares with a Hawaiian lei greeting. The casual ceremony ranks as one of the fastest ways to make the transition from the worries of home to the joys of your vacation. Though the tradition has created an expectation that everyone receives this floral garland when they step off the plane, the state of Hawai'i cannot greet each of its nearly 7 million annual visitors.

If you've booked a vacation with a wholesaler or tour company, a lei greeting might be included in your package, so check before you leave. If not, it's easy to arrange a lei greeting for yourself or your companions before you arrive into Līhu'e Airport. Kama'āina Leis, Flowers & Greeters has been providing lei greetings for visitors to the islands since 1983. To be really wowed by the experience, request a lei of plumeria, some of the most divine-smelling blossoms on the planet. A plumeria or dendrobium orchid lei are considered standard and cost $16.50/person.

Kama'āina Leis, Flowers & Greeters ☎ 808/836–3246 or 800/367–5183 🖷 808/836–1814 ⊕ www.alohaleigreetings.com.

LANGUAGE

Hawai'i was admitted to the Union in 1959, so residents can be sensitive when visitors refer to their own hometowns as "back in the States." Remember, when in Hawai'i, refer to the contiguous 48 states as "the mainland" and not as the United States. When you do, you won't appear to be such a *malahini* (newcomer).

English is the primary language on the islands. Making the effort to learn some Hawaiian words can be rewarding, however. Despite the length of many Hawaiian words, the Hawaiian alphabet is actually one of the world's shortest, with only 12 letters: the five vowels, *a, e, i, o, u,* and seven consonants, *h, k, l, m, n, p, w.* Hawaiian words you're most likely to encounter during your visit to the islands are *aloha, mahalo* (thank you), *keiki* (child), *haole* (Caucasian or foreigner), *mauka* (toward the mountains), *makai* (toward the ocean), and *pau* (finished, all done). Hawaiian history includes waves of immigrants, each bringing their own languages. To communicate with each other, they developed a sort of slang known as "pidgin." If you listen closely, you'll know what is being said by the inflections and by the extensive use of body language. For example, when you know what you want to say but don't know how to say it, just say "you know, da kine." For an informative and somewhat-hilarious view of things Hawaiian, check out Jerry Hopkins's series of books titled *Pidgin to the Max* and *Fax to the Max,* available at most local bookstores in the Hawaiiana sections.

PAYING

Credit cards are widely accepted throughout the island, with the exception of smaller restaurants in some of the more rural areas where only cash and checks are accepted modes of payment. It's best to confirm when you make the reservation if you're unsure.

For guidelines on tipping *see* Tipping *below.*

RESERVATIONS & DRESS

Hawai'i is decidedly casual. Aloha shirts and shorts or long pants for men and island-style dresses or casual resort wear for women are standard attire for evenings in most hotel restaurants and local eateries. T-shirts and shorts will do the trick for breakfast and lunch.

Regardless of where you are, it's a good idea to make a reservation if you can. In some places, it's expected. We mention them specifically only when reservations are essential (there's no other way you'll ever get a table) or when they are not accepted. For popular restaurants, book as far ahead as you can (often 30 days), and reconfirm as soon as you arrive. (Large parties should always call ahead to check the reservations policy.) We mention dress only when men are required to wear a jacket or a jacket and tie.

Online reservation services make it easy to book a table before you even leave home. OpenTable covers most states, including 20 major cities, and has limited listings in Canada, Mexico, the United Kingdom, and elsewhere. DinnerBroker has restaurants throughout the United States as well as a few in Canada. **OpenTable** ⊕ www.opentable.com. **Dinner-Broker** ⊕ www.dinnerbroker.com.

WINES, BEER & SPIRITS

Hawai'i has a new generation of microbreweries, including on-site microbreweries at many restaurants. The drinking age in Hawai'i is 21, and a photo ID must be presented to purchase alcoholic beverages. Bars are open until 2 AM; venues with a

CON OR CONCIERGE?

Good hotel concierges are invaluable—for arranging transportation, getting reservations at the hottest restaurant, and scoring tickets for a sold-out show or entree to an exclusive nightclub. They're in the know and well connected. That said, sometimes you have to take their advice with a grain of salt.

It's not uncommon for restaurants to ply concierges with free food and drink in exchange for steering diners their way. Indeed, European concierges often receive referral *fees.* Hotel chains usually have guidelines about what their concierges can accept. The best concierges, however, are above reproach. This is particularly true of those who belong to the prestigious international society of Les Clefs d'Or.

What can you expect of a concierge? At a typical tourist-class hotel you can expect him or her to give you the basics: to show you something on a map, make a standard restaurant reservation (particularly if you don't speak the language), or help you book a tour or airport transportation. In Asia concierges perform the vital service of writing out the name or address of your destination for you to give to a cabdriver.

Savvy concierges at the finest hotels and resorts can arrange for just about any good or service imaginable—and do so quickly. You should compensate them appropriately. A $10 tip is enough to show appreciation for a table at a hot restaurant. But the reward should really be much greater for tickets to that U2 concert that's been sold out for months or for those last-minute sixth-row-center seats for *The Lion King.*

WORST-CASE SCENARIO

All your money and credit cards have just been stolen. In these days of real-time transactions, this isn't a predicament that should destroy your vacation. First, report the theft of the credit cards. Then get any traveler's checks you were carrying replaced. This can usually be done almost immediately, provided that you kept a record of the serial numbers separate from the checks themselves. If you bank at a large international bank such as Citibank or HSBC, go to the closest branch; if you know your account number, chances are you can get a new ATM card and withdraw money right away. **Western Union** (☎ 800/325–6000 ⊕ www.westernunion.com) sends money almost anywhere. Have someone back home order a transfer online, over the phone, or at one of the company's offices, which is the cheapest option.

cabaret license can stay open until 4 AM. No matter what you might see in the local parks, drinking alcohol in public parks or on the beaches is illegal. It's also illegal to have open containers of alcohol in motor vehicles.

▋ HOURS OF OPERATION

Even people in paradise have to work. Generally, local business hours are weekdays 8–5. Banks are usually open Monday–Thursday 8:30–3 and until 6 on Friday. Some banks have Saturday-morning hours.

Many self-serve gas stations stay open around-the-clock, with full-service stations usually open from around 7 AM until 9 PM. U.S. post offices are open weekdays 8:30 AM–4:30 PM and Saturday 8:30–noon.

Most museums generally open their doors between 9 AM and 10 AM and stay open until 5 PM Tuesday–Saturday. Many museums operate with afternoon hours only on Sunday and close on Monday. Visitor-

attraction hours vary throughout the state, but most sights are open daily, with the exception of major holidays such as Christmas. Check local newspapers upon arrival for attraction hours and schedules if visiting over holiday periods. The local dailies carry a listing of "What's Open/What's Not" for those time periods.

Stores in resort areas sometimes open as early as 8, with shopping-center opening hours varying from 9:30 to 10 on weekdays and Saturday, a bit later on Sunday. Bigger malls stay open until 9 weekdays and Saturday and close at 5 on Sunday. Boutiques in resort areas may stay open as late as 11.

CREDIT CARDS

Throughout this guide, the following abbreviations are used: **AE**, American Express; **D**, Discover; **DC**, Diners Club; **MC**, MasterCard; and **V**, Visa.

It's a good idea to inform your credit-card company before you travel, especially if you're going abroad and don't travel internationally very often. Otherwise, the credit-card company might put a hold on your card owing to unusual activity—not a good thing halfway through your trip. Record all your credit-card numbers—as well as the phone numbers to call if your cards are lost or stolen—in a safe place, so you're prepared should something go wrong. Both MasterCard and Visa have general numbers you can call (collect if you're abroad) if your card is lost, but you're better off calling the number of your issuing bank, since MasterCard and Visa usually just transfer you to your bank; your bank's number is usually printed on your card.

Reporting Lost Cards **American Express** ☎ 800/992–3404 in U.S. or 336/393–1111 collect from abroad ⊕ www.americanexpress. com. **Diners Club** ☎ 800/234–6377 in U.S. or 303/799–1504 collect from abroad ⊕ www. dinersclub.com. **Discover** ☎ 800/347–2683 in U.S. or 801/902–3100 collect from abroad ⊕ www.discovercard.com. **MasterCard** ☎ 800/622–7747 in U.S. or 636/722–7111 col-

lect from abroad ⊕ www.mastercard.com.
Visa ☎ 800/847-2911 in U.S. or 410/581-9994 collect from abroad ⊕ www.visa.com.

TRAVELER'S CHECKS & CARDS

Some consider this the currency of the caveman, and it's true that fewer establishments accept traveler's checks these days. Nevertheless, they're a cheap and secure way to carry extra money, particularly on trips to urban areas. Both Citibank (under the Visa brand) and American Express issue traveler's checks in the United States, but Amex is better known and more widely accepted; you can also avoid hefty surcharges by cashing Amex checks at Amex offices. Whatever you do, keep track of all the serial numbers in case the checks are lost or stolen.

American Express now offers a stored-value card called a Travelers Cheque Card, which you can use wherever American Express credit cards are accepted, including ATMs. The card can carry a minimum of $300 and a maximum of $2,700, and it's a very safe way to carry your funds. Although you can get replacement funds in 24 hours if your card is lost or stolen, it doesn't really strike us as a very good deal. In addition to a high initial cost ($14.95 to set up the card, plus $5 each time you "reload"), you still have to pay a 2% fee for each purchase in a foreign currency (similar to that of any credit card). Further, each time you use the card in an ATM you pay a transaction fee of $2.50 on top of the 2% transaction fee for the conversion—add it all up and it can be considerably more than you would pay when simply using your own ATM card. Regular traveler's checks are just as secure and cost less.
American Express ☎ 888/412-6945 in U.S., 801/945-9450 collect outside U.S. to add value or speak to customer service ⊕ www. americanexpress.com.

▌ SAFETY

Hawai'i is generally a safe tourist destination, but it's still wise to follow the

---

WORD OF MOUTH

Was the service stellar or not up to snuff? Did the food give you shivers of delight or leave you cold? Did the prices and portions make you happy or sad? Rate restaurants and write your own reviews in Travel Ratings or start a discussion about your favorite places in Travel Talk on www.fodors. com. Your comments might even appear in our books. Yes, you, too, can be a correspondent!

---

same commonsense safety precautions you would normally follow in your own hometown. Hotel and visitor-center staff can provide information should you decide to head out on your own to more remote areas. Rental cars are magnets for break-ins, so don't leave any valuables in the car, not even in a locked trunk. Avoid poorly lighted areas, beach parks, and isolated areas after dark as a precaution. When hiking, stay on marked trails, no matter how alluring the temptation might be to stray. Weather conditions can cause landscapes to become muddy, slippery, and tenuous, so staying on marked trails will lessen the possibility of a fall or getting lost. Ocean safety is of the utmost importance when visiting an island destination. Don't swim alone, and follow the international signage posted at beaches that alerts swimmers to strong currents, man-of-war jellyfish, sharp coral, high surf, sharks, and dangerous shore breaks. At coastal lookouts along cliff tops, heed the signs indicating that waves can climb over the ledges. Check with lifeguards at each beach for current conditions, and if the red flags are up, indicating swimming and surfing are not allowed, don't go in. Waters that look calm on the surface can harbor strong currents and undertows, and not a few people who were just wading have been dragged out to sea.

Be wary of those hawking "too good to be true" prices on everything from car

EFFECTIVE COMPLAINING

Things don't always go right when you're traveling, and when you encounter a problem or service that isn't up to snuff, you should complain. But there are good and bad ways to do so.

Take a deep breath. This is always a good strategy, especially when you are aggravated about something. Just inhale, and exhale, and remember that you're on vacation. We know it's hard for Type A people to leave it all behind, but for your own peace of mind, it's worth a try.

Complain in person when it's serious. In a hotel, serious problems are usually better dealt with in person, at the front desk; if it's something quick, you can phone.

Complain early rather than late. Whenever you don't get what you paid for (the type of hotel room you booked or the airline seat you reserved) or when it's something timely (the people next door are making too much noise), try to resolve the problem sooner rather than later. It's always going to be harder to deal with a problem or get something taken off your bill after the fact.

Be willing to escalate, but don't be hasty. Try to deal with the person at the front desk of your hotel or with your waiter in a restaurant before asking to speak to a supervisor or manager. Not only is this polite, but when the person directly serving you can fix the problem, you'll more likely get what you want quicker.

Say what you want, and be reasonable. When things fall apart, be clear about what kind of compensation you expect. Don't leave it to the hotel or restaurant or airline to suggest what they're willing to do for you. That said, the compensation you request must be in line with the problem. You're unlikely to get a free meal because your steak was undercooked or a free hotel stay if your bathroom was dirty.

Choose your battles. You're more likely to get what you want if you limit your complaints to one or two specific things that really matter rather than a litany of wrongs.

Don't be obnoxious. Nothing will stop your progress dead in its tracks as readily as an insistent "Don't you know who I am?" or "So what are you going to do about it?" Raising your voice will rarely get a better result.

Nice counts. This doesn't mean you shouldn't be clear that you are displeased. Passive isn't good, either. When it comes right down to it, though, you'll attract more flies with sugar than with vinegar.

Do it in writing. If you discover a billing error or some other problem after the fact, write a concise letter to the appropriate customer-service representative. Keep it to one page, and, as with any complaint, state clearly and reasonably what you want them to do about the problem. Don't give a detailed trip report or list a litany of problems.

---

rentals to attractions. Many of these offers are just a lure to get you in the door for time-share presentations. When handed a flier, read the fine print before you make your decision to participate.

Women traveling alone are generally safe on the islands, but always follow the safety precautions you would use in any major destination. When booking hotels, request rooms closest to the elevator, and always keep your hotel-room door and balcony doors locked. Stay away from isolated areas after dark; camping and hiking solo are not advised. If you stay out late visiting nightclubs and bars, use caution when exiting nightspots and returning to your lodging.

■ TIP→ Distribute your cash, credit cards, IDs, and other valuables between a deep front pocket, an inside jacket or vest pocket, and a hidden money pouch. Don't reach for the money pouch once you're in public.

TAXES

There's a 4.16% state sales tax on all purchases, including food. A hotel room tax of 7.25%, combined with the sales tax of 4%, equals an 11.41% rate added onto your hotel bill. A $3-per-day road tax is also assessed on each rental vehicle.

TIME

Hawai'i is on Hawaiian Standard Time, five hours behind New York and two hours behind Los Angeles.

When the U.S. mainland is on daylight saving time, Hawai'i is not, so add an extra hour of time difference between the is-lands and U.S. mainland destinations. You may also find that things generally move more slowly here. That has nothing to do with your watch—it's just the laid-back way called Hawaiian time.

TIPPING

Tip cabdrivers 15% of the fare. Standard tips for restaurants and bar tabs run from 15% to 20% of the bill, depending on the standard of service. Bellhops at hotels usually receive $1 per bag, more if you have bulky items such as bicycles and surfboards. Tip the hotel room maid $1 per night, paid daily. Tip doormen $1 for assistance with taxis; tips for concierges vary depending on the service. For example, tip more for "hard-to-get" event tickets or dining reservations.

GETTING STARTED / BOOKING YOUR TRIP / TRANSPORTATION / ON THE GROUND

INDEX

PHOTO CREDITS

Cover Photo *(Na Pali Coast): Kerrick James. 5, Superstock/age fotostock.* **Chapter 1: Experience Kauai:** *7, Dallas & John Heaton/Picture Finders/age fotostock. 8-9 (all), Kauai Visitors Bureau. 11, Superstock/age fotostock. 12 (left), Robert Coello/Kauai Visitors Bureau. 12 (top right), Greg Vaughn/Alamy. 12 (bottom center), Lee Foster/ Alamy. 12 (bottom right), Starwood Hotels & Resorts. 13 (top left), Andre Jenny/Alamy. 13 (bottom left), Photo Resource Hawaii/Alamy. 13 (right), Ty Milford/Aurora Photos. 15, Ty Milford/Aurora Photos. 16 (left), Chad Ehlers/Alamy. 16 (right), Photo Resource Hawaii/Alamy. 17, iStockphoto. 18, Photo Resource Hawaii/Alamy. 20, Kauai Visitors Bureau. 21 (left), Starwood Hotels & Resorts. 21 (right), Mark A. Johnson/ Alamy. 22, Photo Resource Hawaii/Alamy. 23, Travis Rowan/Alamy.* **Chapter 2: Exploring Kauai:** *25, Douglas Peebles Photography/Alamy. 34-36, Douglas Peebles Photography. 37 (top right), Douglas Peebles Photography. 37 (bottom right), iStockphoto. 38, Photo Resource Hawaii/Alamy. 39 (top right), Photo Resource Hawaii/Alamy. 39 (bottom right), SuperStock/age fotostock. 40, Mark A. Johnson/Alamy. 41 (top right), Photo Resource Hawaii/Alamy. 41 (bottom right), Dallas & John Heaton/age fotostock.* **Chapter 3: Beaches:** *61, Andre Jenny/Alamy.* **Chapter 4: Water Sports & Tours:** *79, Mark A. Johnson/Alamy. 96, Ron Dahlquist/HVCB.* **Chapter 5: Golf, Hiking & Outdoor Activities:** *103, Kauai Visitors Bureau. 112, Luca Tettoni/viestiphoto.com. 113, Jack Jeffrey.* **Chapter 6: Shops & Spas:** *121, Beauty Photo Studio/age fotostock. 130 (top), Linda Ching/HVCB. 130 (bottom), Sri Maiava Rusden/HVCB. 131 (top), leisofhawaii.com. 131 (2nd from top), kellyalexanderphotography.com. 131 (3rd, 4th, and 5th from top), leisofhawaii.com. 131 (bottom), kellyalexanderphotography.com.* **Chapter 7: Entertainment & Nightlife:** *135, Douglas Peebles Photography/Alamy. 138, HVCB. 139, Thinkstock.* **Chapter 8: Where to Eat:** *147, Princeville Resort. 157, Polynesian Cultural Center. 158 (top), Douglas Peebles Photography. 158 (top center), Douglas Peebles Photography/Alamy. 158 (center), Dana Edmunds/Polynesian Cultural Center. 158 (bottom center), Douglas Peebles Photography/Alamy. 158 (bottom), Purcell Team/Alamy. 159 (top, top center, and bottom center), HTJ/HVCB. 159 (bottom), Oahu Visitors Bureau.* **Chapter 9: Where to Stay:** *173, Princeville Resort.* **Color Section: Views of the Kalalau Valley from Kalalau Lookout, Kokee State Park:** *Ron Dahlquist/Kauai Visitors Bureau. Naupaka, Limahuli Garden: Kauai Visitors Bureau. Ficus carica roots: blickwinkel/Alamy. Sunset from Kee Beach: Cornforth Images/ Alamy. Mt. Waialeale: Douglas Peebles Photography/Alamy. Sailing a 48-foot cruising yacht off the Na Pali Coast North Shore: Photo Resource Hawaii/Alamy. Surfer: Ty Milford/Aurora Photos. Windsurfing: Douglas Peebles Photography/Alamy. Queen's Bath near Princeville on the North Shore: Russ Bishop/Alamy. Hawaiian sunset: Images Etc Ltd/Alamy. Waimea Canyon: Mark A. Johnson/Alamy. Hula dancers: Danita Delimont/Alamy. Diver with a Hawaiian monk seal: David Fleetham/Alamy. Hiker, Hanakapiai Valley, Na Pali Coast: Cornforth Images/Alamy.*

NOTES

NOTES